OXFORD WORLD'

LEUCIPPE AND (

ACHILLES TATIUS was an inhabitant o
second century CE, and highly unlikel)　　　　 ᴜᴇᴇn (as the later
biographical tradition makes him) a Christian bishop. He may have
also composed scholarly works on language and astronomy, but his
reputation rests primarily upon the brilliantly perverse novel *Leucippe and Clitophon*. This text was influential upon the writers of late
antiquity (including Nonnus, the author of the *Tales of Dionysus*,
and the Byzantine romancers), but his most direct impact upon literary history is mediated through the novels of Fielding and
Richardson.

TIM WHITMARSH is E. P. Warren Praelector, Fellow and Tutor in
Classics at Corpus Christi and Lecturer in Greek at the University
of Oxford. He has published numerous articles on the Greek
novelists and the literary culture of Roman Greece. He is the author
of *Greek Literature and the Roman Empire: The Politics of Imitation*
(2001).

HELEN MORALES teaches Classics at the University of Cambridge
and is a Fellow of Newnham College. She has previously taught at
the University of Reading and at Arizona State University. She has
edited (with Alison Sharrock) *Intratextuality: Greek and Roman
Textual Relations* (Oxford, 2000) and her book *Vision and Narrative
in Achilles Tatius* is forthcoming from Cambridge University Press.

OXFORD WORLD'S CLASSICS

*For over 100 years Oxford World's Classics have brought
readers closer to the world's great literature. Now with over 700
titles—from the 4,000-year-old myths of Mesopotamia to the
twentieth century's greatest novels—the series makes available
lesser-known as well as celebrated writing.*

*The pocket-sized hardbacks of the early years contained
introductions by Virginia Woolf, T. S. Eliot, Graham Greene,
and other literary figures which enriched the experience of reading.
Today the series is recognized for its fine scholarship and
reliability in texts that span world literature, drama and poetry,
religion, philosophy and politics. Each edition includes perceptive
commentary and essential background information to meet the
changing needs of readers.*

OXFORD WORLD'S CLASSICS

ACHILLES TATIUS

Leucippe and Clitophon

Translated with Notes by
TIM WHITMARSH

With an Introduction by
HELEN MORALES

OXFORD
UNIVERSITY PRESS

OXFORD

UNIVERSITY PRESS

Great Clarendon Street, Oxford OX2 6DP

Oxford University Press is a department of the University of Oxford.
It furthers the University's objective of excellence in research, scholarship,
and education by publishing worldwide in

Oxford New York

Auckland Bangkok Buenos Aires Cape Town Chennai
Dar es Salaam Delhi Hong Kong Istanbul Karachi Kolkata
Kuala Lumpur Madrid Melbourne Mexico City Mumbai Nairobi
São Paulo Shanghai Taipei Tokyo Toronto

Oxford is a registered trade mark of Oxford University Press
in the UK and in certain other countries

Published in the United States
by Oxford University Press Inc., New York

First published 2001
First published as an Oxford World's Classics paperback 2003
Reissued 2009

British Library Cataloguing in Publication Data

Data available

Library of Congress Cataloging in Publication Data

Data available

ISBN 978–0–19–955547–5

10

Printed in Great Britain by
Clays Ltd, Elcograf S.p.A.

Contents

For Julie and India

Introduction

'A romance,' Saint-Savin explained to him, 'must always have at its base a misconception—of a person, action, place, time, circumstance—and from that fundamental misconception episodic misconceptions must arise, developments, digressions, and finally unexpected and pleasant recognitions. By misconception I mean things like a living person's reported death, or one person's being killed in place of another, or a misconception of quantity, as when a woman believes her lover dead and marries another, or of quality, when it is the judgement of the senses that errs, when someone who appears dead is then buried, while actually he is under the influence of a sleeping potion; or else a misconception of relation, as when one man is wrongly believed the murderer of another; or of instrument, as when one man pretends to stab another using a weapon whose tip, while seeming to wound, does not pierce the throat but retracts into the sleeve, pressing a sponge soaked in blood.'

(Umberto Eco, *The Island of the Day Before*)

LEUCIPPE AND CLITOPHON AND THE ANCIENT NOVEL

Achilles Tatius' *Leucippe and Clitophon* is a riotous romance of misconceptions: mistaken identities, false reports, and lurid staged murders. An ambitious philosophico-bonkbuster, it tells of the adventures of a young man and woman who fall in love at first sight, elope, and are separated by perils which propel them around the Mediterranean until they are reunited and can marry. It is part of an explosion of prose fiction writing that took place in the first few centuries CE, during the Roman Empire. The 'ancient novel', as the genre has come to be known, is the most significant literary phenomenon of that time. However, a rigid scholarly canon defining what counts as 'Classical', and a tenacious tradition which posited the birth of the novel in the eighteenth century, conspired to consign the ancient novel to a long period of neglect. This new translation of Achilles Tatius rides the crest of a wave of the last few decades' resurgent interest in the ancient novel: its radical representations of gender and cultural identity, its important role in the history of sexuality, and its complex relationship to the modern novel.

Questions of Genre

The terms 'novel' and 'romance' are modern ones and the issue of what constitutes a novel in antiquity, or even whether it makes sense to talk of the 'ancient novel', is highly contentious. In its loosest formulation, 'novel' categorizes an extended work of fiction written in prose. Within this category, convention has given pride of place to seven works, two written in Latin and five in Greek, all most probably in the first five centuries CE. Petronius' *Satyrica* is a magisterial 'Tales from the Land of the Satyrs', written in prose and verse, which survives only in fragments, but whose complex narrative includes parody of epic, meditation on the pleasures of life, and satirical critique of Neronian Rome. It is most famous for its banquet scene, 'Trimalchio's Dinner Party', and for the many later works it has inspired, notably F. Scott Fitzgerald's *The Great Gatsby* and Federico Fellini's film *Fellini Satyricon*. Apuleius' *Metamorphoses* (sometimes known as *The Golden Ass*) is an equally rich and sophisticated account of a man's transformation into an ass and his subsequent adventures, involving, among other things, an exploration of 'curiosity', Platonic readings of myth, and an initiation into the mysteries of the goddess Isis. The five Greek novels are *Chaereas and Callirhoe* by Chariton, *Ephesian Tales* by Xenophon of Ephesus, *Daphnis and Chloe* by Longus, *Ethiopian Tales* by Heliodorus, and *Leucippe and Clitophon* by Achilles Tatius. These works survive intact, but lack of firm knowledge about their dates, contexts, and authors leaves much open to speculation. They have certain elements in common: all feature a young man and woman of the urban elite who fall in love but who are prevented from consummating their desire, and all are centrally interested in chastity and marriage. All but Longus' *Daphnis and Chloe* involve the hero and heroine leaving home, travelling to foreign lands, and being physically separated from each other. All either end in the marriage of the couple or, in the case of Chariton and Xenophon, in the reunion of the hero and heroine whose marriage had been followed by forcible separation. All conspicuously ignore contemporary Rome and are set within idealized Greek contexts. This common repertoire has led to these works being known as the five 'ideal' Greek novels or 'the big five'.

It is often argued that these constitute the genre proper, with other fictitious narratives which do not have a central romantic element or are less 'idealistic' being relegated to 'fringe' literature. In fact, other narratives, together with the surviving fragments and summaries of novels, provide a more diverse picture of ancient prose fiction. *The Story of Apollonius, King of Tyre*, an anonymously authored Latin novel, possibly a translation, adaptation, or epitome of a Greek original, begins with the incestuous rape of a princess by her father, (hardly 'ideal'), and the fragments of the Greek *Phoenician Tales* of Lollianus depict group sex, human sacrifice, and cannibalism. The fragmentary *Iolaus* portrays a young man trying to gain access to a woman by disguising himself as a castrated religious acolyte; *Daulis* features a confrontation between the barbarian commander Daulis and a prophet of Apollo, and *Tinouphis* appears to involve a prophet who is condemned for adultery but is helped to escape by the executioner. There are fictional narratives with historical characters and settings (Chariton's novel is one of these, as is one of the earliest novels, *Ninus and Semiramis*), tales of fantastic journeys (Lucian's *True Stories* and Antonius Diogenes' *The Incredible Things Beyond Thule*), epistolary fiction (such as the *Letters of Chion*), fictional 'eyewitness' reports from Troy (the *Diary of the Trojan War* by Dictys of Crete and *History of the Destruction of Troy* by Dares of Troy), Christian fiction (such as the story of Paul and Thecla and the *Clement Romance*), and Jewish fiction (like the story of Joseph and Aseneth). It is hard to escape the conclusion that what constitutes the ancient novel cannot be demarcated along discrete lines, and that the 'ideal' romance novel is neither the generic standard nor the norm. All of this is important for an understanding of *Leucippe and Clitophon*, because different generic expectations will direct very different interpretations of the novel. Viewed against the four other 'ideal' romances, Achilles Tatius emerges as an *enfant terrible* who 'conducts a prolonged guerrilla war against the conventions of his own genre'.[1] Viewed in the context of other 'Phoenician Tales', however, *Leucippe and Clitophon* may seem more conformist.

The Novel and its Readers

Of course, communities of readers create genres. Who read the ancient novels and what did they make of them? The short answer is that they were read by Greek speakers of the Roman Empire. It is hard to be more precise. Part of the problem is that there is no work of ancient literary criticism, like Aristotle's *Poetics*, which discusses Imperial prose fiction. Unlike epic and tragedy, there is not even a Greek word for novel. The terms used to describe the works are disappointingly vague. The Byzantine intellectual Photius refers to *Leucippe and Clitophon* as *ta dramata*, 'the dramas' or, more prosaically, 'the things done', and other works are referred to in general terms, such as *plasmata*, 'fictions', and *erotika*, 'erotic tales'. It is hard to read this silence. It is quite possible that there were critical works which discussed these texts which simply have not survived. It is also possible that reading novels was thought illicit. The little evidence we have of ancient readers' opinions of the novels is largely negative. Macrobius (*c.* fourth century CE) dismisses the Latin novels to the nursery (*Commentary on the Dream of Scipio from Cicero* 1.2.7) and the third-century polymath Philostratus despises Chariton (if it is the novelist Chariton to whom he is referring) as a nobody who would be forgotten by posterity (Epistle 66). The emperor Julian, writing in the fourth century CE, urges: 'as for

[1] J. R. Morgan, 'The Greek Novel: Towards a Sociology of Production and Reception', in A. Powell (ed.), *The Greek World* (London, 1995), 142.

those fictions in the form of history that have been narrated along-side events of the past, we should renounce them, love stories and all that sort of stuff' (Epistle 89. 301b). More productively, a doctor, writing a century later, prescribes erotic fictions as a remedy for impotence (Theodorus Priscianus, *Euporista* 2. 11. 34). But the rar-ity of these snippets of information makes it risky to afford them individually too much importance.

It is important to be aware that the question of the readership of the ancient novels is a highly politicized issue, and that the theories proposed have often only too clearly revealed the prejudices of modern scholars. When the genre was devalued by Classicists, the readership was most often claimed to have been female; if the nov-els were seen as lowbrow, sentimental, pulp fiction, then it followed that only women and other undiscerning communities of readers would have been entertained by them. At times when scholarship has sought to reclaim the novels as valuable and 'Classical', a largely (or even exclusively) male audience has typically been posited. Recently, more positive reasons have been proposed for a female readership. Focusing on the novels' representations of strong women who wield erotic omnipotence, critics have argued that they are likely to have had a particular appeal to women read-ers. However, attempting to identify what characteristics of a nar-rative might be more attractive to a female than a male reader has proven a hazardous exercise. For one scholar, Achilles Tatius' Melite is one of the characters whose individuality, independence, and humour, demonstrated in her masterful seduction of Clitophon, make her most likely to appeal to women readers. In contrast, another commentator sees in Melite's conquest of Clitophon 'a male orientation which should give pause to theories of a chiefly female readership'.[2]

More telling are literacy rates, which indicate that only a small percentage of elite men and an even smaller percentage of elite women could read. Seven papyri of *Leucippe and Clitophon* have been found, more than of any other Greek novel, but still far fewer than

---

[2] B. M. Egger, 'Women in the Greek Novel: Constructing the Feminine', unpublished Ph.D. dissertation, University of California at Irvine (1990), 75–6; E. Bowie, 'The Readership of Greek Novels in the Ancient World', in J. Tatum (ed.), *The Search for the Ancient Novel* (Baltimore and London, 1994), 134.

works by authors on school curricula, like Homer and Thucydides. This suggests that the novels did not enjoy a wide readership. Mosaics thought to illustrate the novels *Metiochus and Parthenope* and *Ninus and Semiramis* have been found on the floors of a house known as 'The House of the Man of Letters' in Daphne, a part of Antioch in Syria, and are thought to date to about 200 CE (they are now in the Museum of Historic Art in Princeton). Such mosaics were expensive, and reinforce the picture of an elite readership. Fragments of other, less well-preserved mosaics which illustrate the same themes attest to the novels' popularity, and arguments that the scenes might in fact depict mimes with the same characters are unpersuasive. It is significant that both male and female characters in the novels read and write (cf. Leucippe's letter at 5. 18). If Achilles Tatius' internal readership is in any way indicative of his actual readership, then women are likely to be included. Moreover, when Clitophon pronounces that 'the female of the species is rather fond of myths' (5. 5), it is inviting to read this not only as an ironic reflection on the misogynist tale he is about to tell Leucippe, but also as a self-conscious nod to some of Achilles' readers. On balance, then, it seems likely that the readership of the novel was well-educated and largely, but by no means exclusively, male.

Achilles Tatius and his Tradition

We have little secure information about the author, who does not reveal anything in the text of the novel itself.[3] Even his name is in dispute: the vast majority of manuscripts have Tatius, but a few, like the tenth-century encyclopedia *Suda*, refer to him as Statius. His name suggests that he was a Greek with Roman citizenship (Achilles is a famous Greek name and Tatius and Statius are common Roman names). The manuscripts and the Byzantine testimonia agree that he was from Alexandria, the main Mediterranean port of Egypt and, with over 500,000 inhabitants, second only to Rome in economic and cultural importance. This multicultural

[3] All known testimonia on him are collected in E. Vilborg, *Achilles Tatius: Leucippe and Clitophon* (Stockholm, 1955), 163–8.

metropolis, with its famous museum and library, was a vibrant centre of intellectualism and creativity.

The *Suda* writes:

Achilles Statius of Alexandria, the author of the story of Leucippe and Clitophon and of other tales of love in eight books. He finally became a Christian and a bishop. He also wrote on the sphere and on etymology as well as a miscellaneous history of many great and illustrious men. His style in all his works is like that of other authors of love stories. [Or: His style in all these works is like that of his love stories.]

The *Etymology* and *Miscellaneous History* are lost. *On the Sphere* survives in fragments preserved in a commentary on Aratus' didactic poem on celestial phenomena, but uncertainty about the date of the work (possibly third rather than second century CE) has made some scholars doubt its ascription to Achilles Tatius the novelist. The scholiast Thomas Magister calls Achilles a *rhetor*, a professional orator, which is more likely than the *Suda*'s story that he became a Christian and a bishop. The same was claimed for Heliodorus, and was most probably part of a strategy of appropriation of the novels into a Christian agenda, without which they might never have been preserved. Achilles does not appear to have had a great impact upon writers of late antiquity, with the notable exception of Musaeus' poem *Hero and Leander* (*c.* fifth–sixth century CE),[4] but his influence on Heliodorus' novel and Nonnus' fifth-century epic *Dionysiaca* is tangible.

The complex role of ancient prose fiction on the development of the modern 'novel' and its attendant theories of literary fictionality has been the subject of extensive debate, for which the reader is referred to two recent important studies.[5] It is, however, worth mentioning here that extensive appropriation of *Leucippe and Clitophon* is evident as early as the first Byzantine novel, *Hysmine and Hysminias*, written in the eleventh century by Eustathius Macrembolites. Ancient Greek novels first seem to have entered the English literary scene (via France, where Hellenism was very

---

[4] On which see H. L. Morales, 'Constructing Gender in Musaeus' *Hero and Leander*', in Richard Miles (ed.), *Constructing Identity in Late Antiquity* (Routledge, 1999).

[5] M. A. Doody, *The True Story of the Novel* (London, 1996); L. Plazenet, *L'Ébahissement et la délectation. Reception comparée et poétiques du roman grec en France et en Angleterre aux XVI et XVII siècles* (Paris, 1997).

much in vogue) in the sixteenth century. Certainly by the time of Shakespeare's *Comedy of Errors* and *Twelfth Night* motifs of doubling, mistaken identities, and coincidences have become commonplace, and it is perhaps an index of the popularity of such novels in the latter part of the sixteenth century that 1597 marks the date of the first English translation of Achilles' novel: William Burton's *The most delectable & plesant historye of Clitophon and Leucippe*. Some twenty-five years later (1622) in France, Pierre du Ryer adapted the novel into a tragicomedy, *Clitophon and Leucippe*. More recently, Achilles has been represented as achieving his greatest impact on English literary history through the influence of his novel's generic ludicity and literary self-consciousness on writers such as Sterne, Fielding, and Richardson, and their postmodern successors. Alain Robbe-Grillet and Italo Calvino, for example, display a tendency toward generic experimentation as sustained and almost as precocious as that of Achilles.

The Date of the Novel

It is hard to be more precise than to date the novel to the second century CE. Papyri (one found in 1938, another as recently as 1989) show that *Leucippe and Clitophon* was in circulation then. It is usually thought to date to the latter part of that century, probably the last quarter, but Willis argues, from his dating of the Robinson–Cologne papyrus, for possibly not later than the middle of the second century.[6] The key to the novel's date has been sought in the text itself, but here the clues are equally tenuous. The incident with the *boukoloi* (4. 13) has led some to argue that Achilles is referring to a specific event in the war with those bandits which Cassius Dio reports occurred in 172 CE (71. 4. 1). This would place *Leucippe and Clitophon* after 172 CE, but skirmishes with the *boukoloi* were common throughout the second century, and there is no reason to

[6] W. H. Willis, 'The Robinson–Cologne Papyrus of Achilles Tatius', *Greek, Roman and Byzantine Studies*, 31 (1990), 73–102; see also M. Laplace, 'Achilleus Tatios, *Leucippe et Clitophon*: P. Oxyrhynchos 1250', *Zeitschrift für Papyrologie und Epigraphik*, 53 (1983), 53–9, and K. Plepelits, 'Achilles Tatius', in G. Schmeling (ed.), *The Novel in the Ancient World* (Leiden, 1996), 388–90.

believe Achilles was drawing upon one particular war. The claim that Achilles' representation of victorious Byzantines (7. 12) would not be possible had the author known of the city's catastrophe in 194 CE, and that thus the work must be earlier than that date, is equally literalist and unconvincing. Karl Plepelits suggests two reasons for placing the novel after the mid-second century CE. The first is the passage at 2. 18. 3, where it is mentioned that the men who have disguised themselves as women have shaved off their beards. This would only make sense, argues Plepelits, if men normally grew beards. It was not customary to wear a beard from about 300 BCE until the emperor Hadrian (117–38 CE) brought them back into fashion, which suggests a date for Achilles after the vogue had become well established. The second clue lies with the references to the Sun-Gate and the Moon-Gate in the description of Alexandria at the beginning of Book 5. This is the earliest reference to these gates and there are some indications—though it is not conclusive—that they were not known by these names until the mid-second century. Grasping at straws? Our inability to be more precise is frustrating, but what does seem clear is that Achilles wrote in the second century, a period when Greek prose fiction was at its height.

IMAGINATIVE GEOGRAPHY

Leucippe and Clitophon is an ambitious traveller's tale, symptomatic of the expanded horizons of the Roman Empire and its narratives. The characters traverse the Mediterranean, encountering the unknown and glimpsing a wider world. Their journey starts and ends in Phoenicia, travelling through Ionia and Egypt on the way (the towns and cities where they visit are marked on the Map, p. xl). The time in which the novel is set is unclear. It is obviously after the founding of Alexandria (332–1 BCE) and construction of the lighthouse on the island of Pharos (early third century BCE). Some argue for an Imperial setting, possibly that of the author's own time. To identify a specific date, however, seems to ask for too much detective work on the part of the reader, even taking into account that events with a contemporary resonance would have been more obvious to the original readers than to us now. Rather, it seems that the setting is designedly indeterminate.

Is the novel's fascination with other peoples and lands a celebration of diversity or a reaffirmation of Hellenic superiority? Many elements suggest the latter. All of the characters, whether they are natives of Phoenicia, Byzantium, Egypt, or Ephesus, speak in Greek, have Greek names, and demonstrate Greek *paideia* or culture. The exceptions are the *boukoloi*, the bandits who ambush Leucippe and Clitophon. They are described as 'terrifying savages. All were huge, black-skinned (not the pure black of the Indians, more as you would imagine a half-caste Ethiopian), bareheaded, light of foot but broad of body. They were all speaking a barbarian language' (3. 9). Bandits were a real threat in the Roman Empire. Tacitus describes how in Nero's reign the Cilician tribal chief Troxoboris fortified a mountain position, from which base his men launched an attack upon the city; cultivators, townspeople, and traders all suffered (*Annals* 12. 55). But to read Achilles' description as a reflection of reality is grossly to underplay his rhetoric of demonization. The *boukoloi* are caricatures, like other ethnocentric stereotypes of Egyptians elsewhere in the novel (eg at 4. 4: 'Thus it is with an Egyptian: in times of fear, cowardice leads him to servility'). Geographic and ethnographic descriptions reinforce this construction of the alterity of Egypt. The description of the Egyptian clod of earth emphasizes its difference and strangeness (3. 13, and cf. the description of the Nile's duplicity at 4. 12). Despite Achilles' being a native of Alexandria, he perpetuates the ethnocentric stereotypes of Egypt familiar from many centuries' construction of Greek self-definition against the 'barbarian'.

It is this type of construction that contributes to interpretations of Achilles Tatius and the other five so-called 'ideal' novels as an 'outlet for the cultural ideals and formulas of the elite, as another expression of their cultural hegemony'.[7] In ignoring Rome and recreating a nostalgic world where Greece, not Rome, was the supreme power, the novel is part of 'an assertion of Greekness in the form that was possible under Roman control, that is, in the cul-

[7] S. Swain, *Hellenism and Empire: Language, Classicism, and Power in the Greek World AD 50–250* (Oxford, 1996), 109.

tural arena'.[8] It is attractive to see the novel as a having a directed functionalist role, comparable to the role of Greek tragedy in Classical Athenian civic ideology. However, there are certain caveats. First, cultural identity was an extremely complex process in the second century CE, with bi- and multicultural identities rendering a 'Greek' response to 'Roman' rule too crude a formulation.[9] 'Greek' and 'Roman' were by no means always exclusive categories (and everyone living in Roman territory was granted Roman citizenship by the Severan decree in 211 CE). It is highly likely that Achilles Tatius was a Hellenized Roman Egyptian. Moreover, what constituted Greekness was a paraded concern in the literature of this period; it was a heightened time of testing cultural identities, sometimes undermining, sometimes reaffirming traditional categories.[10] It is also the case that focusing on 'Greek' and 'Roman' has tended to occlude other more local cultural affiliations, such as 'Phoenician'.

A Phoenician Tale

Leucippe and Clitophon are Phoenicians, their adventures begin and end in Phoenicia, and Phoenician customs and curiosities are a repeated thematic interest. This directs a reading of the novel as *Phoenicica*, 'Phoenician Tales'. It may even have been circulated under that title, like Lollianus' *Phoenicica*, which appears to have been a common type (Henrichs notes several local histories of the first and second centuries CE called *Phoenicica*;[11] and it was a standard formulation: cf. *Babyloniaca*, *Ephesiaca*, *Milesiaca*, *Aethiopica*). 'Phoenicia' refers to the land of the Phoenician people, which stretched along the East Mediterranean coast from modern Syria to the South Lebanon, and whose boundaries were flexible in

[8] Ibid. 412.

[9] Cf. the articles in S. Goldhill (ed.), *Being Greek Under Rome: Cultural Identity, the Second Sophistic and the Coming of Empire* (Cambridge, 2001).

[10] On the complexity of cultural formations during this period, see T. J. G. Whitmarsh, *Greek Literature and the Roman Empire: The Politics of Imitation* (Oxford, 2001).

[11] Claudius Iolaus, Herennius Philo, and Mochus: A. Henrichs, *Die Phoinikika des Lollianos* (Bonn, 1972), 11; cf. S. A. Stephens and J. J. Winkler, *Ancient Greek Novels: The Fragments* (Princeton, 1995), 314–25.

antiquity. The Phoenician people were also known as Canaanites, but their own name for themselves is unknown. Massively influential on early Greek culture, the Phoenicians were first to introduce alphabetic writing and played an important role in international trade. After the Persian Wars, Phoenicia gradually became Hellenized, a process which increased with Alexander the Great's conquests. By the time of Achilles' novel the cities were integrated into the Hellenistic *koine* or shared culture, but kept their language (Punic) and some of their cultural and religious distinctions. One of these is the purple dye industry for which the city of Tyre was renowned (one of the meanings of the word *phoenix* is 'purple-red'). The mythology behind the discovery of the dye is told by Achilles at 2. 11. Specifically Tyrian origins are also claimed for the introduction of wine to mankind (2. 2). This account highlights the fact that there are different versions of the myth: Attic and Tyrian. The telling of such stories is not simply a celebration of Greek *paideia*, but a striking creation of an alternative, paradedly *Phoenician*, tradition.

It has been observed that the description of the painting of the abduction of Europa at the beginning of the novel can be read through both Greek and Phoenician cultural filters. In Greek myth, Europa, descendant of Phoenix, the eponymous founder of the Phoenicians, was abducted by Zeus, king of the Greek gods, who had turned himself into a bull. The image of the girl on the bull was a popular motif in Greek iconography. However, the painting, which is viewed among the temple offerings in the temple of Astarte in Sidon, is doubly evocative of imagery of the Phoenician goddess who is regularly depicted on a bull, the symbol of her consort Baal. 'The text', argues Daniel L. Selden, 'strategically accomodates both possibilities, so that, depending on the reader's frame of reference, Hellenic or Phoenician, the image can be decoded in two opposing ways.'[12] Far from being univocally Hellenocentric, this line of interpretation suggests, the 'ideal reader' of Achilles Tatius is someone with both Phoenician and Greek perspectives.

Reading the novel as a collection of *Phoenicica* would also have been suggestive of the novel's sensationalist contents. Though the

---

[12] D. L. Selden, 'Genre of Genre', in Tatum (ed.), *Search for the Ancient Novel*, 51.

evidence is exiguous and usually from hostile Christian writers, Phoenicia was associated with sacred prostitution. Tyre and Byblos were reputedly centres for prostitution linked to the cult of the goddess Aphrodite (see Socrates, *Ecclesiastical History* 18 on the ritual defloration of Phoenician virgins, and Saint Augustine, *City of God* 4. 10 on the Phoenicians' prostitution of their daughters before marriage in honour of Venus). It is also suggested, though the evidence is equally questionable, that human sacrifice was practised in Phoenicia. There is material evidence of child sacrifice dating from the seventh to the second centuries BCE in the Tophet region at Carthage.[13] Among the repertoire of rumours in the *Augustan History* about the emperor Elagabalus, who was born in Phoenicia and ruled some time after *Leucippe and Clitophon* was written (218–22 CE), was that he sacrificed human beings (*Elagabalus* 81). Whether or not any of these representations had any basis in fact is less important than the fact that they became part of the mythology of Phoenicia. It is this myth, I suggest, that both Achilles Tatius and Lollianus draw upon to provide the seamier elements of their 'Phoenician Tales'. Both novels feature salacious sexual episodes and descriptions of human sacrifice. Reading *Leucippe and Clitophon* with an awareness of its cultural determinations invites reinterpretation of many details—what are we to make of the phoenix bird who exposes its 'unmentionables'? Or of Leucippe being called a whore?—and crucially illuminates the Phoenicianness of this 'Greek' novel.

STYLE AND SOPHISTRY

Achilles Tatius was writing during the time known as 'The Second Sophistic', the modern name for the cultural characteristics of the first three centuries CE, and which is increasingly used to denote that whole historical period. Sophists were itinerant teachers of knowledge and argument who first flourished in democratic Athens in the fifth century BCE. The term 'Second Sophistic' was originally coined by Philostratus, who uses it to refer to a style of

[13] S. Brown, *Late Carthaginian Child Sacrifice* (Sheffield, 1991).

oratory *in persona*: improvisations based on historical figures (*Lives of the Sophists* 481), but it has come to refer to the resurgence of interest in Greek education and values (*paideia*) under the Roman Empire. The forces behind this glorification of Greece are complex, but factors include increased economic prosperity as a result of the Pax Augusta, and the enthusiasm of Hellenomaniac emperors like Nero and Hadrian. That there was a marked interest in sophistry during this period is not in question, but 'Second Sophistic' is an unhelpful historiographical heuristic. 'Second', in particular, has pejorative associations: 'Sophistry: The Sequel' (same plot, cheaper sets, higher body count?). Many of the theories of the 'origins' of the ancient novel have been influenced by the ideology informing this periodization, and posit the novel as derivative of, or a degraded version of, other genres.[14] Like the novels of Longus and Heliodorus, *Leucippe and Clitophon* is conventionally called 'sophistic' because of its paraded *paideia* and ostentatious use of rhetoric. *Eros* (desire) itself, in Achilles' hands, becomes a sophist: 'a self-taught sophist' (1. 10) and a 'resourceful, improvising sophist' (5. 27 and cf. the note to 1. 10).

Platonic Pastiche

Leucippe and Clitophon draws quite substantially upon the concerns, ideas, and imagery of Plato's *Phaedrus* and *Symposium*, perhaps the two most important and influential discussions of *eros* in ancient Greek literature. *Symposium*, and in particular the character Aristophanes' aetiological tale of *eros*, with its themes of separation, search for, and reunion of lovers, has clearly influenced the narrative pattern of Achilles Tatius and, to varying degrees, the other Greek novelists.[15] The start of Clitophon's narration is preceded by a description of the physical environment where his story will be

[14] Space prevents me from discussing the origins of the novel, but interesting accounts may be found in Stephens and Winkler, *Ancient Greek Novels*, 11–18, and Doody, *True Story of the Novel*.

[15] M. Laplace, 'Études sur le roman d'Achille Tatius, *Leucippé et Clitophon*', unpublished doctoral dissertation, Paris (1988); R. L. Hunter, 'Longus and Plato', in M. Picone and B. Zimmerman (eds.), *Der antike Roman und seine mittelalterliche Rezeption* (Basel, 1997), 15–28.

told (1. 2). The grove, densely populated with thick plane trees, and with a stream of cold water as cool as freshly melted snow, recalls the setting of *Phaedrus*, one of Plato's most elaborate topographies, where Socrates and Phaedrus settle themselves in a place with plane trees and ice-cold water before they too embark on a discussion of *eros* (229a–259b). The novel dramatizes and explores the major concerns of *Phaedrus*—rhetoric, *eros*, and the form, unity and status of written communication.

A little later, Clitophon relates a dream which he had when he was 19 and his family were preparing for his marriage to his half-sister, Calligone (1. 3). In the dream, he appears to have merged into one body with Calligone from the navel downwards. A viraginous woman brandishing a sickle slices through where their flesh is joined, separating Clitophon from the girl. The division of the enjoined body into two separate entities by a splicing through the navel is reminiscent, albeit with a nightmarish twist, of the fable of the original androgyne told by Aristophanes in *Symposium*. Clitophon interprets this dream as prophetic, warning him of what the future holds. At the very outset of Clitophon's narration, then, the expectation is established that the events of his story will, in an imaginative way, correspond to those in Aristophanes' myth.

Leucippe and Clitophon is not, however, a straightforward vehicle for Platonic thought.[16] The novel is a Platonic pastiche, and the narrator Clitophon, whose very name is the title of a dialogue (most probably) written by Plato, shows himself to be 'cultivated' (*pepaideumenos*) even in the most extreme of circumstances. The parodic nature of much of this pastiche is not to be underestimated. On several occasions characters are described as philosophizing or being philosophers. Clitophon describes a discussion about seduction techniques as 'philosophizing about Eros' (1. 12), and later he calls Melite's powerful plea for him to make love with her 'a philosophical exposition' (5. 27). 'Philosophizing' in these two instances does not mean the lofty argumentation, but talking about how to get your beloved into bed. Elsewhere (5. 16; 5. 23; 6. 21; 8. 5) it is used to signify abstinence from sexual activity, a standard joke which played on philosophers' reputation for sexual restraint.

---

[16] As Laplace, 'Études . . .', argues.

These representations of philosophy constitute an irreverently comic frame for the philosophical intertexts. The humour does not preclude philosophical engagement with the text, but does militate against reading the novel as a straightforward philosophical allegory.

Language

Achilles Tatius' style varies widely, from terse, verbless sentences, to florid magniloquence. He writes mostly in Attic Greek: Greek which is stylistically and lexicographically correct according to fifth-century Athenian standards. Atticizing was in vogue in the second century CE, though Achilles is not consistent in his use of this dialect. The Byzantine intellectual Michael Psellus criticizes him for this: 'In certain passages he wishes to raise himself to full height; but he is like a man suffering from gout: he straightaway forgets the *orthios nomos* [correct method] and sticks to his usual habits. For this reason he gives the impression of making inexpert use of language to a considerable degree and of shooting far wide of the mark of Attic correctness.'[17]

Rather than 'inexpert use of language', Achilles' inconsistency should be seen as part of a deliberate eclecticism. His stilted use of strings of short sentences (*apheleia*), sequences of clauses of identical length (*isokola*); and sentences without verbs (*asyndeton*) is in the style associated with the sophist Gorgias. For example, the description of Sidon with which the novel opens begins with six short phrases with no verbs (Tim Whitmarsh naturally supplies 'is'). Also characteristic of sophistic rhetoric is epideictic ('display') oratory, for example Clitophon's 'tragic declamation' at 8. 5. The translation skilfully captures Achilles' mannered style, with frequent homeoteleuton ('similarity of endings'), for example, 'turning incantation into osculation' (2. 7), and elaborate use of alliteration: 'you see how it pounds, pumps and persistently palpitates . . .' (5. 27). Achilles is also fond of puns and wordplay. The translation

---

[17] Text and translation in A. R. Dyck (ed.), *Michael Psellus: The Essays on Euripides and George of Pisidia and on Heliodorus and Achilles Tatius* (Vienna, 1986), 74–7.

'I have seen the tomb of the unknown soldier, but not the groom with the unknown bride' brilliantly captures Melite's witty play on *kenotaphion* and *kenogamion* at 5. 14.

Structure, Description, Digression

Unlike the other surviving Greek novels, which are narrated in the third person, *Leucippe and Clitophon* is presented as Clitophon's auto-biographical narrative, told to the stranger he meets in a temple grove in Sidon. The stranger who begins the narrative remains anonymous; we have a first-person narration within a first-person narration. The narrative is carefully plotted to account for Clitophon's knowledge about other characters' adventures, but he is not always a trustworthy narrator. He gives a very partial account of the couple's misfortunes to Leucippe's father (8. 5), and omits any mention of his infidelity.

The novel is divided into eight books, which, unlike the book divisions in Homeric epic which are later additions, were most probably designed by the author. Book division allows Achilles to use the endings of books for rhetorical impact. Thus Book 2 ends with the debate on sexuality, Books 3 and 4 with descriptions of outrageous animals, and Book 6 with Leucippe's operatic defense of her virginity. One of the narrative's most striking features is its 'proclivity for the parenthetic',[18] the frequency with which the action is suspended and passages of description foregrounded over the story. These differ in form (for example, stories, fables, nuggets of sententious moralizing) and in theme (descriptions of places and objects, dreams, visual perception, animals and women), but are all too often lumped together and dismissed as 'digressions'. A survey of the sententious statements reveals that particular subjects are predominant: *eros*, vision, women, slaves, and barbarians. Sententious passages are overtly prescriptive, assuming a position of mastery over the object pronounced upon. It is telling that laws are laid down about women (not men), slaves, and barbarians, and

---

[18] S. Bartsch, *Decoding the Ancient Novel: The Reader and the Role of Description in Heliodorus and Achilles Tatius* (Princeton, 1989), 3.

that Clitophon often speaks sententiously but Leucippe never does. They often function, therefore, to assert male and Greek superiority, though on occasion this mastery is comically undermined.[19]

The description of a work of art (*ekphrasis*) is an especially popular motif in writing of this period, and was one of the many rhetorical devices taught to students of oratory. Together with the descriptions of vision and the eye, *ekphraseis* in Achilles Tatius are symptomatic of the Roman preoccupation with the visual. With its gladiatorial shows and chariot races, highly theatrical political debates, and emperors who played at being actors, Rome was the consummate 'theatricalised world'.[20] Certain of the objects described by Achilles are paralleled in Roman art. The crystal cup used at the festival of Dionysus whose glass changes colour—from green to red—when wine is poured into it (2. 3) functions like the Lycurgus cup, an exquisite carved goblet from the fourth century CE.[21] The *ekphrasis* of the painting of Perseus and Andromeda (3. 6–8) is evocative of the Capitoline relief of the same subject,[22] but is of particular interest as it is part of a 'painting with two levels', the other portraying Prometheus' punishment by the eagle. The two images are analysed together, 'the very first example of writing about art where two pictures are analysed as a diptych',[23] and thus form a significant episode for art historians.

In places the narrative appears aleatory, as if the author has surrendered the design of the novel,[24] but a closer reading reveals elaborate architecture. The descriptions of pictures and dreams 'are no mere rhetorical showpieces but forge playful and intricate connections with the narrative and its events'.[25] *Ekphraseis* and dreams function proleptically, encouraging the reader to anticipate

[19] For a much fuller discussion of sententiousness in the novels, see H. L. Morales, 'Sense and Sententiousness in the Ancient Greek Novels', in A. R. Sharrock and H. L. Morales (eds.), *Intratextuality: Greek and Roman Textual Relations* (Oxford, 2000).

[20] A. J. Boyle, *Tragic Seneca: An Essay in the Theatrical Tradition* (London and New York, 1997), 112–37.

[21] Photographed before and after being filled with wine in J. Elsner, *Imperial Rome and Christian Triumph* (Oxford, 1998), 48–9.

[22] Ibid. 182–3.

[23] S. Goldhill, *Foucault's Virginity: Ancient Erotic Fiction and the History of Sexuality* (Cambridge, 1995), 21.

[24] S. Nimis, 'The Prosaics of the Ancient Novel', *Arethusa*, 27: 3 (1994), 387–411.

[25] Bartsch, *Decoding the Ancient Novel*, 6–7.

and reinterpret important events in the story. For example, Leucippe's mother's dream of an intruder stabbing her daughter and slicing her from her genitals to her stomach appears to symbolize Leucippe having sex with Clitophon. However, it more literally anticipates the staged murder of Leucippe, where she is stabbed and her stomach lacerated with a knife. The narrative demands an active reader, alert to the conveyance and revision of meaning. Although the novel was initially written on papyrus rolls, it was among the first literary works to be copied onto a codex (leaves of papyrus or parchment bound together in book form), which by the time of the fourth century CE had become the predominant mode of disseminating writing. The codex made it much easier for a reader to look something up or refer back to a passage; it allowed for the sort of engagement with the intricacies of the narrative which Achilles Tatius (and later Heliodorus) requires.

The ending of the novel is a puzzle. At the beginning of the story, Clitophon is in Sidon, relating to the stranger his experiences of love. We are given no indication of why Leucippe is not with him or of how he came to be there and not in Byzantium, to where he is heading at the end of the narrative. The novel begins with the word 'Sidon' and ends with the word 'Byzantium', emphasizing this discrepancy. What has transpired between the events at the end of the novel and Clitophon's arrival in Sidon? Is Clitophon not living happily ever after? We never return to the opening frame and the unnamed narrator, who might be expected to comment on the story and thank Clitophon for telling it. There is no evidence that the original ending has been lost in the manuscript tradition, which would be a convenient, if unimaginative, solution to the difficulty. Nor is attributing the discrepancy to authorial amnesia or the stupidity of the readership (as critics have done) any answer. It is possible that Achilles is following the precedent of Plato's *Symposium*, which also does not return to its opening frame. It has also been suggested, less persuasively, that Clitophon was constrained by generic conventions according to which fictional autobiographical accounts told to strangers are always tales of hardship and suffering, never of happiness and success.[26] For whatever

[26] G. W. Most, 'The Strangers' Stratagem: Self-Disclosure and Self-Sufficiency in Greek Culture', *JHS* 109 (1989), 114–33.

reasons, the effect of the lack of satisfactory closure at the end of the novel is to keep the reader guessing—it is the sting in Achilles' 'swarm of stories'.

MELODRAMA AND MORALITY

For Friedrich Nietzsche, the Greek novels represent 'the final degradation of Greek literary art': 'They toy with the fact of mortality, they gratify our puerile wishes for personal immortality by showing victories of "good fortune" over that fact. In them, the old heroes, emblems of the human condition, become mere individuals, glorified bourgeois lovers rewarded with happy marriages.'[27] The Greek Tyche (like the Roman Fortuna), 'Chance' or 'Fortune' (not necessarily 'Good'), propels the action. She is the divine playwright of the action, 'scripting a new drama' (6. 3). An abstract deity, Tyche began to be anthropomorphized and worshipped widely in the Hellenistic world. She was adopted by cities as their protecting goddess, notably at Antioch, where Eutychides' impressive statue of Tyche was imitated on the coins and iconography of forty-four eastern cities.[28] If the narrative's vicissitudes illustrate the randomness of life, its ending, with the puzzles explained and loose ends tied up, suggests a more deterministic view of the world, a world ruled by Heimarmene, the Stoic concept of Fate. My comments about the Achilles' Stoic aspects are necessarily limited here; suffice it to note several common interests between Stoic writers and the novelists (e.g. marriage, erotic love, and visual perception). Achilles' ending can be read as a victory for Stoicism (though see the previous section on the problem of the ending): Tyche may write the plot, but it is Heimarmene who stages the grand finale.

It has been argued that the Greek romance novels document a social order greatly changed from that of the independent classical city-state, in which the Hellenistic city-dweller, lacking the strong civic identity of his classical counterpart, lived in a world run by

---

[27] Friedrich Nietzsche, *The Birth of Tragedy*, trans. Douglas Smith (Oxford, 2000), 109.
[28] S. Stewart, *Greek Sculpture, Volume 1* (New Haven and London, 1990), 201–2.

Tyche, a world of displacement, randomness, and lack of purpose. Achilles Tatius' focus on the individual ('mere individuals') adrift in the world reflects the isolation of Hellenistic man. However, not only has this isolation been overstressed, but it is important not to read the representation of individuals as betraying a lack of interest in the social and the civic. Indeed, it was common practice for 'terms of kinship and affection', such as marriage, to function as metonyms for the wider social order.[29] The novels' celebration of marriage functions as a celebration of the society whose continuing strength depends on such marriages. Leucippe's father, away fighting for the city of Byzantium, is said to be 'fighting for other men's marriages' (2. 42). The ultimate favouring of the couple who survive Tyche's capriciousness to be united in marriage symbolizes a social as well as an individual triumph.

Characterization

Modern readers may well find the characters in Achilles Tatius' novel irritatingly wooden, unindividuated stereotypes (the chaste heroine, the sexually predatory older woman, the bully, the cunning slave . . .). They lack interior depth, as their emotions are typically externalized and universalized. Like characters in some nineteenth-century melodramas, the cast of *Leucippe and Clitophon* are not psychologically complex, but are strongly characterized. It might be helpful to cast aside expectations of realism, as one might with a melodrama, and view the characters as embodiments of social and moral values. For example, Callisthenes, the rogue who kidnaps Calligone, is characterized as an *akolastos*, a profligate; he is typically spendthrift and impulsive. The *akolastos* is a recognizable type in New Comedy and in the novel. Callisthenes' remarkable change—by the end of the novel he is a reformed character—allows him to get the girl, and provides a cautionary tale against *akolasia*. Conops, the intrusive slave, is also a stereotype: he is a *polupragmon*, a snoop. Like Longus' Gnathon

[29] J. Perkins, *The Suffering Self: Pain and Narrative Representation in the Early Christian Era* (London and New York, 1995), 48.

('Jaws'), Conops is characterized by his large appetite; like Gnathon, he is a figure of fun. To some degree, then, the hyperbole and theatricality of the stereotypes distils the acting out of social relations.

However, readers have judged Melite, the older, sexually experienced woman who seduces Clitophon, as more realistic, more human, than her counterparts Lycaeneon in *Daphnis and Chloe* and Arsace in *Ethiopian Tales*. Indeed, there are touches of realism in Achilles Tatius, like Menelaus using Leucippe's menstrual period as an excuse for her to delay having sex with the pirate chief Charmides (4. 7), which give his narrative a closer affinity with Petronius' *Satyrica* than the other Greek romances. It has even been suggested that the elusive character Satyrus, who appears and disappears without warning and who stage-manages Clitophon's courtship, is a hint that the narrative is, among its many guises, another 'Tale from the Land of the Satyrs'.[30] Perhaps the most striking aspects of the characterization in *Leucippe and Clitophon* are the representations of the hero and heroine. Leucippe is a spirited and resolute heroine, in contrast to Clitophon's often gutless passivity. Leucippe starts out a willing lover, thwarted only by her mother's untimely intrusion, but after an injunction from the goddess Artemis to remain chaste until marriage, she becomes not just virgin, but extra-virgin, defending herself with all the defiance and display of a Christian martyr (6. 21–2).

A New Erotics?

The active role of Leucippe, and the similarities between the ordeals which she suffers and those which befall Clitophon, inform Michel Foucault's interpretation of the Greek novel in the third volume of his immensely influential *The History of Sexuality*, as evincing 'a new erotics', which 'organises itself around the symmetrical and reciprocal relationship of a man and woman, around the high value attributed to virginity, and around the

---

[30] G. Anderson, 'Archilles Tatius: A New Interpretation', in R. Beaton (ed.), *The Greek Novel AD* 1–1985 (London, 1988), 190–3.

complete union in which it finds perfection'.[31] This 'sexual symmetry' (the title of Konstan's development and criticism of Foucault's thesis)[32] is a significant shift from classical pederasty, which was characterized by the inequality of the relationship between the active male lover and his passive male beloved. The ancient novels, suggests Foucault, reflect a historical change in the Roman Empire; a move from pederasty to heterosexuality and from an asymmetrical to a symmetrical erotics. He is right that the novel's celebration of love and marriage broadly reflects the concern in this period to valorize heterosexual conjugality and to depreciate pederasty. However, it is also important not to reduce the complexities of the narrative nor to ignore its ludic and ironic qualities.[33] The homosexual relationships in Achilles Tatius do not play as big a role as the relationship between Leucippe and Clitophon, and their disastrously unhappy endings fashion them as cautionary tales. However, it is a distortion to say they are merely 'episodic and marginal themes'.[34] In fact, one of the most striking aspects of the sexuality debate (2. 35–8), the debate about who make better lovers, boys or women, is that, unlike similar debates (Plutarch, *Dialogue on Love* 3–9; Lucian, *On Love* 25–51), there is no final judgement; no one wins. The question as to which is the better sexual practice (anachronistically put, whether heterosexuality is better than homosexuality) is left open, an indeterminacy which gains increased punch from its position at the very end of the Book. It is also a moot point whether *Leucippe and Clitophon* can be read as an 'odyssey of double virginity'[35] without ignoring Clitophon's previous experience with prostitutes (2. 37, unparalleled in the other novels) and downplaying his 'therapeutic' sex with Melite: 'an honorable, minor lapse that Clitophon allowed himself'.[36] Rather, it seems that Achilles exhibits a comic disregard for any pious laudation of chastity and virginity. Before the intervention of the goddess Isis, Leucippe seemed willing to have sex with Clitophon, and Melite only

---

[31] M. Foucault, *The Care of the Self: The History of Sexuality, Volume 3*, trans. R. Hurley (London, 1986), 228, 232.

[32] D. Konstan, *Sexual Symmetry: Love in the Ancient Novel and Related Genres* (Princeton, 1994).

[33] Cf. Goldhill, *Foucault's Virginity*.   [34] Foucault, *The Care of the Self*, 229.

[35] Ibid. 230.   [36] Ibid. 231.

passes the chastity test in the River Styx on a technicality. Moreover, the inequality of focalization, as the events are narrated from Clitophon's point of view, militates against any true 'symmetry'.

It is through the limited perspective of the first-person narration that the novel's most disturbing scenes are relayed. The reader watches, with Clitophon, as Leucippe is butchered and her guts roasted and eaten (3. 15). Later he watches her being beheaded and retrieves and embraces her headless corpse: 'I am holding the leftovers of your body' (5. 7). False deaths are also staged in Lollianus, the Pseudo-Lucianic *Ass*, Apuleius, and Petronius, but Achilles excels in Grand Guignol grotesquerie. 'Snuff' displays are very Roman. They form part of the repertoire of deadly dramas enacted in the amphitheatre, when prisoners were tortured and killed while acting out mythological scenes. Even though Leucippe survives these dramas, she does so in the second 'false death' only at the expense of another woman's death: a prostitute is killed in her stead. The fact that the woman was a prostitute and that her death affords only a passing expression of regret is part of the novel's bourgeois elitism: real prostitutes and slaves do not fare well in Achilles Tatius.

Violence and voyeurism also characterize the dreams, *ekphraseis*, and myths told throughout *Leucippe and Clitophon*.[37] Containing much of this material in inset narratives is one way of allowing it to be disavowed ('just a digression . . .'). This appears to have been part of a (Christian) reading strategy which sought to rehabilitate Achilles Tatius. Two thirteenth-century manuscripts of *Leucippe and Clitophon* contain part or whole of the following epigram (also found in the *Palatine Anthology* 9. 203, where it is attributed to Photius or Leon the Philosopher):

> The story of Clitophon shows
> A bitter love, but a virtuous life.
> The most virtuous life of Leucippe
> Astonishes everyone. How she was beaten,
> Shaven and abused,
> And the ultimate, suffered death three times.

[37] For Achilles' complex configurations of the gaze, see H. L. Morales, *Vision and Narrative in Achilles Tatius* (Cambridge, forthcoming).

> If you too wish to be virtuous, my friend,
> Do not look at the images which surround the story,
> But first learn of its outcome,
> For it joins in marriage those who loved wisely.

The injunction not to 'look at the images which surround the story' makes it clear that to read Achilles Tatius as a morality tale involves wearing blinkers. Otherwise, the sexualized violence and associations between marriage and rape contained in the *ekphraseis*, dreams, and myths threaten to taint the narrative's happy ending.

One Christian storyteller appears not only to have read the novel as a 'most virtuous life' but also to have created his own version of what 'happily ever after' might involve for Leucippe and Clitophon:

In the northern parts of Phoenicia, lying amongst the many towns pressed up against Mount Lebanon to the south and the north, was a town which stood apart from the rest: Emesa. There, born and bred, lived a man called Clitophon, distinguished for his family wealth, second to none amongst his fellow citizens and, in intelligence, sharper by far than others. He had, moreover, a wife called Leucippe who was, in all else, a woman befitting such a husband—upright in character and unsurpassed in the exceptional beauty of her appearance—except for one thing alone: she was unfortunately sterile. Because of this she was being constantly subjected to reproaches from her husband and so lived in a state of misery, careworn and wishing all manner and means of deliverance from these bonds.[38]

Deliverance comes in the shape of a Christian monk, Onouphrios, who baptizes her. Leucippe immediately falls pregnant, and when her son, Galaction, is born, she dedicates him to Christ. When he reaches maturity, Galaction meets a young woman called Episteme whom he converts to Christianity. They spend their time preaching the word of Christ, but are persecuted for their beliefs. Tortured to death, they become martyrs. The ultimate happy ending—of sorts—in the 'most virtuous life' of Leucippe and Clitophon.

---

[38] *Patrologia Graeca* 116. 94, translated in S. MacAlister, *Dreams and Suicides: The Greek Novel from Antiquity to the Byzantine Empire* (London and New York, 1996), 110–11.

Many thanks indeed to Joseph Smith of San Diego State University for designing the map, and to Anthony Boyle, Tim Whitmarsh, and the anonymous reader for the press for their helpful comments and suggestions.

Note on the Translation

This is the second English translation of *Leucippe and Clitophon* to appear in the last fifteen years. Some may question the need for a new translation, when Jack Winkler's brilliant, flamboyant rendering has already made it unnecessary for readers to trudge through the Loeb edition's flat and occasionally inaccurate prose.[1] With the ultimate aim of creating a fluently readable 'version' of the text, Winkler allows himself a very free rein, omitting or adapting difficult phrases, sneaking in new jokes and references to contemporary literature, and even at times outpunning Achilles. This translation has a different set of aims. Not that it lays claim to greater 'accuracy': any translation that traverses the vast chasms of cultural and linguistic difference lying between ancient Greek and millennial English necessarily fashions a new text. All translation is appropriation. This statement, however, does not entail the conclusion that 'anything goes'. The challenge of rendering ancient Greek in English is to respect the 'otherness' of the original, to keep alive the ongoing dialectic between the expectations of a modern novel-reading audience and the bizarre (and occasionally unpalatable) idiom of its ancient forebear. The present translation does not claim to be 'closer' to the original, but it does resist the temptation to smooth out Achilles' literary texture into a belles-lettristic patois, seeking instead to convey the genuine oddness of one of antiquity's most conspicuously cracked geniuses. Where Achilles' prose style goes over the top into hackneyed absurdity, so does this translation; where it goes through a bald patch, so does this; where it is crabbed and awkward, so is this.

I have, moreover, sought to provide English equivalents for Achilles' puns (where I have been frustrated, I have indicated this

---

[1] J. J. Winkler, *Achilles Tatius, Leukippe and Kleitophon*, in B. P. Reardon (ed.), *Collected Ancient Greek Novels* (Berkeley, 1989); S. Gaselee, *Achilles Tatius* (Cambridge, Mass, 1917, rev. 1984).

in the notes). For the awfulness of some of these, I crave the reader's indulgence. With literary students in mind, I have also endeavoured to retain as much consistency of vocabulary as possible to mark the webs of metaphor and theme spun across the text. One area where this has been extremely difficult is in the translation of the sexual vocabulary. For *eros*, the Greek word meaning 'lust/desire/passion', 'love' is the obvious, but inadequate, English equivalent. 'Love' denotes an inwardly motivated, creative force of benevolent attachment to another; *eros* is a violent, destructive passion that strikes a person from outside, causing her or him to experience a profound sexual longing for another. At times, though, Achilles' use of the vocabulary of *eros* does convey feelings of tenderness and consideration. For this reason, it is impossible to use the same English word for *eros* in every instance: 'desire' is the most frequent translation, but 'passion' and 'love' do also put in appearances. *Eros*, moreover, is also the god Eros: the phrase '*eros* gripped her' could refer either to a sudden passion or to a visitation of the god, and Achilles constantly elides the distinction between the two. (Greek literary texts of Achilles' age did not use capitalization to distinguish between proper names and nouns.) Similarly, the language of virginity, marriage, and adultery is impossible to render accurately. The primary referent of the word *parthenos* is an unmarried young woman, a 'maiden'; but an unmarried girl ought, in ancient Greek culture, to be sexually inexperienced, and so the word also means 'virgin'. Achilles employs the word in both senses, and exploits the ambiguity (and also experiments with the extraordinary—to ancient Greeks—notion of a male *parthenos*: see 5. 20; 8. 5). Similarly, *gamein*, 'to marry', is used in the sense of 'to have sex with'. In such cases, I have simply done my best to convey ambiguities and plays on words.

Although the division of the text into eight books was (probably) the choice of the author, the subdivision of the eight books into numbered chapters was not. The chapter numbers are retained here for ease of reference rather than as a guide to units of sense. In fact, the subdivisions are at times fairly arbitrary, and this translation frequently buries the transition to a new chapter in the middle of a paragraph. The Greek text on which this translation is based is that of Garnaud, but I have consulted Vilborg's extensively, and have been rather eclectic in my choice of readings (specialists will have little difficulty spotting the deviations from Garnaud).[2]

I am extremely grateful to those who have read the translation in its entirety and commented on it, and in particular to Richard Hunter, Julie Lewis, and Helen Morales.

[2] J.-P. Garnaud, *Achille Tatius d'Alexandrie, Le Roman de Leucippé et Clitophon* (Paris, 1991); E. Vilborg, *Achilles Tatius, Leucippe and Clitophon* (Göteborg, 1962; Stockholm, 1965).

Select Bibliography

This bibliography contains works referred to in the Introduction and some suggestions for further reading. It makes no claims to completeness: for a fuller bibliography on Achilles see Helen Morales, *Vision and Narrative in Achilles Tatius* (Cambridge, forthcoming). *The Petronian Society Newsletter*, edited by Gareth Schmeling, gives updated bibliographies, book reviews, and news items about the ancient novels. It can be accessed at www.chss.montclair.edu/classics/petron/NGPSNNOVEL.HTML.

The most usable Greek text of Achilles Tatius is the Budé edition of J.-P. Garnaud, *Achille Tatius d'Alexandrie. Le Roman de Leucippé et Clitophon* (Paris, 1991), and there is an excellent lexicon by J. N. O'Sullivan, *A Lexicon to Achilles Tatius* (Berlin and New York, 1980).

Anderson, G., *The Second Sophistic: A Cultural Phenomenon in the Roman Empire* (London and New York, 1993).

Bakhtin, M., *The Dialogic Imagination: Four Essays*, ed. Michael Holquist; trans. Caryl Emerson and Michael Holquist (Michigan, 1981).

Bartsch, S., *Decoding the Ancient Novel: The Reader and the Role of Description in Heliodorus and Achilles Tatius* (Princeton, 1989).

Bowersock, G. W., *Fiction as History* (Berkeley and Los Angeles, 1994).

Bowie, E., 'The Readership of Greek Novels in the Ancient World', in Tatum (ed.), *The Search for the Ancient Novel*, 435–59.

—— and Harrison S. J., 'The Romance of the Novel', *Journal of Roman Studies* (1993), 159–78.

Boyle, A. J., *Tragic Seneca: An Essay in the Theatrical Tradition* (London and New York, 1997).

Brown, S., *Late Carthaginian Child Sacrifice* (Sheffield, 1991).

Cooper, K., *The Virgin and the Bride: Idealized Womanhood in Late Antiquity* (Cambridge, Mass. and London, 1996).

Doody, M. A., *The True Story of the Novel* (London, 1996).

Dyck, A. R. (ed.), *Michael Psellus: The Essays on Euripides and George of Pisidia and on Heliodorus and Achilles Tatius* (Vienna, 1986).

Eco, U., *The Island of the Day Before* (= *L'Isola del Giorno Prima*), trans. William Weaver (London, 1995).

Egger, B. M., 'Women in the Greek Novel: Constructing the Feminine', unpublished dissertation, U. of California at Irvine (1990).

Elsner, J., *Imperial Rome and Christian Triumph* (Oxford, 1998).

Foucault, M., *The Care of the Self: The History of Sexuality, Volume 3*, trans. R. Hurley (London, 1986); = *Le Souci de Soi* (Paris, 1984).

Fusillo, M., *Il Romanzo Greco: Polifonia ed Eros* (Venice, 1989).

Goldhill, S., *Foucault's Virginity: Ancient Erotic Fiction and the History of Sexuality* (Cambridge, 1995).

—— (ed.), *Being Greek Under Rome: Cultural Identity, the Second Sophistic and the Coming of Empire* (Cambridge, 2001).

Hägg, T., *The Novel in Antiquity* (Oxford, 1983).

Henrichs, A., *Die Phoinikika des Lollianos* (Bonn, 1972).

Hunter, R. L., 'Longus and Plato', in M. Picone and B. Zimmerman (eds.), *Der antike Roman und seine mittelalterliche Rezeption* (Basel, 1997), 15–28.

Konstan, D., *Sexual Symmetry: Love in the Ancient Novel and Related Genres* (Princeton, 1994).

Laplace, M., 'Achilleus Tatios, *Leucippé et Clitophon*: P. Oxyrhynchos 1250' *Zeitschrift für Papyrologie und Epigraphik*, 53 (1983), 53–9.

—— 'Études sur le roman d'Achille Tatius, *Leucippe et Clitophon*', unpublished doctoral dissertation, Paris (1998).

MacAlister, S., *Dreams and Suicides: The Greek Novel from Antiquity to the Byzantine Empire* (London and New York, 1996)

Morales, H. L., 'The Taming of the View: Natural Curiosities in *Leukippe and Kleitophon*', *Groningen Colloquia on the Novel*, vol. 6 (1995), 39–50.

—— 'Constructing Gender in Musaeus' *Hero and Leander*', in Richard Miles (ed.), *Constructing Identity in Late Antiquity* (Routledge, 1999), 41–69.

—— 'Sense and Sententiousness in the Ancient Greek Novels', in A. R. Sharrock and H. L. Morales (eds.), *Intratextuality: Greek and Roman Textual Relations* (Oxford, 2000), 67–88.

Morgan, J. R., 'Make-believe and Make Believe: The Fictionality of the Greek Novels', in C. Gill and T. P. Wiseman (eds.), *Lies and Fiction in the Ancient World* (Exeter, 1993), 175–229.

—— 'The Greek Novel: Towards a Sociology of Production and Reception', in A. Powell (ed.), *The Greek World* (London, 1995), 130–52.

—— and R. Stoneman (eds.), *Greek Fiction: The Greek Novel in Context* (London and New York, 1994).

Most, G. W., 'The Strangers' Stratagem: Self-Disclosure and Self-Sufficency in Greek Culture', *JHS* 109 (1989), 114–33.

Nietzsche, F., *The Birth of Tragedy* (= *Geburt der Tragödie*), trans. Douglas Smith (Oxford, 2000).

Nimis, S., 'The Prosaics of the Ancient Novel', *Arethusa*, 27: 3 (1994), 387–411.

Perkins, J., *The Suffering Self: Pain and Narrative Representation in the Early Christian Era* (London and New York, 1995).

Plazenet, L., *L'Ébahissement et la délectation. Reception comparée et poétiques du roman grec en France et en Angleterre aux XVIe et XVIIe siécles* (Paris, 1997).

Plepelits, K., 'Achilles Tatius', in G. Schmeling (ed.), *The Novel in the Ancient World* (Leiden, 1996), 387–416.

Reardon, B. P., *The Form of Greek Romance* (Princeton, 1991).

—— (ed.), *The Collected Ancient Greek Novels* (Berkeley, 1989).

Selden, D. L., 'Genre of Genre', in Tatum (ed.), *The Search for the Ancient Novel*, 39–64.

Stephens, S. A., 'Who Read Ancient Novels?', in Tatum (ed.), *The Search for the Ancient Novel*, 405–18.

—— and J. J. Winkler, *Ancient Greek Novels: The Fragments* (Princeton, 1995).

Stewart, S., *Greek Sculpture, vol. 1* (New Haven and London, 1990).

Swain, S., *Hellenism and Empire: Language, Classicism and Power in the Greek World, AD 50–250* (Oxford, 1996).

Tatum, J. (ed.), *The Search for the Ancient Novel* (Baltimore and London, 1994).

Vilborg, E., *Achilles Tatius: Leucippe and Clitophon* (Stockholm, 1955).

—— *Achilles Tatius: Leucippe and Clitophon. A Commentary* (Goteborg, 1962).

Whitmarsh, T. J. G., *Greek Literature and the Roman Empire: The Politics of Imitation* (Oxford, 2001).

Willis, W. H., 'The Robinson–Cologne Papyrus of Achilles Tatius', *Greek, Roman and Byzantine Studies*, 31 (1990), 73–102.

Chronology of the Ancient Novel

Dates are all CE, and most are necessarily estimates.

GREEK

early 1st cent.?	Anon., *Ninus and Semiramis* (fragmentary).
1st cent.?	Chariton, *Chaereas and Callirhoe*
	Anon., *Letters of Chion*
	Anon., *Joseph and Aseneth.*
2nd cent.?	Xenophon of Ephesus, *Ephesian Tales*
	Anon., *Acts of Paul*
	Achilles Tatius, *Leucippe and Clitophon.*
late 2nd cent.?	Longus, *Daphnis and Chloe*
	Antonius Diogenes, *The Incredible Things Beyond Thule* (fragmentary).
3rd cent.?	Anon., *The Clement Romance.*
late 4th cent.?	Heliodorus, *Ethiopian Tales.*

The following cannot be dated with any confidence at all:

> Lollianus, *Phoenician Tales*
> Anon., *Tinouphis*
> Anon., *Daulis*
> Anon., *Iolaus*
> 'Dares of Troy', *History of the Destruction of Troy.*

LATIN

1st cent.?	'Dictys of Crete', *The Diary of the Trojan War.*
mid-1st cent.?	Petronius, *Satyrica.*
2nd cent.	Apuleius, *Metamorphoses* (*The Golden Ass*).
3rd cent.?	Anon., *The Story of Apollonius, Prince of Tyre.*

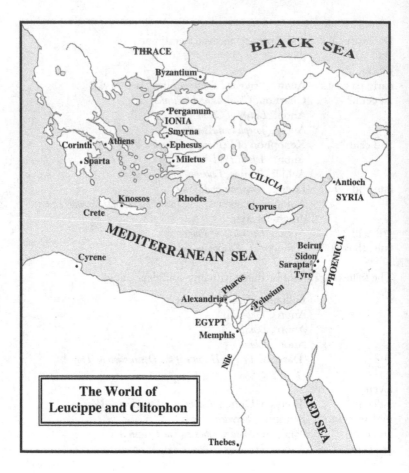

THRACE

BLACK SEA

Byzantium

Pergamum
IONIA
Smyrna
Ephesus
Miletus

Corinth Athens
Sparta

CILICIA

Antioch

SYRIA

Knossos Rhodes

Cyprus

Crete

MEDITERRANEAN SEA

Beirut
Sidon
Sarapta
Tyre

PHOENICIA

Cyrene

Pharos

Alexandria Pelusium

EGYPT
Memphis

Nile

RED SEA

The World of
Leucippe and Clitophon

Thebes

Achilles Tatius
Leucippe and Clitophon

Book 1

[1] Sidon is a city on the sea. The sea is the Assyrian,° the city is the Phoenicians' mother-city, and its people fathered the Thebans.° In the folds of a bay lies a twin harbour, broad and gently enclosing the sea: where the bay bellies out down the flank of the coast on the right, another mouth has been carved out, an alternative channel for the influx of the tide. Thus a second harbour is born from the first, so that trading vessels can winter there in the calm, while they can pass the summer in the outer part of the bay.

It was there that I arrived, a survivor of a severe storm. When I had made my thank-offerings for my rescue to the Phoenicians' goddess (whom the Sidonians call Astarte°), I undertook a tour of the rest of the city, and was browsing among the sacred dedications when I saw a votive picture,° a landscape and seascape in one. The picture was of Europa, the sea was the Phoenician, and the land Sidon. On the side of the land was a meadow and a troupe of maidens; in the sea a bull was gliding over the surface, and a beautiful maiden was seated on his back, sailing on the bull towards Crete. The meadow° was matted with a multitude of flowers, and a phalanx of trees and bushes intermingled with them. The trees were clasped together, and their leaves were intertwined; the branches coupled their foliage with one another, and the embrace of the foliage formed a vault over the flowers.

The artist had also depicted the shade under the leaves, and here and there the sun gently trickled through down onto the meadow, wherever the painter had parted the thatch of the leaves. The entire meadow was bounded at its perimeter, garlanded by the leafy vault. The flower-beds had been allowed to grow in rows under the leaves of the foliage: narcissi, roses, and myrtle. Water was streaming from the middle of the pictorial meadow, some spurting up from beneath the soil, and some dribbling around the blooms and bushes. A man was pictured° using a mattock to irrigate the soil, hunched over one trench and opening a channel for the stream. At the edge of the meadow, on the parts of the land that jutted out into the sea, the artist had arrayed the maidens. The maidens' mien betrayed at once pleasure and terror. Wreathes were bound around their temples, but their hair ran loose down over their shoulders. Their legs were entirely bare, with no skirts around their calves (girdles drew their skirts up to the knee), nor sandals on their feet. Their faces were wan, their cheeks set in a half-smile, and their eyes stared wide open towards the sea. Their mouths gaped a little, as if they were actually about to give out a shriek of terror, and their arms were outstretched towards the bull. They were stepping into the edge of the sea, enough for the wave to lap over their feet a little; they seemed both to desire to pursue the bull and to fear to enter the sea.

The colour of the sea was twofold, reddish towards the land and deep blue towards the open sea. There was spume portrayed, and also crags and waves: the crags stood proud of the land, spume whitened the crags, the wave climaxed and dissolved into spume around the crags. The bull was depicted cresting the waves in the middle of the sea, while the wave rose like a mountain where the bull flexed his bulging limb. The maiden sat in the middle of the bull's back, not astride him but side-saddle, keeping her feet together on his right. She clasped his horn with her left hand, as a charioteer would the reins, and the bull inclined a little in that direction, steered by the pressure of her hand. A tunic enveloped her upper body, down to her most intimate part; from there down, a skirt concealed the lower parts of her body. The tunic was white, and the skirt was purple. Her body was just about visible through her clothing: her navel was deep, her belly taut, her waist slender, and the slenderness gave way to broadness towards her loins. Her breasts protruded gently from her chest (the girdle that fastened her tunic enclosed her breasts, but the tunic mirrored her body). Her hands were each at full stretch, one on his horn and the other on his tail, and with these she gripped either end of her veil, which was spread out above her head, encircling her shoulders. The folds of her cloak were taut, bulging in every direction (and that was how the artist depicted the wind). She was seated on the bull as if on a ship at sea, using her cloak as if it were a sail.

Dolphins were dancing around the bull, cupids were playing. You might have said that the picture was even moving. Eros was leading the bull: Eros, represented as a little boy, had unfurled his wings and strapped on his quiver, and was wielding his torch. He was turned towards Zeus, smiling surreptitiously as though mocking him because it was he who had caused Zeus to turn into a bull.

[2] I admired the whole of the picture, but, being myself under the influence of Eros, I inspected Eros leading the bull with particular attention.

'What power that boy wields over heaven, earth and sea!'° I exclaimed.

At these words of mine, a young man also standing nearby spoke up:

'Yes, I should know! Eros has dealt me enough blows.'

'What blows would they be, my friend?' I asked. 'To judge by the look of you, it is not long since your initiation into the god's cult.'

'That is a swarm of stories° that you are stirring up,' he said. 'My tale is like a fictional adventure.'

'Do not hold back,' I cried, 'I beg you, by Zeus and by Eros himself! It will give me all the more pleasure if your tale is indeed like fiction.'

And with these words, I took him by the hand and led him to a neighbouring grove,° where the plane trees grew thick and plentiful, and the water flowed by cool and clear, just as it comes from freshly melted snow. I sat him down there on a low bench, and sat myself next to him.

'Well, it is time to hear your story,' I said. 'A setting such as this is delightful, and just right for erotic fiction.'

[3] This is how he began:

I am of Phoenician stock, my fatherland is Tyre, and my name is Clitophon. My father is called Hippias, and his brother is called Sostratus, although they are only brothers to the extent that they share a father (my uncle's mother was from Byzantium, and my father's from Tyre). Now this uncle, who inherited a large estate from his mother, spent his whole life in Byzantium. My father lived in Tyre. I never knew my mother: she died when I was young. As a result, my father took another wife, who bore my sister Calligone.

And although my father wanted to bring us two closer by marrying us to one another, the Fates, who rule over mortals, were saving another wife for me . . .

The gods often like to reveal the future to mortals at night, not so that we might deliver ourselves from suffering (for destiny is insuperable), but so that we might endure such suffering more easily: a sudden and unexpected onset tends to paralyse and submerge the soul with the immediacy of its attack, whereas that which is foreseen before it strikes dissipates in advance through gradual familiarization the full force of the pain. When I was in my nineteenth year, and my father was preparing to celebrate our nuptials the following year, Fortune set the drama in motion. I had a dream in which my lower parts were fused up to the navel with those of my bride, while from there we had separate upper bodies. A huge, terrifying woman with a savage countenance appeared: her eyes were bloodshot, her cheeks rugged, and her hair made of snakes.° She was wielding a sickle in her right hand, and a torch in the other. This creature attacked me with furious passion: raising her sickle she brought it down on my loins, where the two bodies were joined, and lopped off my bride.

Although I jumped out of bed in terror at this shock, I told no one; privately, though, I was filled with grim foreboding. Then the following events took place. As I said, my father had a brother, Sostratus, and a messenger came from him with a letter from Byzantium, with the following words:

From Sostratus to his brother Hippias: greetings! My daughter Leucippe and my wife Panthea are on their way to you, for a war with the Thracians is pressing the Byzantines. Please keep my family's most treasured assets safe until the war is decided.

[4] When my father read this, he leapt up and ran out of the house in the direction of the sea. A little later he returned, followed by an enormous throng of slaves and serving-girls, whom Sostratus had sent to accompany the women. In their midst was a tall woman, expensively dressed. When I had aimed the shafts of my eyes at her, a maiden on her left suddenly came into my view, and the vision of her face struck my eyes like lightning. She looked like a picture I had once seen of Selene° on a bull: her eyes were bliss-

fully brilliant; her hair was blonde, curling blonde; her brows were black, unadulterated black; her cheeks were white, a white that blushed towards the middle, a blush like the purple pigment used by a Lydian woman to dye ivory.° Her mouth was like the bloom of a rose, when the rose begins to part the lips of its petals.

As soon as I saw, I was done for: beauty pricks sharper than darts, and floods down through the eyes to the soul (for the eye is the channel of the wounds of desire). All kinds of reactions possessed me at once: admiration, awe, terror, shame, shamelessness. I admired her stature, I was awestruck by her beauty, I was terrified in my heart, I gazed without shame, I felt ashamed at having been captivated so. I tried to force myself to tug my eyes away from the girl, but they resisted, tugging themselves back there again, as if towed by the lure° of beauty. In the end, the eyes won.

[5] The women took their lodgings in our house. My father made over part of the house to them, then saw about supper. When it was time, my father had arranged it so that we were drinking together on couches that had been allotted in twos: he and I on the middle couch, the two mothers on the left, and the maidens on the right. When I heard of this splendid arrangement, I almost ran up to my father and kissed him for placing the maiden on the couch under my eyes. With the gods as my witnesses, I had no idea what I ate: I was like someone eating in a dream. Once I had rested my elbow on the couch and reclined, my entire gaze was focused upon the girl, although I tried at the same time to be surreptitious as I gazed. And that constituted my dinner.

When we had finished our dinner, a slave, a servant of my father's, tuned up his lyre and entered. At first, he began to play the strings by twanging them loudly with his bare hands, but then he softened the tune a little, his fingers whispering over the strings. After this, he now began to sound the strings with a plectrum, and after a short burst on the lyre, he sang to the melodies. He sang Apollo's reproach to Daphne° for resisting his advances, and of how he pursued her, and was on the point of seizing her when the girl metamorphosed into a shrub, and of how Apollo wreathed himself with the shrub's leaves. This song inflamed my soul all the more, for erotic stories fuel the appetite. Even if you school yourself into self-control, an example incites you to imitate it, especially when that example is a divine one; in which case, any shame that you feel at your moral errors becomes an outspoken affront to the station of a higher being. This was how I counselled myself: 'You see, Apollo too desires, and he too desires a maiden. *He* feels no shame at his lust, but hunts the maiden; whereas *you*, you are hesitant and embarrassed, and you practise an untimely self-control. Do you think yourself superior to a god?'

[6] When evening came around, the women went off to sleep first, and we men a little later. The others had measured their bliss by their bellies;° but I departed savouring the banquet of my eyes, stuffed with the girl's face, and drunken with desire,° having sated myself with undiluted gazing. When I reached the room where I generally passed the night, I could not get to sleep,° either. To be sure, it is a rule of nature that diseases and bodily wounds are more painful by night and besiege us all the more when we are resting, stirring our sufferings (for the wound has the leisure to fester when the body is at rest).° But wounds of the soul are much more traumatic when the body is still. For, while by day the eyes and the ears are encumbered by multiple distractions and mitigate the full force of the disease, diverting the soul and depriving it of the leisure to suffer, when the body is restrained in rest, the soul, now alone, is tossed on the waves of ruin. All the emotions hitherto dormant burst out: the woes of the grieving, the cares of the troubled, the fears of the endangered, the fire of lovers. Around dawn, sleep took grudging pity on me, and granted me a little respite, although even then the girl would not leave my soul. All my dreams were of Leucippe. I was talking with her, frolicking with her, eating with her, touching her, and having more successes than I did by day: for I even kissed her, and the kiss was real, so that I set about abusing the slave for his ill-timed attempts to wake me and for having spoilt so sweet a dream.

When I arose, I deliberately began to amble around the inner parts of the house in full view of the girl. All the while I held a book, and hunched over it to read; but whenever I reached her door, I peeked up surreptitiously. After several circuits of the course I had drenched myself with desire° thus inspired by the sight of her, and I left with a sickness in my soul. For three days, those fires of mine blazed.

[7] I had a cousin Clinias, an orphan, young, but two years older than myself. He had been initiated into the cult of Eros, and the object of his desire was a boy. He competed so vigorously for the boy's affection that, when the latter had gazed in admiration at a horse Clinias had bought, he actually gratified him and gave it to him there and then. For this reason, I used to tease him mercilessly for his irresponsibility, in that he wasted his time with love, and that he was enslaved to erotic pleasure. He used to smile at me and shake his head, saying, 'Mark my words, you too will be a slave one day.'

It was straight to him that I went.° I greeted him and sat down beside him.

'Clinias,' I said, 'I have given you satisfaction for my teasing: I too have been enslaved.'

At this, he clapped his hands and burst out laughing; then he stood up and kissed my face, which showed all the signs of a lover's sleeplessness.

'You are in love,' he said, 'you truly are in love. Your eyes tell the whole story.'

As soon as he had spoken, Charicles (that was his boyfriend's name) came running up in distress.

'Oh Clinias,' he said, 'I am done for!'

Clinias joined in his wailing, as if he were a mere extension of his boyfriend's soul. With a tremulous voice, he spoke:

'Speak up: your silence will kill me! What is your trouble? Whom must we fight?'

'My father is arranging a marriage for me,' said Charicles, 'and, what is more, a marriage to an ugly girl, which doubles the trouble I must live with. After all, a woman is a wretched thing, even if she be pretty; but if she be cursed with ugliness too, the trouble is doubled. But my father is eager to bond the families because he is eyeing up their money. Oh, woe is me! I am being engaged to her wealth, to be sold into marriage!'

[8] On hearing these words, Clinias now turned pale. He began to beg the lad to refuse the marriage, slandering the entire female species:°

'Is your father already giving you up to marriage? What crime have you committed to justify such bondage? Do you not know the words of Zeus:

I shall give mankind a bane in exchange for fire, wherewith all
Might rejoice in their hearts, embracing their bane?°

'Such is the pleasure provided by women, which has similar
properties to the Sirens:° women too kill with the pleasure of their
song. You can gauge the scale of the evil from the very trappings of
the wedding: the cacophony of the flutes, the crashing of doors, the
waving of torches. Anyone who observed such a fracas would say,
"The poor, unfortunate groom! It looks to me as if he is being sent
off to war!"

'If you were an uncultured bumpkin, you would not know of the
plays about women. But *you*, you could even lecture others about
all the lying fictions with which women have filled the stage:
Eriphyle's necklace, Philomela's banquet, Sthenoboea's slander,
Aerope's theft, Procne's murder.° If Agamemnon desires the
beauty of Chryseis, he brings a plague down on the Greeks; if
Achilles desires the beauty of Briseis, he procures his own suffering;
and if Candaules has a beautiful wife, Candaules is murdered by
his wife.° Why, Helen's nuptial flame lit another flame, which fell
upon Troy; and how many suitors did the nuptials of Penelope,
"Penelope the chaste", destroy? Phaedra killed Hippolytus for love
of him, Clytemnestra killed Agamemnon for want of love. O
women, you stop at nothing! If they love, they kill; if they do not
love, they kill. Handsome Agamemnon was doomed to die,
Agamemnon, whose beauty was heavenly, who was "as to his eyes
and head like unto Zeus who rejoiceth in thunder",° and it was
that head—O Zeus!—that his wife lopped off.

'These are the accusations that you might level against beautiful
women. So far, the misfortune is tolerable, since beauty offers some
consolation for the troubles, that is to say a stroke of luck in a streak
of misfortunes. But, as you say, if she is not even attractive, the disaster is doubled. How could anyone endure it—and a lad so handsome, at that? I beg you, by the gods, Charicles, do not succumb to
slavery yet, do not lose your bloom before your adulthood—for
this is another misfortune of marriage to add to the others, that it
withers a boy when he is in his prime. Please, Charicles, do not
wither yourself just yet! Do not allow a lovely rose to be plucked by
an ugly farmer!'

'Leave it to the gods, and to me', said Charicles. 'There are a few days until the date of the marriage, and a lot can happen even in one night. We shall seek a solution at our leisure. In the meantime, I am off for a ride. Since you presented me with that fine horse, I have not yet enjoyed your gift. The exercise will lighten the pain in my soul.'

With these words, he set off on his final journey, destined to ride that horse for the first and last time.

[9] I recounted to Clinias how the plot of my own story had unfurled: the affliction, the viewing, the lodging in our house, the meal, the girl's beauty. As I reached the end, I felt I was making a fool of myself:

'I cannot bear the pain, Clinias', I cried. 'Eros has attacked me in full force, and he harries the very sleep from my eyes. Everything that I see is a vision of Leucippe. No one before has ever suffered such misfortune: the cause of *my* suffering even shares a house with me!'

'Rubbish', replied Clinias. 'You are a very lucky lover. You do not have to contend with the doors to another's house, nor to arrange for a go-between: Fortune has handed you your beloved in person, picking her up and planting her in your house. After all, for another lover, the mere glimpse of a well-guarded girl suffices, and that lover counts it the greatest blessing even if he manages to get lucky with his eyes; while more blessed lovers are happy if they simply manage a few words. But you see her continually! You listen to her continually! You eat and drink with her! And you complain, with luck like that? You are an ungracious recipient of Eros' gifts. You do not understand the value of the sight of the beloved: it yields more pleasure than the act itself. You see, when two pairs of eyes reflect in each other, they forge images of each other's body, as in a mirror. The effluxion of beauty° floods down through the eyes to the soul, and effects a kind of union without contact. It is a bodily union in miniature, a new kind of bodily fusion.

'The act itself, too, will, I predict, be performed before long: continual association with your beloved is the best starting-point on the road to seduction, for the eye serves as the go-between of amorous feelings, and mutual familiarity is the most effective route to gratification. If wild beasts are tamed by familiarity, then woman too will be similarly softened, indeed much more easily. What is more, a lover of the same age has a certain allure for a girl. The natural impulses of that ripe age, coupled with the consciousness of being courted, often generate a reciprocal desire.° Every maiden wishes to be beautiful, enjoys being courted, and is grateful to her suitor for testifying to her beauty. If no one has courted her, she cannot yet believe that she is beautiful. So I have but one piece of advice to you: let her believe that she is desired, and she will soon imitate your desire.'

'How might this prophecy be fulfilled?' I asked. 'Tell me how to start out. You have been an initiate for longer than me, and you are already more familiar with the mysteries of Eros. What am I to say? What am I to do? How should I get my girl? I do not know the routes.'

[10] 'In these matters,' replied Clinias, 'you should seek no advice from any other: the god is a self-taught sophist.° It is the same as with newly born babies: no one teaches them how to feed, but they master the art of their own accord, and they know that their food lies in their mother's breasts. Likewise, a young man who is pregnant with his first desire° also needs no instruction to give birth to it. Whensoever the birth-pangs strike, and fate's appointed time arrives, you will unerringly discover a means of parturition, though it be your first pregnancy. The god himself will be your midwife. But you should also hear and learn all the general rules, which do not depend on lucky breaks. Take care not to use erotic language to the girl: it is the act that you should aim to achieve, and in silence. Boys and maids are equally shy: even if they are inclined towards the pleasures of Aphrodite, they do not want to hear about what they are undergoing. They think that the shame lies in talking about it. Now mature women, *they* enjoy talking about it, but a maiden is different. She puts up with the border skirmishes of reconnoitring lovers, and tends to acquiesce suddenly with a nod; but if you mount a full-scale assault, and ask her outright to perform the act, you will stun her ears with your voice. She will blush, condemn your words, and consider them an affront. Even if she is willing to promise you gratification, she will be ashamed to do so. You see, the pleasure she derives from your words leads her to think that she is actually experiencing the act, and not simply listening to your attempts.

'If, though, you have more success via the other approach, by breaking her in gently, then maintain for the most part the silence of a mystery-cult. A lover's kiss is a silent command when given to a beloved who is willing to surrender, but a sign of capitulation when she is unpersuaded. And if you obtain some guarantee of action, often, when they come to the act, even if they are still willing, they want it to look as if they have been forced, seeking to deflect the charge of shameful consent by claiming coercion. So do not waver if you see her resisting, but observe *how* she resists. You will need to have mastered the principles then, too: if she struggles, do not force her (she is unpersuaded as yet); but if she now softens, assume the directorial role, in case you ruin the entire play.'

[11] 'What an excellent start you have given me on my journey, Clinias', I said, 'I pray I get there! But I am still afraid that success might mark the beginning of bigger troubles, spurring me on to greater desires. So what am I to do if my suffering increases? I could not marry her: I am pledged to another girl. My father is pressurizing me into this marriage, and his request is not unreasonable: that I should marry a girl who is not a foreigner, nor ugly—nor indeed is he selling me to raise money, as in Charicles' case. In fact, he is giving me his own daughter, and—O gods!—I thought she was beautiful enough until I saw Leucippe! But as it is, I am blind to her beauty, and have eyes for Leucippe alone. I am on the border between two countries at war: Eros is marshalled against my father. The one is standing, and his weapon is shame; the other lounges, brandishing his torch. How am I to deliver my verdict? Fate and nature are at war. I want to judge in your favour, father, but I have a more dangerous adversary: he is torturing the judge, he stands fully armed in the dock, he wields his torch as he is being tried! If I disobey him, father, his very flames consume me!'

[12] We were philosophizing about Eros in this vein when suddenly one of Charicles' young slaves ran up. His expression heralded disaster, to the extent that Clinias cried out at the mere sight of it:

'Something terrible has happened to Charicles!'

As he spoke, the slave burst out simultaneously:

'Charicles is dead!'

At this news, Clinias lost the power of speech, and stood immobile. The words had struck him like a whirlwind. The slave told the story:

'It was on your horse, Clinias, that he was sitting. First of all, he took it for a gentle ride; after two or three circuits he decided to stop riding, dropped the reins, and began to stroke the sweating beast from his seated position. As he was wiping the sweat from the saddle there was a sudden noise from behind, and the horse panicked, leapt upright, bolted, and began to gallop senselessly. It gnashed at the bit and threw back its neck, hair bristling, and flew through the air, spurred on by fear. Its front hooves were bounding, its back hooves racing, eager to outpace the front ones, as if in pursuit. This contest between the hooves meant that the horse was bending itself double, bucking up and down in response to the efforts of each pair, and tossing its back like a ship in a storm. Poor, ill-starred Charicles was bowled from his seat, whirled by this equestrian wave, now sliding towards its tail, now tumbling towards its neck. The storm-waves were wrecking him. No longer could he keep hold of the reins, and he committed himself wholly to the gusts of the horse's stampede: he was Fortune's prisoner. At full gallop, the horse charged off the road and bounded into a wood. Immediately, it dashed poor Charicles into a tree. He was launched from the saddle as if he had been flung by a catapult. His face was lacerated by the tree's branches, and he suffered as many cuts as the branches had points. The reins were tangled around him, and would not release his body; in fact, they pulled him in the opposite direction, dragging him down the path of death. The horse panicked all the more when he had fallen, and, finding the body in its path, it began to trample the poor boy, kicking at him for restraining his flight. As a result, no one who saw him would even recognize him.'

[13] At these words, Clinias was struck dumb with terror for a short while. Then, as the effects of the shock wore off, he let out a resounding howl and ran off at speed towards the corpse. I set off in pursuit, offering all the consolation I could. At that point, Charicles was carried back on a bier, a most pathetic, pitiable spectacle. He was one big wound, and no one present could restrain his tears. His father led the lamentation with a distressed wail:

'How fine you were when you left me, my son—and look at you on your return! Ah, iniquitous equitations! And your death was not even shared by me! Nor is the sight of your corpse even lovely! Of others at least a trace is preserved when they die, whereby to recognize them: even if the bloom of a man's face is ruined, he yet retains its image, and consoles the mourner with an imitation of sleep, for Death may have snatched away the soul but he preserves the man in the body. But in your case, Fortune has destroyed this too at the same time. To me, you have died a double death,° both in body and in soul. Thus is even the shadow of your likeness dead: your soul has fled, and not even in your body do I see you. Tell me, my son, when are you to marry? When am I to perform the nuptial sacrifice, O horseman and groom (frustrated bridegroom, and sorry horseman)? Your bridal bedding will be your tomb,° my son, and death will be your wedding; your wedding march will be your dirge, and this lamentation will be your hymns. It was another kind of torch that I hoped to light for you, my son, but that one wretched Fortune extinguished along with you; she lights instead the torches of doom. Ah, a miserable kind of torch-parade is that! Your nuptial torch-parade has turned into a funeral.'

[14] Such were his father's groans. In the other corner, Clinias was soliloquizing (the lover and the father were holding a competition in lamentation):

'I have destroyed my master. Why did I choose that kind of gift to give him? Did I have no golden bowl, so that he could make his libations when he was drinking, and use my gift for his relaxation? Ah, woe is me! I sought to gratify that handsome lad with a beast, and even beautified that wretched beast with breast-buckles, frontlets, silver cheek-plates, and golden reins. Alas, Charicles! I decked your murderer with gold! Ah horse, most savage of beasts! Wretch, ingrate, insensitive to beauty! Though he was wiping off your sweat, and promising you a double ration, and complimenting your running, you killed him, in spite of his compliments. You took no delight in being mounted by such a body, such a rider was no luxury in your eyes: you dashed his beauty to the ground, loveless beast! Oh alas, woe is me! I bought you your murderer, the slayer of your manhood!'

[15] After the burial, I immediately set off hurriedly to see the girl, who was in the ornamental garden of our house. The garden

was in fact a grove, a substantial affair, a pleasure to the eyes. Around the grove was a wall, which was quite high. Each of the four lengths of wall was overshadowed by a troupe of columns, and within the perimeter, beneath the columns, paraded the trees. Branches abounded, interlocking, one on top of another: leaf caressed leaf, beside frond embracing frond, beside fruit coiling around fruit, so intimate was this kind of mingling of trees. Ivy and smilax grew around some of the trees, the sturdier ones. The smilax hung from the plane trees, thickening them with its tender thatch, while the ivy wound itself around the firs, absorbing the tree with its embraces. The tree formed a stay for the ivy, the ivy a garland for the tree. On either side of the trees, vines, supported by canes, abounded with leaves. The fruit was ripe and sprouting, and dangled through the gaps between the canes like locks of the reed's hair. The ground sparkled in the pale, marbled shade as the leaves on high fluttered in the wind beneath the sun. The flowers, with their intricate hues, displayed in turn their beauty: the earth's purple flower,° the narcissus, and the rose. Now the rose and the narcissus have identical calyces, in outline at any rate, like a floral bowl; but the colour of the rose's petals where they part around the calyx of the flower is blood-red, while the lower part is milky white, whereas the narcissus is like the rose's lower parts all over. The violet has no calyx at all, and its colour is like the effulgence of a calm sea. In the midst of the flowers a fountain was spurting, and a square conduit for its stream had been traced around it by human hand. The water served as a mirror for the flowers, so that the grove seemed to be doubled, part real and part reflection.

There were birds, too. Some were tame, spoilt by human nurture, and were feeding around the grove; others were free of wing, and frolicked around the peaks of the trees, either singing their birdsongs or exalting in the array of their feathers. The singers were cicadas and swallows, and they sang respectively of the love of Eos and the feast of Tereus.° The tame birds were the peacock, the swan, and the parrot. The swan was feeding around the water's springs, the parrot was suspended in a cage fixed around a tree, and the peacock trailed his fan among the flowers. The spectacle of the flowers gleamed in rivalry with the plumage of the birds—a garland of feathers.

[16] Now since I was keen to break the girl into the ways of desire, I struck up conversation with Satyrus,° taking advantage of the opportunity afforded by the bird; for, as it happened, Leucippe was strolling with Clio and had come to a halt in front of the pea-cock,° since, again by chance, at that time the bird had fanned out his glory and staged a show of his feathers.

'The bird's actions, you know,' I said, 'are not without design. He is in love, you see: whenever he wishes to seduce his beloved, he glorifies himself like this. Do you see that hen near the plane tree?' I pointed out the female. 'She is the one to whom he's displaying his glory, his feathery meadow. The male's meadow is the more florid, for nature has sown gold on his feathers, and deep purple runs in a circle around an identical circle of gold, forming an eye on the plumage.'

[17] Satyrus grasped the gist of my words, and, to provide me with a pretext for speaking further on the subject, replied:

'Are you really saying that Eros has so much strength that he can actually hurl his brand as far as the bird kingdom?'

'Not only the bird kingdom', I said. 'After all, there is nothing marvellous in that: like them, he has wings. No, he can reach snakes, plants, and (in my opinion) stones! For example, the mag-net desires iron: if she only sees him and touches him, she attracts him towards her as though she has an erotic flame inside her. Is this not a kind of kiss between the desirous stone and her beloved, the iron? Wise men tell a story about plants, a story that would be called an allegory if the countryfolk did not tell the story too. They say that there are various instances of plant desiring plant, but this desire particularly afflicts the palm tree. There are, they say, male and female palms. The male lusts after the female, and if the female is uprooted from the patch where the male is planted, the lusting male pines. The countryman understands what is upsetting the plant. He goes up to a point of vantage over the land and looks in the direction in which the palm has bowed (for it inclines towards its beloved). When he has ascertained this, he treats the plant's malady: he takes a shoot from the female palm and grafts it into the heart of the male. Thus he revives the soul of the plant, and life is breathed into its dying body, which recuperates, rejoic-ing in the embrace of its beloved. It is a botanical marriage.

[18] There is also another kind of marriage, a transmarine marriage of waters.° The lover is a river in Elis, the beloved a spring in Sicily. The river flows through the sea as though it were a plain. The sea does not destroy the sweet lover with its salty surge, but parts to make way for his course, and the parting of the sea acts as a channel for the river; in this way it escorts the Alpheus to his bride, Arethusa. Thus it is that whenever the Olympic Festival takes place, and many people cast all sorts of gifts into the eddies of the river, he immediately bears them to his beloved, a river's dowry.

'Yet another mystery of desire arises,° this time among snakes, and not just a mutual desire in snakes of the same species, but even between different types of snake. The viper, a terrestrial snake, is stung with desire for the lamprey, also a snake but a marine one (with the form of a snake but the habits of a fish). Now, whenever they wish to unite in marriage, the male goes to the seashore and whistles towards the sea a code for the lamprey: she recognizes the password and emerges from the waves. But she does not come out towards her groom immediately, for she knows that he bears death in his teeth: she climbs up onto a crag and waits for her groom to clean out his mouth. So they both stand looking at each other, the lover on the mainland, the beloved on her island. When the lover has spat out the cause of his bride's fear, and she has seen his death discharged onto the ground, only then does she descend from the rock and emerge onto the mainland to enfold her lover and fear no more his kisses.'

[19] During this exposition, I was eyeing the girl to see how she reacted to hearing about desire. She seemed to be signalling that the experience was not without a certain pleasure. The effulgent beauty of the peacock seemed to me a lesser thing than Leucippe's countenance, for the beauty of her form was vying with the flowers of the meadow: her face gleamed with the complexion of narcissus, the rose bloomed forth from her cheeks, violet was the radiance that shone from her eyes, the clusters of her locks coiled more than ivy. Thus was the brilliant meadow that lay on Leucippe's face.

After a short while, she set off to go, as it was time for her to play the lyre. To me, though, she seemed still present: though departed, she had left behind her image in my eyes. So Satyrus and I congratulated ourselves, I for my storytelling and Satyrus for having provided me with the pretexts.°

Book 2

[1] Congratulating ourselves along the way, we strolled towards the girl's room under the guise of wanting to listen to her lyre-playing (for I did not have the strength to refrain from seeing her even for a short time). First, she sang of the battle between the boar and the lion in Homer.° Then she struck up another sweet tune, inspired this time by the tender Muse, a song in praise of the rose. If you stripped away the meanderings of the melody and recounted the narrative shorn of its tune, the narrative would run as follows:

If Zeus had wished to set a king over the other flowers, the rose would have been king of the flowers. The rose is the embellishment of the earth, the adornment of the plants, the eye of the flowers, the flush of the meadow, an astonishing beauty. It exhales desire, procures Aphrodite, thick with fragrant leaves and luxurious with fluttering petals, its petals laughing in the West wind.

This was her song. I thought that I could spy the rose on her lips, as if someone had enclosed the outline of the calyx within the shape of her mouth. [2] As soon as she stopped her playing it was once again time for supper. It was, at that time, the festival of 'Dionysus of the Vintage'.° The Tyrians consider that Dionysus is a local god, since the story of Cadmus is a Tyrian myth. They have a fable explaining the origin of the festival: that no one on earth had wine before the Tyrians, neither the dark wine with its fragrant bouquet nor that of the Biblian vine, nor the Thracian wine of Maro, nor the Chian wine from the Laconian cup, nor the island wine of Icarus.° All of these have emigrated from Tyre, they say, and the original mother of wines was born there. There was, so the myth goes, a certain hospitable shepherd, such as the Athenians claim Icarius° to have been (and it was, they say, the latter who was responsible for the subsequent elaboration of the myth into its apparently Attic form). Dionysus visited this herdsman, who set down before him all that the earth and the udders of cows bring forth; for their beverage they shared the cows' drink, since the fruit of the vine did not yet exist. Dionysus complimented the shepherd on the warmth of his welcome, and proffered him the cup of friendship. The drink was wine. As he drank it, its pleasure drove him into a fit of ecstasy, and he said to the god:

'Tell me my friend, whence came this crimson liquid? Where did you find blood so sweet? It is not the liquid that flows on the earth: that produces but a slender pleasure as it slips down into the chest, whereas this drink pleasures the nostrils even before it reaches the mouth, and, though it is cold to the touch, it exhales a fiery pleasure from below when it bounds down to my belly.'

'This is the liquid of the autumn,' replied Dionysus, 'this is the blood of the cluster.'

The god led the herdsman to the vine. Taking hold of one of the clusters, he crushed it and pointed to the vine, saying:

'This here is the liquid, and this is its fountainhead.'

This is how wine came to humankind, according to the Tyrian version.

[3] On this day they celebrate the festival in honour of Dionysus My father, then, was in a good mood, and amongst the other more lavish preparations he set out a mixing-bowl dedicated to the god, second only to that of Glaucus of Chios.° The whole object was fashioned from rock-crystal. In a circle around it ran a crown of vines, growing out of the very bowl; grapes dangled around it everywhere, each unripe for as long as the bowl remained empty, but when wine was poured in the grapes began to darken and ripen the green cluster. Dionysus was engraved upon it near the clusters, so as to cultivate the vine for his wine.

As the drinking progressed, I now began to gaze upon Leucippe, shamelessly even. Once Eros and Dionysus, two forceful gods, have gripped the soul, they drive it to ecstatic shamelessness, the one burning it with his usual flame, the other providing the fuel in the form of wine (for wine is the food of desire). Now she too plucked up the courage to gaze upon me more attentively. We carried on like this for ten days, but we achieved and dared nothing more than visual stimulation.

[4] I confided everything to Satyrus, and asked him to be my ally. He told me that he had worked it out for himself before I had told him, but had been reluctant to ask me, in case I wished to cover it up (for if a man with a furtive desire is exposed, he despises the man who exposes him).

'Fortune has already provided for us of her own accord', he said. 'I have become intimate with Clio (who is entrusted with her chamber), and she considers me her lover. I shall win her gradually over to our side, so that she can work together with us to get the act done. Your task is to make an attempt on the girl, and not just with your eyes: you must also speak more penetrating words to her. Then draw up your second battery: touch her hand, massage her finger, and sigh as you do so. If she submits to these actions of yours and endures them, your next task is to call her your mistress and to kiss her neck.'

'By Athena,'° I replied, 'these are persuasive pedagogic preparations for the act! But I fear I may prove a feeble athlete of desire, given my timidity.'

'My good friend,' he said, 'Eros admits of no feebleness. You observe the military nature of his accoutrements, the bow, the quiver, the missiles, the flame: all manly things, and crammed with courage. And you are cowardly and timorous with a god such as that inside you? Be sure not to betray the god! Now, I shall provide you with the starting-point: I shall make a particular point of distracting Clio whenever I see a suitable opportunity for you to engage the girl all on her own.'

[5] With these words, he went outside. Left alone, and whipped up by Satyrus, I began to train myself for a daring attempt upon the girl:

'How long will your silence last, O man without manhood? Why this cowardice in a soldier in the service of a manly god? Are you biding your time until the girl makes an attack upon you?'

Then, however, I rejoindered:

'Why do you show no self-control, you wretch? Why does your desire not follow your duty? There is another beautiful maiden inside for you: *she* is the one you should be desiring, *she* the one you should be beholding, and *she* the one it is open to you to wed.'

I thought myself persuaded; but Eros spoke up in opposition, as if from the depths of my heart:

'So you really are arming yourself to resist me, my daredevil friend? I can fly, I can shoot and burn: how can you escape? If you shield yourself against my bow, you will be unable to do so against my flame; and even if you should extinguish that flame with your self-control, I shall use my very wings to catch up with you.'

[6] While I was indulging in this dialogue, I failed to notice that I was standing next to the girl, who had approached unseen. On seeing her I immediately turned pale, and then scarlet. She was alone: not even Clio was with her. Even so, I found myself dazed and incapable of speech.

'Greetings, mistress', I said.

She smiled sweetly, and her smile was a coded signal that she had understood why I had said 'Greetings, mistress'.

'I, your mistress? Don't say that.'

'Why not? After all, a certain one of the gods has sold me into servitude to you, as Heracles was sold to Omphale.'°

'Are you referring to Hermes?° It was to him that Zeus entrusted the sale of Heracles.' (She said this with a laugh.)

'Hermes? What is this nonsense? You know very well what I mean.'

As I was weaving my words in and out of hers, luck came to my aid. [7] It had happened that on the previous day at around midday the girl had been plucking her lyre, with Clio also seated by her side in attendance, while I was strolling by. Suddenly, a bee had flown out from somewhere and stung Clio on the hand. She had screamed, and the girl had leapt up, put down the lyre, comforted her while taking stock of the wound, and told her not to worry: she would, she said, stop her pain by chanting two spells; she had been taught by an Egyptian woman how to deal with wasp- and bee-stings. As she had chanted, Clio had said that the pain was gradually relieved. Now, as it happened, on this occasion a wasp or bee had flown nearby, buzzing in a loop around my face. I seized upon the idea, and clapped my hand upon my face, pretending to have been afflicted and to be in pain. The girl came up to me, drew away my hand, and asked me where I had been stung.

'On the lip', I replied. 'Why do you not chant your spell, dearest?'

She drew near and placed her mouth upon mine for the spell: she began to whisper something, brushing the surface of my lips. I in turn began to kiss silently, concealing the sound of the kisses, while she parted and joined her lips with the whisperings of the spell, turning incantation into osculation. And then I threw my arms around her and began to kiss her openly. She recoiled.

'What are you doing?' she cried. 'Are you also reciting a spell?'

'It is my enchantress that I am kissing,' I replied, 'because you cured my pain.'

She understood my meaning and smiled, so I spoke up boldly:

'Alas, dearest, I have been wounded again, and more grievously: the wound has plunged down into my heart, and needs your spell. You too must have a bee on your lips: you are full of honey and your kisses wound me. I beg you, chant your spell again, and do not aggravate the old wound by racing through the spell at speed.'

With these words, I clasped her more forcibly and began to kiss more freely. She acquiesced, with a show of resistance. [8] Then we saw her servant approaching in the distance and we separated, I unwilling and suffering, she—well, I do not know what her emotions were. I had found some relief now, and I was full of expectation. I could feel the pressure of her kiss upon me as though it were a real presence there, and I preserved it carefully, guarding the kiss like a pleasure-hoard. A kiss is the foremost sweetness, for it is born of the most beautiful of body-parts, the mouth, which is the organ of speech, and speech is the image of the soul. When lips meet and mingle, when they loose forth pleasure down below, they draw souls up towards the kisses. I know not of any time before when my heart had been so joyous: then it was that I first learned that nothing can rival for pleasure the kiss of desire.

[9] When it was time to drink, we all once again set about drinking as before. Satyrus was our wine-waiter—and he made arrangements for Eros, exchanging our cups, giving mine to the girl and hers to me, offering them to both of us when he poured the wine and after mixing in the water. I watched for the place on the cup where the maiden's lip touched it as she drank, and glued my own there when I drank, sending her a telegraphed kiss as I kissed the cup. When she noticed, she perceived that I was kissing even the shadow of her lip. Satyrus gathered the cups in again and exchanged ours. Then I saw that the girl too was now imitating my actions and drinking in the same way, and my joy was now all the

greater. This happened a third time and a fourth time, and for the rest of the day we drank kisses to one another in this way.

[10] After the banquet, Satyrus approached me and said:

'Now is the time to harden your manhood: the girl's mother, as you know, is unwell and resting alone, and the girl will take her usual stroll before turning in for the night on her own, with only Clio accompanying her. I shall distract Clio for you by engaging her in conversation.'

After these words, we prepared our allotted ambushes, he for Clio and I for the girl. It went according to plan: Clio was diverted, the maiden was left alone on the path. I waited for the moment when the daylight was mostly faded, and, emboldened by my first encounter with her, like a soldier already victorious and contemptuous of the war, attacked. The arsenal inspiring my optimism was, after all, fully stocked at that time: wine, desire, expectation, her isolation. Without a word, as if the act that I sought had been agreed upon, I simply took the girl in my embrace and began to kiss her. But just as my attempts were beginning to pay off, there was a sudden noise behind us, and we leapt up in a panic. She headed off in the one direction towards her room and I in the other, deeply aggrieved at having missed the opportunity for so excellent an achievement, and cursing the noise. Thereupon Satyrus waylaid me, grinning broadly: apparently he had been watching all our actions whilst hiding behind a tree in case anyone should come upon us. It was he who had made the noise, because he had seen someone approaching.

[11] When a few days had passed, my father set about organizing my wedding, sooner than he had previously intended. A sequence of dreams was disturbing him, in which he was conducting our marriage, but, as soon as he lit the torches, the flame went out. For this reason, he was in even more of a hurry to unite us. The ceremony was being planned for the following day. He had bought for his daughter everything she needed for the marriage: a choker of polychrome stones and a dress entirely of purple,° with gold where other dresses have purple. The stones vied with each other: the ruby was a rose in a stone, the amethyst's purple flushed next to the gold. In the centre were three stones, their colours shading into one another. The three stones had been fused

together, so that the base of this single stone was black, the middle part was white but interpenetrating the black, and, next to the white, the remainder of the stone at the peak was a blazing red. Around the stone ran a chaplet of gold, the very image of a golden eye. The dye used for the purple part of the dress was nothing run-of-the-mill: it was of the kind that, in the Tyrians' mythology, the shepherd's dog discovered,° and that up until this very day they use to dye the robe of Aphrodite. There was, they say, a time when this embellishing purple dye was hidden away from the world of mortals: it was concealed in the hollow recess of a tiny shell. A fisherman landed this catch. First of all, he imagined it to be a fish; but when he saw the rough shell, he cursed his catch and threw it away thinking it to be marine detritus. A dog, though, discovered this godsend and crunched into it with his teeth: the blood of the murex dribbled around the dog's mouth, and the blood dyed his muzzle, weaving purple strands into his lips. When the shepherd saw the bloodied lips of the dog, he tried to wash away the dye with seawater, thinking it was a wound; but the blood simply glowed a deeper purple, and when he touched it with his hands the purple coloured his hand too. And so the shepherd grasped the nature of the shellfish, that nature had planted within it a pigment of great beauty. He took a flock of wool and sank it into the shell's cleft, probing its mysteries. The wool was bloodied like the dog's muzzle: then it was that he learned how purple may be represented. Taking some stones he cracked the outer wall that encased the pigment, revealing its inner sanctum, and discovered the treasure-hoard of dye.

[12] At this time, then, my father was conducting the sacrifices preliminary to the wedding. When I heard of this I was done for, and began to cast around for some stratagem that would allow me to postpone the marriage. A sudden commotion in the men's quarter of the house disturbed my reflection. This is what had happened. When my father had performed the sacrifice and the victims lay on the altar, an eagle had swooped down from on high and snatched away the offering. Efforts to scare it off had been in vain: the bird had gone, bearing its quarry. The event had occurred in a flash, and the eagle had flown out to sea and out of view.° Well now, this did not seem a good omen, and they post-

poned the wedding for that day. My father summoned prophets and soothsayers and recounted the portent to them; they replied that we should go to the seashore (since that was the direction in which the bird had flown) at midnight and sacrifice to Zeus Xenios.° Because of the way these events turned out, I lauded the eagle beyond all bounds, saying that he was rightly the king of birds. And the fulfillment of the portent was not long in coming.

[13] There was a young man of Byzantium called Callisthenes, a wealthy orphan,° but prodigal and extravagant. When he heard that the daughter of Sostratus was beautiful, although he had never seen her, he wanted to make her his wife. His desire was based on hearsay: the wantonness of the licentious is so great that even with their ears they wallow in erotic pleasure, and they suffer through mere words the effects that wounded eyes usually administer to the soul. Well, this man approached Sostratus before the war befell the Byzantines, and pressed his suit for his daughter. Sostratus, however, refused out of disgust at his uncontrolled lifestyle. Callisthenes was incensed, partly because he thought his honour impugned by Sostratus and partly because his desire was unfulfilled: before he knew it he had worked himself into a dreadful state, picturing the girl's beauty to himself and envisaging the invisible. He plotted, therefore, to avenge himself upon Sostratus for the insult and to satisfy his own appetite.

The Byzantines have a law° that anyone who abducts a maiden and is the first to make a woman of her may treat the rape as a marriage. This was the law he had in mind, and he set about discovering an opportunity to commit his act. [14] Then the war broke out, and the girl was sent to stay with us. He learned all of this, but not a whit did his plotting wane. The following event came to his aid. The Byzantines received an oracle that ran as follows:

> There is an island city, its descendants named of a plant,
> Joined to mainland by both causeway and strait,
> Where Hephaestus enjoys possession of grey-eyed Athena;
> Thither I bid you bear sacrifices to Heracles.°

They were bewildered about the meaning of the oracle, but Sostratus (who was the commander of the war, as I mentioned°) said:

'It is time for us to send sacrifice to Heracles at Tyre: all the elements in the oracle correspond to that place. The god said that it was "named of a plant": the island is the home of the Phoenicians, and the "phoenix"° is a plant. The land and the sea compete for the city: the sea drags her one way and the land the other, but she is rooted to both, for she sits on the sea without renouncing the land. A narrow neck° binds her to the mainland, as if it were the island's throat. She has no roots underneath the sea, and the water flows underneath: a "strait" flows under the "causeway". It is a novel spectacle, a city in the sea and an island on the land. As for "Hephaestus enjoying Athena":° the riddle is alluding to the olive tree and the fire, which live in close proximity in our part of the world. The place is a sacred space within an enclosure, where an olive tree flourishes with luxuriant branches, but fire also grows alongside it and shoots up sheets of flame around the sprigs. The soot from the fire fertilizes the plant. This is the "love" between fire and plant: in this sense, Athena does not resist Hephaestus.'

Chaerephon, who was joint commander but Sostratus' senior, and also Tyrian (on his father's side), extolled him, saying:

'You have interpreted the oracle thoroughly and excellently. Yet it is not only the nature of fire that deserves our wonder, but also that of water. I myself have observed such mysteries. For example, the water of the Sicilian spring° carries fire intermingled with it: you will see flames bounding up from its depths, but the water is cold as snow to your touch. Neither is the fire quenched by the water nor the water scorched by the fire: there is a treaty in the spring between water and fire. Another example: there is a river in Spain,° no better than any other river at first sight; but if you wish to hear the water singing, you should pause a while and strain your ears. For if a light breeze should fall upon its eddies, the water is played upon like a string, the gust becomes the water's plectrum, and the river sings like a lyre. There is also a lake in Libya that imitates the soil of India.° The maids of Libya know its secret: the water contains treasure. The treasure is stored thus in its depths, ensconced in the river's mud, and there lies the fountain of gold. So the maidens plunge into the water a pole smeared with pitch, and unbar the gates of the river. The pole does to the gold what a hook does to a fish: it captures it. The pitch serves as a bait to the catch, since whatever is made of gold (and only that) adheres to it on contact, and the pitch draws the catch up onto dry land. This is how they fish for gold from the river in Libya.'

[15] After these words, Chaerephon approved the sacrificial expedition to Tyre, and the people assented. Now, Callisthenes had inveigled his way into the number of the sacred ambassadors. Soon he had disembarked at Tyre, and when he discovered my father's address he lay in ambush for the women. These left the house to see the procession, which was a grand affair. Much incense indeed was burned during the procession, and many were the flowers woven into garlands. The incense consisted of cassia, frankincense, and saffron, and the flowers of narcissi, roses, and myrtle: the scents exhaled by the flowers vied with the fragrance of the incense. As the breeze rose up into the aether it intermingled the fragrances, the breath of bliss.

The sacrificial victims were many and varied, but outstanding among them were the oxen of the Nile. An Egyptian ox excels not only in size but also in colour. In size, it is vast in every respect: it is thick of neck, broad of back, capacious of belly; its horns are neither paltry like those of the Sicilian nor ugly like those of the Cyprian, but they rise up erect from their temples, with a gradual curve in from either side, bringing the tips to the same distance from one another as between the bases of the horns. This sight is the very image of the crescent moon. As for their colour, it is that praised by Homer in the horses of Thrace.° The bull processes with its neck upright, as if this performance displayed its kingship over the other beasts. If there is any truth in the myth of Europa,° it must have been an Egyptian bull that Zeus imitated.

[16] Now, as it chanced, my mother was unwell at that time. Leucippe, under the pretext of also being ill, remained in the house (we had arranged a place to meet whenever most people were out), and so it happened that my sister had left the house together with Leucippe's mother. Callisthenes had never seen Leucippe, and so on seeing my sister Calligone he took her for Leucippe, since he recognized Sostratus' wife. He made no enquiries, for he had been snared by the sight of her, but pointed the girl out to his most trusted servant and bade him assemble a band of robbers to kidnap her in the way he detailed: there was to be a festival during

which, so he had heard, all the maidens are accustomed to meet on the shore. With these words, then, he left, having discharged the sacred duties entrusted to him.

[17] He owned a private ship, which he had arranged in advance to have brought from home, in case he should succeed in his attempt. When the other sacred envoys sailed away, he coasted at a small distance from land, so that he might at the same time seem to be following his fellow citizens and avoid being detected (if his vessel was near Tyre) after the abduction. When he reached Sarapta,° a Tyrian village lying on the shore, he bought in addition a small boat that he gave to Zeno (as his servant was called), preparing it for the abduction. Zeno, who had the nature of a brigand (and, in any case, a doughty constitution), swiftly recruited as pirates some fishermen from the aforementioned village and set sail for Tyre. The boat lay in ambush in a small harbour belonging to Tyre, an island lying a small way from the city said by the Tyrians to be the tomb of Rhodope.°

[18] Prior to the festival that Callisthenes was anticipating, the business with the eagle and the prophets occurred. On the following day we made our preparations for the nocturnal sacrifice to the god. All of this was observed by Zeno. When it was late into the evening, we set out and he pursued. Just as we arrived at the lip of the sea, he raised the arranged signal and the boat suddenly set sail shorewards; when it came into view there were ten young men aboard. They had eight accomplices secreted on land in advance, wearing women's clothes and with their beards shaved from their chins, each carrying a sword in the folds of his clothes. They themselves also joined in the sacrifice, so as to provoke as little suspicion as possible: we thought that they were women. When we started building the pyre they suddenly rushed upon us with a shout and put out our torches. We were terrified and fled in panic, whereupon they bared their swords, snatched my sister, and put her on board the boat; then, embarking themselves, they took wing like a bird. Some of us fled without knowing or seeing anything that was going on, while others saw what happened and cried out:

'Pirates have got Calligone!'

The boat, though, was already well out to sea. When they put in at Sarapta, Callisthenes saw the signal from a distance and sailed out to meet up with them. He took the girl and set sail at once. I myself was both reanimated by this extraordinary collapse of my wedding and dismayed that an event such as this had befallen my sister.

[19] After an interval of a few days, I asked Leucippe:

'How long are we to stop at kisses, dearest? The beginning of the story was fine, but let's now add the truly erotic part. Come, let us agree a pact of fidelity. After all, once Aphrodite has initiated us into her mysteries, well, there is not one of the other gods who can overrule her.'

By repeating these sentiments to her like a spell I prevailed upon her to receive me into her boudoir that night. Clio, her chamber-maid, was an accomplice. This is how her chamber was arranged: there was a large space encompassing four rooms, two on the right, two on the left, with a narrow passage running between them to provide access to the rooms. A single, locked door stood at the entrance to the passageway. Such were the women's quarters. The inner two rooms opposite one another were occupied by the maiden and her mother, while, of the outer two nearer the door, the one next to the maiden's was occupied by Clio, and the other served as a storeroom. When she had put Leucippe to bed, her mother invariably locked the door to the passage from the inside. Someone else used to lock it from the outside and pass the keys through the opening, and she would take them and guard them; then, around dawn, she would summon the servant detailed for this task, and pass the keys back out again so that he could unlock it. Now Satyrus had arranged for a duplicate set of keys to be made. After he had tried the lock and found that it opened, he prevailed upon Clio (with the full consent of the girl) to do nothing to impede the plot. That was the arrangement.

[20] Among their slaves was a fellow who was interfering, garrulous, gluttonous, and anything else you might want to call him, by the name of Conops. It seemed to me that he was observing our actions from afar. He particularly suspected that we might be up to some nocturnal intrigue (which was in fact the case); and so he stayed awake well into the evening with the doors of his room wide open, and as a result it was difficult to avoid his attention. For this reason, Satyrus tried to befriend him, teasing him, calling him

Gnat-man° and punning laughingly on his name. Conops, though, saw through Satyrus' trick, and although he pretended to reply with some jokes of his own, he made it clear from his jokes that his mind was made up, and there was no chance of a rapprochement. He replied to Satyrus:

'Alright then, since you are mocking me and my name, I shall tell you a fable about a gnat.° [21] There was a lion who was complaining repeatedly to Prometheus° on the grounds that he had made him large and handsome, he had armed his jaws with teeth, reinforced his paws with claws, and made him mightier than the other animals; "But even as I am," he used to claim, "I am afraid of the cock."

'Prometheus stood next to him and said: "Why these pointless accusations against me? All my skills, everything I could fashion has gone into you; your soul has but this one weakness."

'And so the lion used to weep for himself, chiding his own cowardice, until finally he resolved to die. While he was so minded, he met with an elephant. He greeted him and stood in conversation with him. Seeing that the latter was constantly moving his ears, he asked him: "What is wrong? Why on earth does your ear never stop moving, even for an instant?"

'The elephant replied as follows, for as it happened a gnat had just flown in his direction: "Do you see this little buzzing thing? If it enters my ear-duct, I am dead."

'"What reason, then," said the lion, "is there for me to die, given that I am more fortunate than the elephant, to the same degree that a cock is mightier than a gnat?"

'So you see how much power a gnat has: it even terrifies an elephant.'

Satyrus recognized the threat encoded in his words, and smiled gently.

'Listen, I too have a story,' he said, 'the one about the gnat and the lion: I heard it from one of the philosophers. As for the elephant in your story, I leave him to you.

[22] 'A jumped-up gnat was once addressing a lion: "So, you think you can rule over me too, as you do over the other animals? Yet you are by nature neither more handsome nor stronger nor bigger than me. First of all, in what does your strength consist? You

tear with your claws and you bite with your teeth. Is that not what a woman does in a fight? Then, what sort of size and beauty is this that adorns you? A broad chest, firm shoulders, and a thick mane around your neck. Can you not see that your rear is a disgrace? *My* range, on the other hand, covers the entire atmosphere, all the space that my wings can command; and my beauty is the mane of the meadow grasses, which are to me like clothes that I don when I wish to rest from my flying. To catalogue my manly attributes would be no laughing matter: every last part of me is an instrument of war. I array myself for battle to the sound of the bugle, and my mouth is both bugle and missile, so I am both bugler and archer. I am my own bow and my arrow: I shoot my winged self through the air, and where I hit I inflict a wound as if from a missile. The victim of my blow lets out a sudden scream and looks around for his assailant, but though I am there, I am not: I flee and resist at one and the same time; I use my wings to gallop around the man, and laugh as I watch him dancing about with his wounds. But the time for words has passed: let battle commence!"

'With these words he fell upon the lion, attacking his eyes and any other part of his face not covered by mane, flying around him to the accompaniment of his buzzing. The lion, increasingly enraged, whirled around in every direction and snapped at the air; but at this the gnat only treated his anger all the more as a game, and began to bite him, even on the very lips. Whenever the lion turned to the part where the pain was, craning back to the place where the wound had been inflicted, the gnat, like a wrestler feinting with his body before moving into a hold, would slip through the lion's teeth, even flying through the midst of his jaws as he shut them. The teeth would clatter down into each other, missing their prey. Well, finally the lion tired of using his teeth to shadow-box with the air, and stood there, exhausted by his rage. The gnat circled around his mane piping his victory ode. When he widened the wheels of his flight in this extraordinarily ostentatious display of his, though, he accidentally became ensnared in the threads of a spider's web—and the spider spotted his landing. When it transpired that there was no longer any means of escape, he cried out in distress:

' "What a fool I am! I challenged a lion, but it was the slender fabric of a spider that caught me." '

Concluding his story, Satyrus said:

'So you see, it is time that you too began to be afraid of spiders.'
And he laughed as he said this.

[23] After an interval of a few days, Satyrus (who knew that
Conops was the slave of his belly) bought a drug that induced deep
sleep, and invited him to a party. The latter suspected a trick, and
was reluctant at first, although he did in fact give in, under the
compulsion of that excellent belly of his. He came around to
Satyrus' quarters, and then was about to depart after dinner when
Satyrus poured a quantity of the drug into his final cup. Conops
drank it, and after a short interval (but long enough for him to
reach his room), he fell down and lay there in a drug-induced slum-
ber. Satyrus ran to me and said:

'Conops is lying fast asleep: over to you! See to it that you play
the part of Odysseus° well!'

As he was speaking, we arrived at the doors guarding my
beloved. He remained outside while I entered, Clio admitting me
without a sound. I felt a double tremor, of simultaneous pleasure
and fear: my fear of the danger was perturbing the hopes of my
soul, while my hope of success was overwhelming my fear with
pleasure; thus the hopeful part of me was terrified and the anxious
part ecstatic. But no sooner had I entered the girl's chamber than
the girl's mother experienced the following event. She was disturbed by a dream, in which a brigand carrying a naked blade°
kidnapped her daughter and carried her off; then he laid her down
on her back and cut open the middle of her belly with the knife,
starting down below at her most intimate parts. At this, Pantheia
bolted out of bed just as she was, and raced, racked with fear, into
her daughter's chamber (which was, after all, nearby), just as I had
lain down. I heard the noise of the doors opening and immediately
bolted out of bed, but she was already beside the couch. Realizing
my predicament, I bounded out of the room and ran out through
the doors. I was trembling and disturbed when Satyrus met me.
Then we turned to make our escape under cover of darkness,
before reaching our rooms.

[24] Pantheia first of all fell to the ground in a swoon; but when
she came round, she simply beat Clio on the side of the head and
grabbed her by the hair, screaming to her daughter:

'You have wrecked my hopes for you, Leucippe! Alas, Sostratus! While you are fighting to protect the marriages of others in Byzantium, you have been routed in Tyre and someone has looted your own daughter's marriage! Alas, wretched girl! It was not such a marriage as this that I hoped to see. You should have stayed in Byzantium! Better to have been raped in the way of war, better even that it had been some triumphant Thracian who raped you! In that case the coercion would have removed the stigma of shame° from the calamity. But as things stand, miserable girl, your misfortune is compounded by ill repute. Even the phantasms of my dreams misled me, and the dream I saw was not of the more truthful kind:° the stroke that actually pierced your belly was more disgraceful, an unluckier prick than that of the knife. Nor did I even catch sight of the man who defiled you, nor do I even know how this calamity came about. Alas for my woes! Surely he was not—horrors!—a slave?'

[25] The maiden, emboldened now that she realized I had escaped, spoke up:

'Do not slander my virginity, mother. I have done nothing to justify such talk; nor do I even know whether the figure was a deity, the manifestation of a local hero, or a brigand. I was lying here in terror, terrified even to the point of inability to scream, for terror is the shackle of the tongue. One thing alone I know, mother: that no one has besmirched my virginity.'

At this, Pantheia fell back to the floor and began to wail again.

As for us, now that we were back on our own ground, we began to consider what was to be done. The best course seemed to be to escape before day broke and Clio revealed the whole plot under torture.° [26] So, having taken this decision, we set to work. After giving our night-porter the excuse that we were going out to see a sweetheart, we went to Clinias' house. It was already the middle of the night, and so his night-porter was reluctant to let us in. Clinias, who had his room on the upper floor, heard us discussing our predicament and ran down in agitation. Meanwhile, we saw Clio behind us running at great speed: she had decided to abscond. And so, at the same time as Clinias heard what had happened to us, we heard how Clio had got away, and Clio in return heard what we planned to do. We came indoors and recounted to Clinias what had happened, and how we had decided to escape. Clio said:

'I shall escape with you, too: if I wait here until dawn, death awaits me—and that death will be more desirable than the accompanying tortures.'

[27] Clinias now grabbed hold of my hand and took me aside from Clio.

'I think I have come up with the best plan', he said. 'Smuggle Clio away, and we shall stay put for a few days; if we think it best, we shall make preparations and leave. After all, according to your story, the girl's mother even now has no idea whom she surprised, and there will be no one to convict you if Clio disappears from view. You may even persuade Leucippe to escape with you.'

He added that he too would join us in our travels. We agreed to this. He handed Clio over to one of his own slaves and told him to put her on a boat, while we stayed there and took thought for the future. Finally we decided to make trial of Leucippe, and, if she was willing to escape with us, to go ahead; but, if not, to stay there and hand ourselves over to Fortune. So, after a brief sleep through what remained of the night, we returned home at dawn.

[28] Pantheia, meanwhile, had risen and started making preparations for the torture of Clio, ordering her to be summoned. When she was nowhere to be found, Pantheia hurried back to her daughter.

'Will you not reveal what plot underlies the story? Look: now Clio has escaped, too!'

Leucippe was all the more emboldened, and said:

'What more do you want me to tell you? What further evidence do you want me to produce that could be weightier than the truth? If there be a test for virginity, apply it to me.'

'That', said Pantheia, 'would cap it all—that our misfortune should be witnessed publicly, too!'

With these words she jumped up and ran out of the room.

[29] Finding herself alone and overburdened with her mother's words, Leucippe felt the full range of emotions: distress, shame, fury. She was distressed at having been found out, she felt ashamed at being reproached, she was furious at being mistrusted. Shame, grief, and anger are the soul's three waves: shame pours in through the eyes and washes away their freedom, grief ranges around the breast and quenches the fire that animates the soul, while anger,

barking° around the heart, floods our reason with the foaming waves of mania. Language is the author of all these emotions: it seems to fire a missile towards its mark and hit, causing wounds and all sorts of arrow-marks in the soul. One of its arrows is abuse, and the wound thereby caused is anger; another is exposure of accidents, and from this arrow grief ensues; and the final one is castigation of immoralities, and this wound they call shame. All these arrows share something in common: bloodless is their laceration, though deep their penetration. And there is but one remedy for all of them, namely, to retaliate against one's assailant with the same weapons. Language, the arrow of the tongue, is counteracted by the arrow of another's tongue: it checks the heart's ardour and withers the soul's dolour. If, however, one is forced by inferior station to retaliate in silence, the silence makes the wounds more painful: the wave-pangs brought on by the waves that are stirred by language, since they have failed to spit forth their foam, become dilated and swell up around one another. Troubles of this magnitude, then, filled Leucippe—and she was unable to sustain their assault.

[30] Meanwhile, as it happened, I had sent Satyrus to the girl to test the issue of flight. Before listening to Satyrus, she cried:

'By the gods, whether foreign or local, I beg you! Snatch me away from my mother's eyes, anywhere you like! If you run away and leave me, I shall weave a noose for myself and use it to end my life.'

When these words were reported to me, I set aside most of my anxiety. After an interval of two days, at a time when my father happened to be out of town,° we set about preparing for our flight. [31] Satyrus had some of the drug that he had used to put Conops to sleep left over, and when he was ministering to us he secretly poured some into the last cup, which he took to Pantheia. She rose, headed to her room, and immediately fell asleep. Leucippe had another chambermaid, whom Satyrus plunged into sleep using the same drug (for as soon as she had taken charge of the chamber, he had feigned desire for her too). In pursuit of a third quarry, he went after the night-porter, and struck him down too with the same potion.

A fine coach was waiting for us outside the gates, organized by Clinias, who was waiting in it ahead of us. When all were asleep,

around the first watch of night,° we crept out without a sound,
Satyrus leading Leucippe by the hand. This was possible because
Conops, who had been lying in wait for us, was by chance out of
the house for that day, on an errand for his mistress. Satyrus
opened the doors and we advanced. When we reached the gates,
we climbed into the coach. There were six of us in all: Clinias, his
two slaves, and us. We started driving towards Sidon.° During
approximately the second watch of the night, we reached the city
and immediately turned our course towards Beirut, thinking we
would find a ship anchored there. Our luck held: when we arrived
at the harbour of Beirut we found a boat putting out to sea, on the
very point of releasing its hawsers. Without even asking where it
was sailing, we began shifting ourselves and our belongings from
land to sea. The time was just before dawn. The ship was sailing to
Alexandria, the great city on the Nile.

[32] My first reaction on seeing the sea, and that the boat was
not yet sailing but sitting in the harbour, was of joy. Next, when
they decided that the wind was favourable for sailing, there was a
great commotion on the boat, as sailors ran around, the helmsman
shouted orders, and the guys were hauled about. The yardarm was
swung around, the sail lowered into place, the boat bobbed out to
sea, they weighed in the anchors, and the harbour was left behind.
We watched from the boat as the land slowly receded, as if it was
itself sailing away. We sang paeans and uttered many a prayer,
invoking the gods of salvation,° piously asking them to make the
journey a safe one. The wind, meanwhile, was growing stronger,
and the sail was billowing, driving the boat along.

[33] It happened that a certain young man was occupying the
pitch next to us. When it was time for breakfast, he asked us cour-
teously to join him. Satyrus waited upon us. We put out what we
had and shared breakfast; then we shared our stories, too. I was the
first to speak:

'Where are you from, young man? What should we call you?'

'My name is Menelaus,' he said, 'and my family is from Egypt.
What is your situation?'

'My name is Clitophon and this is Clinias. We are both
Phoenicians.'

'So what is the reason for your journey abroad?'

'If you tell me yours first, you shall then hear my story.'

[34] Menelaus, then, spoke up:

'In summary, the story of my journey tells of the evil eye of Eros and an ill-starred hunt.° I was smitten with desire for a handsome boy, and the boy was fond of hunting. I often tried to restrain him, but I could not stop him. Since I could not dissuade him, I decided to join in the hunt myself. We hunted, then, on horseback, and at first we enjoyed good fortune, while we pursued the smaller kinds of beasts. Suddenly, a boar bounded out of the wood, and the boy set off in pursuit. The boar, though, whirled about face and ran at him head on. The boy would not get out of the way, though I shouted and screamed: "Pull the horse up! Rein him aside! That beast is vicious!" But the boar charged, and started hurtling in his direction at high speed. They clashed, and a shaking terror seized me as I watched. Fearing that the boar might get in first and gore the horse, I fitted my javelin to its thong and released the weapon before taking proper aim. The boy, however, swung into its path and received the force of the blow! What feelings do you think I felt in my soul? If, that is, my soul was still with me at all: my living state resembled anyone else's death. What was more piteous, he reached his hands out to me while he still had a little breath left, and held me. even as he died, the victim of my murder showed no hate to me, but gave up his soul while embraced by the hand that murdered him.

'The lad's parents took me to court. Not that I resisted; in fact, when I entered the dock, I made no defence, proposing for myself instead the death-penalty. The jurors pitied me and passed the sentence of a three-year exile. That period is now over, and I am returning once again to my homeland.'

As he was speaking Clinias wept, 'apparently for Patroclus',° but in fact recalling Charicles.

'Are you weeping for my sufferings,' Menelaus asked, 'or has some such event accounted for your exile too?'

With a groan, Clinias recounted the story of Charicles and the horse. I then told mine. [35] Then, seeing Menelaus altogether downcast as he reminisced about his sufferings, and Clinias weeping quietly in memory of Charicles, and wanting to coax them out of their grief, I struck up a conversation aimed at erotic entertainment.

(Leucippe was not, of course, present: she was sleeping below deck.)
With a knowing smile, I said to them:

'Clinias always beats me by such a margin! He wanted to deliver
his oration against women,° as usual, and his delivery will be
greatly facilitated now that he has found an erotic ally. I have no
idea why desire for males is all the rage these days.'

'Is it not because it is far superior to the other kind?' replied
Menelaus. 'There is, after all, much more simplicity in boys, and
their beauty is a keener spur towards pleasure.'

'Keener?' I replied. 'How can anything be so, when it disappears just as soon as it has peeked out? It allows the lover no enjoyment of it, but acts just like the draught of Tantalus:° often it
disappears even as it is being drunk, and the lover leaves without
having found a way to drink. While it is still being drunk, it is
snatched away before the drinker is satisfied. It is impossible for a
lover to leave a boy without a certain pain mixed in with his pleasure: it leaves him still thirsting for more.'

[36] 'You do not know the crucial point about pleasure,
Clitophon', he said. 'That which is unfulfilled always generates
longing. The delights of something that is experienced over a
period wilt through satiety; whereas something snatched is ever
fresh and blooms all the more, since the pleasure it provides is
unaged. Longing amplifies beauty all the more that it is diminished
by time. This is the reason why the rose is more attractive than
the other plants, because its beauty is soon gone. I consider that
there are two kinds of beauty that wander among mortals, the one
heavenly and the other vulgar,° just like the goddesses who lead
these two processions. The heavenly type is distressed at being
chained to mortal beauty and seeks to flee swiftly heavenwards,
while the vulgar has been cast down here, a long-term visitor in the
corporeal world. If we must also cite a poet as witness to beauty's
ascent to heaven, listen to the words of Homer:

> Him the gods took up to pour wine for Zeus
> Thanks to his beauty, so he might be with immortals.°

No woman (for Zeus has also consorted with women) has ever
ascended to heaven for her beauty: no, Alcmene's fate is suffering
and exile, Danaë's a chest on the sea, and Semele became fuel for

the flames.° But if he desires a Phrygian boy,° he grants him access to heaven, so that he can live beside him and pour out nectar for him. The former servant°—a woman, I believe—was stripped of this honour.'

[37] 'But surely,' I interjected, 'women's beauty would seem to be heavenly precisely in that it does not dissolve quickly: indestructibility and divinity, after all, are closely linked. Anything that moves in the realm of the perishable, in imitation of mortal nature, is not heavenly but vulgar. Yes, Zeus desired a Phrygian boy and took this Phrygian up to heaven; but the beauty of women brought Zeus himself down from heaven. It was for a woman's sake that Zeus once lowed,° for a woman that he once performed a satyr's dance;° for another woman, he even converted himself into gold!° I grant you, Ganymede may play wine-waiter to the gods; but you should remember that Hera also drinks with the gods, so Zeus' wife has the boy as her servant. As for the manner of his rape, I pity that too: a flesh-eating bird swooped down upon him, and he was kidnapped and violated like a tyrant's victim. A most disgraceful spectacle this, a lad hanging from the bird's claws. Now as for Semele, it was no flesh-eating bird that snatched her up to heaven, but fire. You should not be too quick to disbelieve that someone could ascend to heaven through fire: that is how Heracles ascended.° And if you mock Danaë's imprisonment in a chest, why so silent about Perseus?° And as for Alcmene, well, Zeus' gift to her (for her sake he robbed the world of three days°) was in itself enough to make her happy.

'Now, if we must leave the realm of mythology and speak of the very pleasure of the act—well, my own experience with women is limited,° extending only to intimacy with those who put Aphrodite up for sale. Perhaps someone else who has been initiated might be able to comment in somewhat greater detail; but I shall speak nevertheless, moderate though my experience be. A woman's body is doughy when you embrace it, her lips soft when you kiss them. This is why she can hold her companion's body perfectly enfolded in her embraces, in her very flesh, and he is enveloped by pleasure. She places kisses onto your lips like the imprint of a seal. She kisses with art, and her techniques sweeten the kiss: for she is not content to kiss with her lips alone, but attacks with teeth as well, nibbling around her lover's mouth and kissing with bites. A hand on the breast, too, has its own particular pleasure. When Aphrodite's peak is reached, the pleasure stings her into a frenzy: she goes crazy, her mouth gaping wide as she kisses. All this time tongues have been weaving in and out of one another, and they too are pressed into the job of kissing, in so far as they can: your job, meanwhile, is to increase the pleasure by opening your mouth.

'And as she comes in sight of Aphrodite's own finishing-post the woman naturally pants with blazing pleasure: when her gasp is driven up by erotic exhalation as far as the lips of the mouth, it meets with the roaming kiss as it seeks to penetrate down below; the kiss is whirled around and blended with the gasp, then it follows it back down and strikes a blow to the heart, which is convulsed by the kiss and begins to palpitate. Were the heart not bound to the innards, it would pursue the kisses and tear itself upwards.

'Boys' kisses, though, are immature and uneducated; their embraces are unlearned, Aphrodite works lazily with them, there is no pleasure to be had.'

[38] Menelaus replied:

'Well, as far as I can tell, you are no inexperienced youngster but an old hand in Aphrodite's game! What an array of minutiae about women you have showered upon us! But now it is your turn to listen, to the boys' case. With women, all is artificial, be it pillow-speak or technique. Even if she looks beautiful, there is some multi-talented dexterity with make-up behind it. Her beauty consists in perfumes, hair-dye, or even in kissing: strip her of most of these tricks and she looks like the jackdaw stripped of his wings in the fable.°

'Boys' beauty, though, is not tended by watering it with the fragrances of perfumes, nor by any deceitful and alien odours: the sweat of boys smells sweeter than any female perfume. Even before Aphrodite's bouts begin, he can go to the wrestling-gym to join with another and interlace bodies openly: such embraces carry no shame. What is more, a boy's sexual clinches are not softened by doughy flesh. Bodies rub firmly against one another in these athletics of pleasure.

'Yes, a boy's kisses lack the ingenuity of a woman's. He does not trump up some lascivious deceit with his lips but kisses in the way he knows: his kisses spring not from art but from nature. Here is an image for a boy's kiss: if nectar were to solidify and take the form of a lip, you would receive such kisses as this. Your kissing would never be satisfied: no matter how much you swallowed you would still thirst for kisses, and you would not withdraw your mouth until the very pleasure drove you to flee from those kisses.'

Book 3

[1] During our third day of sailing, the fine weather that we had
had in abundance deserted us, and a sudden fog enveloped us.
Daylight disappeared. The wind blew up from the sea against the
prow of the ship, and the helmsman gave the orders to swing
around the yardarm. The sailors set energetically about rotating it:
on the one side they drew in the sail above the yard, using sheer
force, since the extreme violence of the wind's onslaught inhibited
their efforts at hauling; while on the other they kept just enough of
the sail spread as before for the wind to be of assistance to the rota-
tion. The vessel's hull lay at an angle on beam ends, and on the
other side the deck was upended, rising steeply everywhere: as the
wind assaulted it, the ship seemed to most of us in constant danger
of capsizing altogether. So we all relocated to the higher parts of
the ship, aiming both to relieve the weight upon the part that was
being submerged and to force the ship gradually to equilibrium by
the exertion of additional pressure. This gained us no advantage,
though: the ship's deck, towering up, lifted us more successfully
than we could lower it. For a while, we wrestled to restore the ship
to equilibrium, as it rocked with the waves; then, suddenly, the
wind switched to the opposite side of the ship. The vessel was
almost submerged: the side that had been leaning into the waves
leapt up with a sharp jerk, while the other side (where the ship had
been at its highest) crashed down into the sea. A mighty scream
arose from the ship, followed by shouting and a speedy reversion
to our former location. The same thing happened to us three
times, four times, many times more, and we all shared in the ship's
wanderings. Before we could finish changing position in the first
place, we had to start on the second lap.

[2] And so we carried our baggage the width of the ship all day
long, exhausting ourselves with endless racing in this quasi-
marathon, constantly anticipating death (which was, in all proba-

bility, not far off). At around midday we lost the sun completely: we could only see each other in a kind of moonlight. Flames of lightning flew, and the heavens bellowed with thunder; the air reverberated with crashes, and the waves, warring down below, reverberated in response; the sound between heaven and sea was of sundry winds hissing. The air blared with bugle-sounds.° The cables flapped around the sail, producing a 'thwack' as they clattered against it; equally terrifying was the splitting of the timbers, and the thought that the vessel might gradually break up as the bolts gave way. A wicker awning was stretched over the ship, since torrents of rain were flooding down: we ducked under the awning as if it were a cave and waited there, casting away all hope and handing ourselves over to Fortune. A succession of enormous rollers welled up from every direction and crashed into each other, some at the ship's fore, others aft. The ship was constantly being now raised towards the peaks of the swelling sea, now dropped into the intervening troughs: the peaks of the waves were like mountains, the troughs like chasms. Those waves, meanwhile, that struck us athwart from either side were still more terrifying, since the sea climbed right into the ship and poured in through the wicker, covering the entire vessel. As a wave rose high, touching the very clouds, it looked high as a mountain facing the vessel in the distance; as you watched it approach, you felt sure the ship would be gulped down. It was like a battle between the winds and the waves.

Thanks to the rolling of the ship we were unable to keep to the same spot. Noises arose from all quarters, intermingling: waves roared, gusts blustered, women shrieked, men screeched, sailors barked. There was wailing and lamentation everywhere. Then the helmsman gave the order to throw our cargo overboard. Gold and silver were treated no differently from any old trinket: we hurled everything overboard just the same. Even many of the merchants hurriedly joined in the throwing, carrying with their own hands those items in which they had invested their hopes. The ship was now completely empty of cargo, but the storm was not to be appeased by such libations.

[3] Finally the helmsman gave up the struggle: he released the rudder from his hands and handed the vessel over to the sea. Then he made ready the lifeboat, and, ordering the sailors to embark, he

initiated the evacuation. They immediately leapt out in quick succession. That marked the beginning of a dreadful event, a hand-to-hand battle. Those who had clambered aboard were already trying to cut the cable that attached the lifeboat to the vessel. Each of the passengers started making vigorous attempts to jump ship when they saw the helmsman hauling in the cable, but the sailors were making efforts from the lifeboat to prevent them coming on board. They had with them axes and daggers, and they made threats to strike anyone who boarded. Many on the ship also armed themselves as best they could, one retaliating by seizing a section from an old oar, another some of the ship's thwarts. The law of the sea was force. It was a novel form of sea battle: those on the lifeboat were using their axes and daggers to strike those trying to leap on board, fearing that the boat might sink with the number of boarders; while the others were trying to jump at the same time as raining down blows with their cudgels and oars. Some touched the very tip of the boat and slipped down, while others who were boarding were now wrestling with those on the lifeboat. Any bond of friendship or respect disappeared: each looked to his own safety with no thought for altruism. Thus it is that great dangers dissolve even the laws of friendship.

[4] Then a certain well-built young man on the ship grabbed the cable and hauled in the lifeboat. When this was now close to the ship, each prepared to leap on board if it should approach any nearer. Two or three succeeded, although not without injury, but many plunged headlong from the ship into the sea in their attempts to leap, for the sailors soon cut the cable with an axe and unshackled the lifeboat, to sail wherever the wind took them. Those on the ship, meanwhile, cursed them and prayed that the boat would sink. The vessel rolled and tumbled as it danced in the waves, before colliding invisibly with an underwater reef and breaking up altogether. When the ship slid back down the reef, the mast collapsed athwart, smashing one side of the ship and submerging the other. Those who were overwhelmed and drank the brine straightaway could have counted this the less extreme fate in the midst of such calamities, in that they were spared the time in which to fear death. A protracted death at sea kills even before the deathly blow is dealt, for when the eye confronts the enormity of

the sea, it extends fear beyond any horizon, and this also increases the misery of death (for the dread of death is proportionate to the expanse of the sea).

Some who tried to dive in were dashed against the reef by the waves and mangled; many also fell onto shivered timbers and were impaled like fish;° still others tried to swim for it, half-dead though they were. [5] Now, when the ship was shattered, some good spirit saved part of the prow for us: Leucippe and I sat astride this and followed the currents of the sea. Menelaus and Satyrus, along with some of the other passengers, chanced upon the mast, climbed on, and began to swim. We also saw Clinias nearby, paddling astride the yardarm, and we could hear him shout: 'Hold onto that timber, Clitophon!' As he spoke, a wave engulfed him from behind, and we screamed. At the same time, a wave was travelling towards us, too; but, luckily, when it approached it dipped underneath us and passed, so that the timber was merely lifted up high on the crest of the wave, and we could see Clinias once more. I wailed:

'Have mercy, lord Poseidon! Call a truce with the last remainders of your shipwreck! Many are the deaths we have already suffered out of fear. If you wish to slay us, do not part us in death: let a single wave engulf us. If it is our fate to become fish-food, let it be a single fish that consumes us, and a single belly that holds us, so that we may lie buried together, even if it is inside a fish.'

A short while after this prayer, the worst of the wind around us abated and the savagery of the waves was diffused. The sea was thick with corpses. Menelaus and his company were carried ashore fairly quickly by the tides, and the shores were those of Egypt. At that time, the whole of the coastal region was under the control of pirates. We, on the other hand, put in by some chance at Pelusium° in the early evening, and began to praise the gods out of relief at touching dry land. Then, however, we began to bewail Clinias and Satyrus, whom we thought lost.

[6] There is in Pelusium a temple dedicated to Zeus Casius.° The cult statue is of a boy, looking rather like Apollo because of his similar age. His hand is stretched out and bears a pomegranate (the pomegranate has a mystic meaning°). We were told that the god was an oracle, and so we addressed him in prayer, asking him for an indication about Clinias and Satyrus. Then we made a tour

of the temple. In the inner chamber of the temple we saw a painting with two levels, signed by the artist, Euanthes.° The painting
represented Andromeda and Prometheus,° both chained. This
was the reason, I suppose, why the artist had combined the two
subjects onto one canvas, but the situations depicted by the pictures were also akin in other respects: each victim had a rock as a
prison; each had a beast as a torturer (his coming from the air, her's
from the sea); their rescuers were both Argives, and related to each
other,° Heracles in the one case (who shot the bird sent by Zeus),
Perseus in the other (who contended with the sea-monster sent by
Poseidon). Heracles, though, was firmly planted on the ground
when he shot, while Perseus was suspended by wings in the air.

[7] The rock was hollowed out enough to fit the maiden. This
cleft seemed to say: 'No human hand made me: this painting is the
spontaneous creation of nature!' For the artist had roughened the
pleats of the stone, just as it is when the earth has given birth to it.
She was crouched in this shelter: the spectacle resembled a novel
kind of graven image if you focused on her beauty, or an
impromptu grave if you focused on the chains and the monster. In
her face were combined beauty and fear: the fear resided in her
cheeks, while the beauty bloomed from her eyes. Yet her pallid
cheeks were not altogether without colour, tinged as they were with
a gentle blushing; nor were her florid eyes without anxiety, resem-
bling as they did violets in the first stage of wilting. Such was the
comely fear with which the artist had embellished her. Her hands
were spread out over the rock, each fastened to it by a clamp that
shackled them from above, and dangling like clusters of grapes
from the wrist.° The pure white of the girl's arms shaded into a dis-
coloured bruising: her fingers looked as if they were dead. Thus
was she bound, awaiting death. She stood there dressed in bridal
clothes, done up as if she were a bride for Hades.° Her robe was
full-length, her robe was white: the weft was delicate like a spider's
web, woven in the style not of sheepswool but of the moths' wool
that Indian women tease down from the trees and weave into
strands.° The monster rose up from below to face the girl, cleaving
the sea in two: most of its body was shrouded in waves, and only its
head stood clear of the sea. Beneath the briny wave, the outline of
its shadowy back was drawn so as to be visible: its protuberant

scales, its sinuous neck, its spinous crest, its twisting tail. Its jaws
were enormous and capacious, an all-encompassing hole reaching
down to a point where the shoulders met; and at that point the
belly immediately took over.

   In the mid-point between the monster and the maiden was drawn
Perseus, descending from the air. He was entirely naked as he
descended to do battle with the beast, except for a mantle around
his shoulders and winged sandals on his feet. His head was protected
by a cap, which signified the helmet of Hades.° In his left hand he
wielded the Gorgon's head,° which he held out like a shield. Even
when represented by pigments, she was terrifying: her eyes were
gaping and her hair bristling from her temples, the serpents erect.
Even in a painting this was a threatening sight. This, then, was the
weapon in his left hand. In his right hand he was armed with a double weapon, split between a sickle and a sword. The hilt for each
blade shared a common point of origin down below, and up until
halfway the weapon was a sword; thereupon it diverged into two,
the one part sharpening in a line, the other curving. The part that
sharpened remained a sword as before, while the part that curved
became a sickle, so that with a single blow the one blade could drive
home the lethal stab and the other could complete the decapitation.
This was how the scene was set for Andromeda.°

   [8] Next to it was the Promethean scene. Prometheus was
bound by both iron and stone, while Heracles was armed with
both bow and spear. A bird was feasting on Prometheus' belly. It
stood there prising it apart: the belly had already been prised
apart, but the bird's beak was buried in the trench, seemingly digging further into the gash in search of the liver. The latter was just
visible, inasmuch as the artist had sundered the trench of the
wound. The tips of the bird's claws were sunk into Prometheus'
thigh. Prometheus himself was hunched in agony at this, one side
of his body doubled up as he raised his thigh towards it; in this way,
he only brought the bird closer to his liver. The other leg had been
stretched out downwards in the opposite direction with a jerk, in a
straight line that narrowed towards the toes. The rest of his posture
also indicated his pain: his eyebrows were contracted and his lips
pursed, revealing his teeth. A pitiable spectacle, as though the very
painting were suffering.

Heracles, though, was in the process of releasing him from his woes: he stood there in the act of shooting Prometheus' torturer, arrow fitted to the bow, the handle extended in his left hand as he thrust it forwards, right hand drawn back to his breast, his elbow flexed behind as he drew back the string. All the details—bow, string, and arrow—were alike poised in contracted tension: the stringing of the bow had arched it, the hand had doubled up the string, and the hand was bent in against the breast. Prometheus could barely contain his simultaneous hope and fear. He was gazing both at the wound and at Heracles: he wanted to devote his full attention to the latter, but half of his gaze was distracted by the pain.

[9] So, we spent two days here recovering from our trials before hiring an Egyptian ship (with some of the little money that we happened to have stowed in our belts) and making the voyage up the Nile towards Alexandria.° We had decided to spend some time there in the hope that our friends might have travelled there, and that we might perhaps find them. When, however, we reached a certain town we suddenly heard a great cry. 'Herdsmen!'° called out the captain, and began to turn the ship around so as to sail back in the opposite direction. The banks were suddenly filled with terrifying savages. All were huge, black-skinned (not the pure black of the Indians, more as you would imagine a half-caste Ethiopian), bare-headed, light of foot but broad of body. They were all speaking a barbarian language.

'We're done for!' cried the helmsman. He brought the ship to a halt, as this was the narrowest part of the river, and four of the bandits climbed on board. They took everything on the ship, and carried off our money; then they bound us and locked us in a cell before leaving guards to watch over us and departing, with the intention of bringing us before their king (as they styled the chief bandit) on the following day. This involved two days' travel, as we learned from our fellow captives.

[10] When night fell, we lay down, tied up as we were, and the guards fell asleep. Then, as was finally possible, I began to weep for Leucippe. I counted up all the troubles that I had brought upon her and wailed deep in my soul, concealing the sound of my wailing by internalizing it:

'O gods and spirits,' I wept, 'if there be any truth to your existence and if you hear me: what crime can we have committed grave enough for us to be immersed in so many troubles in the space of a few days? Now you have placed us in the hands of Egyptian bandits, so that we cannot even expect compassion. Had the bandit been Greek our voices could have broken down his resistance, our prayers could have softened him. Speech often procures compassion; for when the tongue is mandated by a grieving soul to appeal for clemency it softens the raging souls of its audience. But as things stand, what language are we to use for our appeals? What oaths should we offer? Even if someone acquired more eloquence than the Sirens,° he could not get through to this murderer. Must I make my supplication with mere nods, must I play charades for my appeal? Alas for my misfortunes: now I shall have to mime my lamentation! Yet even if it overflows with calamity, I feel less pain for my own situation; but yours, Leucippe—where can I find the mouth to wail, the eyes to weep for that? Ah, how faithful you are to the pact of our love, how staunch towards your unfortunate lover! And what fine trappings for your wedding! A prison for a nuptial chamber! The earth for your bed! Ropes and knots for your necklaces and bracelets! And there is the man to give you away: that bandit sitting outside! It is a dirge that they are singing for you, not a wedding hymn. It was a mistake to proclaim our gratitude to you, O sea: I reproach your benevolence. You were kinder to those you killed; us you have rescued, but consigned to more of a death. You begrudged us a non-piratical death.'

[11] Such was my silent lament, but I was unable to cry, a peculiarity of eyes in times of major crisis. In moderate disasters the tears run in abundance, appealing for clemency to persecutors on behalf of their victims and phlebotomizing sufferers' pain like a pustular sore; but amid extreme suffering even tears desert one, forsaking the eyes. For when the tears well up, grief confronts them and halts them when they are at their peak, then heads them off and escorts them down with it. The tears, diverted from their journey to the eyes, flood down to the soul and exacerbate its wound.

Leucippe had not said a word, so I said to her:

'Why so quiet, dearest? Why do you not speak to me?'

'Because,' she replied, 'I have lost my tongue, ahead of losing my life.'

[12] During this discussion, dawn stole up on us. A man with long, wild hair arrived on horseback. The horse too was hairy, with no trappings, saddle, or face-protector (as is the way with bandits' horses). He had come from the chief bandit.

'My orders,' he said, 'are to take any maiden among the captives to be sacrificed to the god, an offering to purify the army.'

They immediately turned to Leucippe, who grabbed hold of me and hung on, screaming. The bandits set about tugging and beating: the tuggers tugged Leucippe, and the beaters beat me. They slung her up and carried her off, then bound the rest of us and began to march us slowly. [13] When we had advanced two stades° from the settlement, we heard a great shrieking and the sound of a trumpet, then a detachment of soldiers, all armed, manifested itself. When the bandits saw this, they put us in their midst and waited to resist the onslaught. After a while, it became clear that they were fifty in number, some with full-body shields, others with light bucklers. The bandits, far superior in number, began picking up clods of earth and pelting the soldiers. An Egyptian clod is more dangerous than any stone, since it is heavy, jagged, and irregular, the irregularities caused by sharp stones. As a result, when one is used as a missile it causes a double injury in the same place: it bruises like a stone and cuts like a spear. The soldiers, though, took these rocks on their shields and made light of this barrage.

When the bandits tired of throwing, the soldiers opened up their ranks and light-armed men charged from the midst of the heavily armed, each bearing a spear and a sword. They hurled their spears as they ran, and not a single one missed its target. Then the heavily armed infantry charged. It was a tough battle, with slashes, wounds, and slayings on either side. The experience on the soldiers' side made up for the shortfall in numbers. Those of us who were prisoners looked around for a struggling section of the bandit army, then grouped together and broke through their ranks, hurtling out towards their opponents. At first the soldiers did not realize who we were and tried to despatch us; but when they saw that we were unarmed and bound they divined the truth and received us into the middle of their army, keeping us out of harm's way by sending us towards the rear. Then the massed cavalry also charged. When they approached, they stretched out into a line and encircled the bandits with horses, and, constricting them in this way, they began to all but massacre them. Some of the bandits lay dead, others fought on though they were half-dead; the rest were captured.

[14] The time was around mid-afternoon. The general took each one of us separately and asked who we were and how we had been captured. All of us gave our various accounts, and I told my story. When all his questions were answered he invited us to follow him, promising to arm us, since he had decided to wait for the entire army to join him, and then to attack the brigands' capital. There were said to be tens of thousands of them. I asked him for a horse, as I had been trained into an excellent horseman. When one was produced, I rode a circuit, performing all the military manoeuvres in a perfect dressage: even the general declared himself extremely impressed. Indeed, he invited me to dine with him that day, and over dinner he asked me about myself, expressing pity when he heard the reply. A man who listens to another's troubles is somehow drawn through sympathy into compassion. Compassion, moreover, often procures friendship, for the soul is softened by grief at what it hears, and, by gradually attuning itself to this tale of suffering, transforms pity into friendly feelings and grief into compassion. At any rate, this was the effect of my story upon the general, so that he too was provoked to tears. But there was nothing more we could do: Leucippe was in the hands of bandits.

He also gave me an Egyptian batman to see to my needs. [15] On the following day, he made preparations to cross over the divide, attempting to fill in the trench that lay in our path. We could see the bandits standing in an enormous armed force on the other side of the trench. There was also an improvised altar made of clay and, next to it, a coffin. Two figures led out a girl with her hands tied behind her back. I could not tell who they were, as they were wearing armour, but the girl I recognized as Leucippe. Then they sprinkled holy water over her head and led her in procession right around the altar. Someone played the flute over her, and the priest began to chant what was in all probability an Egyptian hymn: the shape of his mouth and the twisted contortions of his face suggested a hymn. Then a signal was given and the assembly retreated a long way from the altar. One of the two young men laid her on her back and tied her down to some pegs driven into the earth (just as the artists represent Marsyas° tied to a tree). Then he took his sword and plunged it in below her heart; twisting it downwards, he ruptured her belly. Her innards leaped out at once. Tearing them out with his hands he placed them upon the altar. When they were roasted, each man cut off a portion and ate it.

The general and his army were watching and cried out at each one of these rites, averting their eyes from the spectacle. I, on the other hand, beyond all expectation, simply sat there as a spectator. My reaction was one of pure shock: this unbounded calamity had thunderstruck me. Perhaps the myth of Niobe° is no lie: she too may have experienced something like this when she lost her children, and given the impression through her immobility of having turned into stone. When the sacrament was over, or so I thought, they placed the body into the coffin and left it there with a lid placed over the top. Then they demolished the altar and retreated without looking back, following the oracular pronouncements of their priest.

[16] By the time evening had drawn in the entire trench had been filled. The soldiers crossed over and pitched camp a little beyond the trench, and then saw about their supper. The general attempted to console me, but I was in a state of devastation. About the first watch of night I checked that all the guards were sleeping and set forth with my sword, intending to immolate myself over the coffin. When I approached it I drew my sword, saying:

'Miserable Leucippe, unluckiest person in the whole world: I bewail you not only for your death, and because you died in a strange land, and because of the violent mode of your sacrifice, but also because this business makes a mockery of your suffering, because you were sacrificed to purify these irredeemably defiled creatures, because they carved you up while you were still living—alas!—and watching the whole carving process, because they took the inner mysteries of your belly and served them out in portions, and because your resting-place is on this wretched altar and in this coffin. Your corpse has been laid out here, but where are your innards? If fire had consumed them, the calamity would have been less intense; but as it is, your innards' inhumation has become these robbers' alimentation! Ah, you miserable torchlit altars! Ah, what a novel form of mystic meal! And the gods gazed down from above on such offerings as these, without quenching the flames: this fiery pollution was tolerated, and it elevated the burnt aroma to the gods! So, Leucippe, accept the only fitting libation I can offer you.'

[17] With these words I raised my sword, intending to sacrifice myself by plunging it into myself, when I spied in the moonlight two figures running in my direction with great haste. I paused, thinking that they were bandits, hoping to die at their hands. Then they drew near, and both called out to me. It was Menelaus and Satyrus! Even though I had seen these men unexpectedly alive, and dear friends at that, I could not embrace them, nor was I over-come with joy, so stunned was I with grief at the calamity. They seized hold of my right hand and tried to wrench away the sword.

'By the gods,' I cried, 'don't begrudge me an honourable death, still less a remedy for my pains! I can live no longer, even if you force me to do so, now Leucippe has been slaughtered as she has. This sword you may wrench from me, but the sword of grief is planted firmly within me and little by little minces up my soul. Do you wish it to be a deathless death that slays me?'

Menelaus replied:

'If that is the reason for your death-wish, then now is the time to hold back the sword. Leucippe will now be resurrected before your eyes.'

I stared at him.

'Are you still mocking me,' I asked, 'even at a time of such despair? An excellent way of showing how mindful you are of Zeus Xenios!'°

He tapped on the coffin, and said:

'Well then, since Clitophon will not believe . . . Hey! Leucippe! If you are alive, prove it!'

As he spoke he beat on the coffin some two or three times. From deep down, and extremely faintly, I heard a voice! I was immedi-ately seized by trembling, and turned to look at Menelaus, think-ing he must be a miracle-worker. At the same time he opened the coffin, and Leucippe climbed out from down below. Ye gods, what a fearful, chilling spectacle! Her entire belly had been carved open, and was bereft of viscera. She threw herself upon me, I flung her arms around her, and the two of us fell to the ground as if we were one. [18] After struggling to regain my composure I said to Menelaus:

'Will you not tell me what is going on? Is this not Leucippe that I can see? Is it not she whom I hold, and whose voice I hear? What were those spectacles I beheld yesterday? Either they were a dream, or this is. But see! This must be a living, breathing kiss, since this is Leucippe's sweetness.'

'And now,' said Menelaus, 'her innards will now be restored to her and her stomach will be resealed: you will see her wound disappear. But . . . cover your face, for I call upon Hecate° to perform this act!'

I believed him and covered it. He began his mumbo-jumbo, reciting some formula or other: as he did so, he unpeeled the miraculous device from Leucippe's stomach and made her as good as new. Then he said:

'You may reveal your face.'

I was hesitant and fearful, thinking that Hecate really was there, but I did nevertheless remove my hands from my eyes and behold Leucippe whole. Still more amazed at this, I asked Menelaus:

'Menelaus, my excellent friend, if you are some divine apostle, tell me, I beg you: what land am I in? What on earth are these phenomena I am witnessing?'

'Menelaus,' said Leucippe, 'stop scaring him. Tell him how you trumped those bandits.'

[19] So Menelaus replied:

'You know I am of Egyptian descent, since I told you this beforehand, on the ship. Well, most of my holdings were around this district, and I am well acquainted with the local officials. When we were shipwrecked and the tide subsequently cast me ashore on the Egyptian coast, I was captured (along with Satyrus) by the bandits who patrol that region. As I was being led to the chief bandit, some of the bandits recognized me, released me from my bonds, reassured me, and invited me to join their cause on equal terms. I asked them to give me Satyrus as a servant.

'Only', they replied, 'if you first display to us some deed of daring.'

At that time they received an oracle telling them to purify their den by sacrificing a girl and, after the sacrifice, tasting her liver; then they were to transfer what was left of her corpse to a coffin and retire, allowing the enemy army to capture the land where the sacrifice had taken place. You can tell the rest, Satyrus: it is your story from now on.'

[20] Satyrus spoke up:

'As we walked towards the camp, master, I was weeping and wailing now that I had found out about Leucippe. I begged Menelaus to use any means to save the girl. Some good spirit came to our aid. By chance, the day before the sacrifice we happened to be sitting by the sea,° grieving and pondering these matters, when some of the bandits spotted and attacked a ship that had unknowingly erred from its course. When those on board the ship realized where they had ended up, they tried to about sail; and then, when the robbers caught up with them first, they turned to self-defence. This was down to one of their number who was a vocal performer of Homeric songs in theatres:° he kitted himself and his neighbours out in Homeric props, and with these props they attempted to join battle. They confronted the first arrivals extremely robustly, but when more bandit boats sailed up the ship was sunk and the men who fell out slaughtered. Without the bandits noticing, a chest floated away from the wreck and was carried towards us by the current. Menelaus rescued it and withdrew a certain distance. I was there too, as I guessed that there was something important inside. He opened up the chest, and we saw a cloak and a sword. Its hilt was the length of four palms but the blade attached to the hilt was tiny, no longer than three fingers' length. Menelaus picked up the sword, and when he inattentively lowered the blade-segment, that paltry sword shot out to the same length as the hilt, as if from a compartment in the hilt! When he lifted it up again, the blade once again retracted inside. That poor wretch, no doubt, used this for his fake slaughters in the theatres.

[21] 'So I said to Menelaus: "If you are willing to prove yourself a hero, god will be on our side: we shall be able to save the girl without the bandits' knowledge. I shall tell you how. We shall take the softest sheepskin we can find and sew it into the shape of a purse the same size as a human stomach; then we shall fill it with

animal innards and blood and sew up this bastard belly so as to stop the guts from falling out too easily. Then we shall fit the girl with this prop, tying ribbons and girdles around her clothing and concealing the prop by binding it onto her. What's more, the prophet's words certainly profit our secret plan: it was enjoined that she should be dressed in a robe and stabbed in the belly, through the robe, by a blade. You can see how the mechanism in this sword works: if you press it against someone's body, it retreats into the hilt as though it were being sheathed. The audience thinks that the blade is being plunged into the body, but in fact it has shot up into the compartment in the hilt, leaving only the tip: enough to slice through the bastard belly as the hilt reaches the skin of the victim. If you withdraw the blade from the wound, the sword gradually slips back down from the compartment the more that you raise the hilt up high: the audience is similarly taken in, for it appears as if the length that is actually descending out of the hilt is rising from the sacrificial cut. The bandits will not spot the art that lies behind these effects, as the sheepskin will be carefully concealed; the innards will leap out at the moment of sacrifice, and we shall remove them and place them on the altar. Thereafter the bandits will not approach the body, and we shall place it in the coffin. You heard the chief bandit say a short while ago that you had to display some deed of daring to them: it is up to you to approach him and volunteer this display."

'With these words I began to beg Menelaus, calling on Zeus Xenios,° reminding him we had shared hospitality over the table and shared the experience of shipwreck. [22] This excellent fellow replied, saying: "This is a mighty ordeal; but danger undergone for a friend's sake is noble, even if death is required."

'"I think," I said, "that Clitophon is also alive. When I asked, the girl told me that she had left him tied up with the bandits' captives; while those bandits who escaped and met up with their chief said that all their prisoners had escaped to the enemy camp. So he will be grateful to you for your compassionate rescue of this poor girl from such horrors."

'These words clinched it. Fortune also played her part: when Menelaus was on the very point of speaking to the chief on the subject of the sacrifice (I was devising the props at the time), the latter, inspired by some deity, interrupted: "It is our custom," he said, "that our new initiates should preside over religious rites, especially in cases of human sacrifice. Well, it is your turn: prepare yourself for the sacrifice tomorrow. Your servant will also need to be initiated at the same time as you."

' "By all means", said Menelaus. "We are keen to be second to none in your band. But we shall have to prepare the girl ourselves, so that she is suitable for slicing up."

' "The victim is all yours", replied the chief.

'We privately prepared the girl in the aforementioned way. We encouraged her to take heart, going through the whole plan, adding that she had to remain in the coffin for the whole day, even if she woke up too early: if anything should occur to hold us up, we said, "save yourself and run away to the camp!" With these words we led her to the altar. You saw the rest for yourself.'

[23] When I heard this, the whole spectrum of emotions seized me. I had no idea what I could do to repay Menelaus for his deeds. I went for the most common means, throwing myself at his feet in homage, prostrating myself before him as if he were a god. My soul was gripped by complete pleasure.

Since Leucippe's side of things had turned out well for me, I asked:

'And Clinias? What happened to him?'

'I do not know,' said Menelaus. 'Immediately after the shipwreck I saw him clinging onto the yardarm, but I do not know where he has ended up.'

At this I wailed, even in the midst of my joy: some deity had no doubt begrudged me pure pleasure. Clinias, whose disappearance was due to me; Clinias, who was, after Leucippe, master of my life: of all men, it was him that the sea had retained, to deprive him of not only his life but also a decent burial. O cruel sea, you begrudged us a benevolent theme throughout the whole drama!

We left for the camp in a group, entered my tent, and passed the remainder of the night. The rank and file were fully aware of what had happened. [24] As soon as dawn broke, I took Menelaus to the general and told him the full story. He was as delighted as we were. He befriended Menelaus and quizzed him about the extent of the enemy's forces. Menelaus replied that the entire adjacent village was brimming with desperadoes, and that an army of bandits had flooded in to join them: they must have totalled around ten thousand.

'Yes,' replied the general, 'but our five thousand are enough to fight twenty thousand of theirs. Our numbers will be swelled presently by the arrival of two thousand others from the outposts set up around the delta and Heliopolis° against the barbarians.'

As he was speaking, a slave ran in saying that a messenger had come from the Delta with a message from the camp there: the two thousand men were staying put for five more days; the barbarian strikes had been ended, but when they had been on the point of setting off, the holy bird had paid a visit to them, bearing its father's tomb; so it was altogether necessary to postpone the expedition by the given number of days.

[25] 'What bird is this,' I asked, 'that has merited so much respect? And what on earth is meant by this "tomb" that it carries?'

'The bird is called the phoenix,° although it comes not from Phoenicia but from Ethiopia. It is as big as a peacock; as far as complexions go, though, a peacock would come second in a beauty-contest. Its wings are a combination of gold and purple. It boasts of being the servant of the Sun; and its head proves it, crowned as it is with a handsome ring, this circular crown being the very image of the sun. Its colour is deep crimson like roses, and its aspect delightful. Its plumage is streaked with sunbeams, which rise like the rays of dawn along its wings.

'It is apportioned to the Ethiopians as long as it lives, and the Egyptians at its death. When it dies (which it does after a long period), its child carries it to the Nile, after improvising a tomb as follows. It takes a lump of the most fragrant myrrh, enough for a bird's tomb, bores into it with its beak, and hollows out the middle: the final product becomes the resting-place for the corpse. It commits the bird to the coffin and fixes it there, sealing the gap by plugging it with clay. Then it flies along the Nile bearing this fabrication. Other birds follow in a troupe, looking like sentinels, and the bird resembles a king on a state visit. They fly straight to Heliopolis without deviation, the goal of the dead bird's migration. The phoenix positions itself on a lofty site and receives the ministers of the god. An Egyptian priest approaches, carrying a book from the inner sanctum of the temple, and uses a description there to ratify that the bird is not counterfeit. But the bird knows that it is the object of scepticism, and flashes the secret mysteries of its body, displays the corpse, and pronounces a kind of funeral oration. The priests of the Sun receive from it the corpse of the bird and bury it. So, in life it is an Ethiopian because of its Ethiopian alimentation; but in death it becomes an Egyptian because of its Egyptian inhumation.'

Book 4

[1] On learning of the disposition of the enemy troops and the hold-up to his reinforcements, the general decided to retreat to the garrison from which they had originally set out and await the arrival of the others. I was billeted with Leucippe in a house a little way beyond the general's quarters. When I entered, I grabbed her into my arms, trying to put my manhood to use. She refused.

'How long will we go without Aphrodite's rites?' I cried. 'Think of all the extraordinary events that have occurred, the shipwreck, bandits, sacrifices, and deaths! Let us take the opportunity while Fortune's seas are calm, before some crueller fate prevents us!'

'No,' she said, 'it would now be against divine law for that to occur. For Artemis° appeared to me in a dream the night before last while I was weeping at the thought of my sacrifice. "Do not cry, now", she said. "You will not die, for I shall be there to succour you. You shall remain a virgin until I lead you up the aisle; and none other than Clitophon will wed you.' I was certainly irritated by the delay, but equally titillated by my expectations for the future.'

When I heard about her dream, I recalled having seen a similar vision: on the previous night, I had dreamt I saw a temple of Aphrodite, with the goddess' cult-statue within; when I approached to pay my devotions, the doors slammed shut. I was crestfallen, but a woman who looked like the statue appeared to me and said:

'It is not permitted for you to enter the temple for the time being. If you wait a brief period, though, I shall not only open up for you, but even make you a priest of the goddess.'

I recounted this dream to Leucippe, and subsequently refrained from my attempts to coerce her. When I started trying to match it up with Leucippe's dream, however, I began to be more than a little disturbed.

[2] It was at this time that the eyes of Charmides (that being the general's name) alighted upon Leucippe, and the origins of his eyeing were as follows. It happened that some of the men had caught a river beast, a real spectacle: the Egyptians call it the horse of the Nile.° It is indeed a horse, as its name indicates, in terms of its belly and feet (except in the case of the hoof, which is cloven). Its size is that of the largest ox; its tail is short and without hair— which also goes for its entire body. Its head is round and far from small, its jowls like a horse's. Its snout flares out broadly, and it exhales fiery gases as if from a fiery fount. Its jaw is as broad as its jowls. Its mouth opens as far as its temples. It has bent, canine teeth, like a horse's in appearance and arrangement but three times as big.

[3] The general invited us to behold the spectacle, and Leucippe was also present. While all our eyes were on the beast, the general's were on Leucippe. He was immediately captivated; and so, wishing us to prolong our sojourn with him for as long as possible so that he could gratify his eyes, he sought to weave elaborate pretexts, giving us a catalogue first of the beast's attributes, then of the means of its capture. It is, he said, a most voracious beast, capable of munching through an entire field of crops; and it is hunted by subterfuge, in the following manner. The locals observe its routines, then they dig a trench and cover the top with reeds and loose earth. Below this reedy contraption, he said, they set a deep-sunk wooden cage with the gates in its roof wide open; then they lie low and wait for the beast to fall in. When it treads upon this device, it immediately plummets and the cage welcomes it into its new den. The hunters thereupon rush out and fasten the gates on the roof. This is how they trap their prey, he said, since if it were a contest of strength no one could summon the force to master it.

'Amongst all its mighty qualities,' he continued, 'its hide in particular, as you can see, is hard and will not allow it to be wounded by a blade. It is, so to speak, an Egyptian version of the elephant: it is second only to the Indian elephant in terms of might.'

[4] 'So,' said Menelaus, 'you must have seen an elephant at some point?'

'I should say so', replied Charmides. 'I have also heard from reliable sources about the extraordinary nature of its birth.'

'We on the other hand', I said, 'have never to this very day set eyes upon one, except in paintings.'°

'Allow me to tell you,' he said, 'since time is at our disposal. The mother's pregnancy lasts an extremely long time: she spends ten years moulding her fetus. After this lengthy cycle of years is complete she gives birth, by which time the parent is elderly. This is why, I suppose, its frame is so large, its might so irresistible, its lifespan so long, and its death so slow in coming (for they say that it lives longer than Hesiod's crow°). The elephant's jaw is comparable to an ox's head. If you saw it you would say that its mouth had a pair of horns: these are the curved teeth of the elephant. Midway between the teeth rises its proboscis, like a trumpet in appearance and size. It responds to all the elephant's needs. It forages for the beast's food, probing for whatever is edible in front of it: anything that is elephant-fodder it immediately snatches up and, angling back towards its jaw, serves up to the mouth as sustenance; anything more dainty that it spies, it encompasses by wrapping itself tightly around this prey, before lifting it up in its entirety and offering it up to its master as a gift. The latter is an Ethiopian° seated on its back, a novel kind of elephant-jockey. The elephant is timorously submissive to him, recognizes his voice, and allows him to whip it (the whip used is an iron axe).

'And I once witnessed a novel spectacle. A Greek man put his head into the middle of the elephant's head: the elephant had opened his mouth wide open and was exhaling his breath around the man within. I marvelled at both phenomena, the intrepidity of the man and the humane temper of the elephant. The man said that he had even given the beast a reward, for the breath it exhaled on him was practically identical to the aromatic spices of India, and was also a cure for headaches. Now the elephant knows of its restorative powers, and does not open its mouth for free: like a quack doctor, it demands its payment first. If you pay up, it agrees and fulfills its side of the bargain, unfurling its jaws, opening wide and admitting the human as far as is desired. It knows it has sold its odour.'

[5] 'How is it', I said, 'that such an ugly beast could have such a pleasant fragrance?'

'Because', replied Charmides, 'its diet is equally fragrant. The land of the Indians, you see, lies next to the sun: the Indians are the first to see the god rise, its light strikes them hotter, and their bodies retain the mark of scorching. There grows in Greece a bloom° of the colour of an Ethiopian: in India, it is not a bloom but a leaf, like the leaves of the bushes that grow here. The leaf hides away its fragrant breath, making no display of it, either because it is reluctant to advertise its pleasures too ostentatiously to those who are in the know, or because of a grudge against the inhabitants. When it travels a little way from home, though, and crosses the mountains, it shows forth the pleasure it once hid away: it metamorphoses from a leaf into a bloom and invests itself with fragrance. This is the black rose of India. Elephants feed on it, just as our oxen feed on grass. Since the elephant is fed on this from the moment of its birth, its whole body exudes the fragrance of this food, and it emits this most fragrant breath from deep inside: this is the fountainhead of its breath.'

[6] When we had finished discussing with the general and gone our separate ways, after a rather brief interval (for a wounded man cannot stand his fiery affliction), he sent for Menelaus, took him by the hand and said:

'I know how constant your friendship is with Clitophon, because of what you have done for him. You will find mine no worse. I want to ask a favour from you: it will be no trouble for you, but it will save my life if you agree. Leucippe has done for me. Please, save me! She owes you for rescuing her. There will be fifty gold pieces in it for your service, and for her as many as she desires.'

'You can keep your gold,' said Menelaus in reply, 'save it for those who sell their favours: I am a true friend, and shall do my best to help you out.'

With these words he departed, before approaching me and telling me everything. We set to discussing the best course. We decided to trick him. To resist would have been parlous, in case he brought force to bear; to escape would have been hopeless, with the entire area teeming with bandits, and given the number of soldiers he commanded. [7] So, after a brief period, Menelaus went off and said to Charmides:

'The act is all but performed. At first, the woman strongly refused, but when I insisted and reminded her of the favour she owed me, she acceded. She has one request, a fair one: could you grant her a few days' grace, "just until I get to Alexandria," she says, "since this is a village and everything that goes on is observed by numerous witnesses." '

'This favour of yours will be a long time in coming,' replied Charmides. 'Who in war holds back from fulfilling his desire? Does a soldier in the midst of battle know whether he will live or die? Many indeed are the roads to death. Pray to Fortune for my safety and I shall wait. For now I shall advance to a war against the Herdsmen; but another war is being fought over the territory of my soul. The soldier is sacking my citadel with his bow, with his arrows. I am beaten! I am bristling with arrows! Call the doctor, man, quick! The wound is agonizing! I shall light flames to throw at the enemy, but Eros has lit other brands to use on me. This is the flame you must quench first, Menelaus! Making love is a lucky omen before making war: may Aphrodite send me on my way to Ares!'°

'But you take the point,' replied Menelaus, 'that it is not easy for her to keep a secret from her husband while she is here, especially when he himself is under the influence of Eros.'

'Well now,' replied Charmides, 'that is no problem: we can get rid of Clitophon.'

At this, Menelaus realized how urgent were Charmides' feelings, and began to fear for me, so he quickly invented an excuse.

'Would you like to hear the real reason for the delay?' he asked. 'Actually, she began her time of the month yesterday, and religious law forbids her to sleep with any man.'

'In that case we shall wait', said Charmides, 'for three or four days from now. That will be enough. But I would ask her for what I *am* permitted to have. Let her come before my eyes and exchange words with me: I wish to hear her voice, to hold her hand, to touch her body. These things can console those afflicted by desire. It is also permitted for her to kiss: her womb cannot have forbidden *that*.'

[8] Menelaus left and reported these words to me. I cried out in response that I should sooner die than stand by and watch Leucippe's kiss be signed over to another man.

'What', I protested, 'is sweeter than a kiss? With Aphrodite's act come satiation and culmination°—but it is all reduced to nothing if you take away the kisses from it. A kiss, on the other hand, neither satiates nor culminates, but is ever renewed. The mouth is the source of the three finest things: respiration, speech, and kissing. Though we kiss each other with the lips, the wellspring of pleasure lies in the soul. Believe me, Menelaus—in this time of emergency I am about to divulge secret mysteries—when I say that I too have had nothing but kisses from Leucippe. She remains a virgin: my kisses alone have made a woman of her. If someone is to snatch these too from me—well, I cannot put up with the violation. No adulterer shall steal her kisses from me!'

'In that case,' replied Menelaus, 'we need the best plan we can find—and the quickest. A man with a passion can put up with striving for success for as long as he has hopes of succeeding; but if he is desperate, his appetite changes its focus, and he takes it on himself, using every resource he can muster, to repay whatever stands in his way with equal measures of pain. If he also has the power to act without fear of recrimination, the part of his soul uncurbed by timidity aggravates the part impelled by acerbity. And this tricky situation is compounded by the need to act fast.'

[9] While we were deep in consideration, someone ran in excitedly and said that Leucippe had been walking when she had suddenly fallen to the ground, her eyes spinning. We leaped to our feet, ran to her, and saw her lying on the ground. I went up to her and asked her what was the matter. When she saw me, she leaped to her feet, her eyes bloodshot, and struck my face. When Menelaus also tried to restrain her, she struck him too, using her leg this time. We realized that the problem was some madness, and so we grabbed her forcibly and tried to get the better of her. She struggled with us, with no thought to conceal the parts that a woman would not wish to be seen. There was soon uproar around the camp, and as a result even the general himself came running and observed the events. At first, he suspected that this malady was some trumped-up excuse, and stared menacingly at Menelaus; but when the truth gradually dawned upon him, he too was somewhat affected by pity. So they carried her back and bound the poor girl with rope. When I saw her with bonds around her hands, I begged Menelaus, once the crowd had dispersed:

'Free her,' I cried, 'for pity's sake, free her! Those delicate hands will not tolerate bonds. Leave me alone with her, and I shall embrace her and make myself her bond. Let me hold her while she rages! For what reason is there for me to stay alive? Leucippe is unaware of my presence! She lies before me bound, and I, shameless I, am unwilling to free her, though it lies within my power! Is it for this that Fortune saved us from the bandits, so that you could become the toy of madness? Oh, how unlucky we are whenever good luck comes our way! We escaped from our fears at home, to meet with bad luck at sea; we survived the sea; we were saved from the bandits; all because we were being kept for this madness! If your sanity returns, dearest, I for one fear that the god will devise some new calamity for you. Who has suffered more divine persecution than us? We fear even good fortune! But may your sanity only return and may you come to yourself again, and Fortune is welcome to devise some new game.'

[10] During this speech of mine, Menelaus was trying to console me, telling me that such afflictions were not permanent and were quite common at the age when youth reaches its boiling-point: when the blood, which is everywhere young and fresh, bubbles up to a great climax, it often bursts out of the vein and swamps the brain, submerging the faculty that inspires reason.° For this reason, he said, we should send for doctors and arrange for her to have treatment. So Menelaus approached the general and asked him to summon the camp surgeon. He was glad to agree, for lovers rejoice in the duties assigned them by Eros. When the doctor arrived, he said:

'For now, let us get her to sleep: that way we shall reduce the savagery of the affliction from its present climactic state, for sleep serves as a cure for any illness. Afterwards I shall apply the rest of the treatment.'

He gave us a small prescription of medicine about the size of a seed of vetch, and told us to dissolve it in olive oil and smear it upon her forehead. He also said that he would prepare another medicine to purge her womb. So we did as we had been told, and a little while after she had been besmeared she fell asleep for the rest of night, until dawn. I, meanwhile, was awake for the entire night, sitting beside her and weeping. Looking at the bonds, I said:

'Alas, dearest! You are bound even while you sleep: you cannot even enjoy sleep in freedom. What must your dreams be? Are you sane in your sleep at least, or are your dreams mad too?'

When she awoke, she once again began to scream incomprehensibly. The doctor arrived and started to administer the rest of the treatment.

[11] At this point, an emissary arrived from the satrap° of Egypt with a letter for the general. The message, in all probability, urged him to war: at any rate, he ordered all his men to arm themselves to fight the Herdsmen. Each man rushed out with all speed at once: first they went to the armoury, then they joined their captains. When the general had given this order and instructed them to pitch camp, he remained alone. The army, on the other hand, marched out to fight the enemy at dawn the following day.

The situation of the village before them was as follows. The Nile flows down from Egyptian Thebes, and continues to flow as before as far as Memphis (and a little way beyond: the name of the village that lies at the point where the great river ceases is Cercasorus).° Thereupon it fragments around the land and three rivers are born from one, two of which spread out on either side, while the remaining one continues to flow as it did before it was divided, forming the land into deltoid shapes. Not even each of these rivers manages to flow all the way to the sea: they bifurcate variously around cities (and these offshoots are bigger than Greek rivers). Although the water is everywhere diffused, it does not lose its capacity to be sailed on, drunk, and farmed. [12] The mighty Nile is everything to the locals: river, land, sea, and lake. What a novel spectacle! A ship serves as a mattock, an oar as a plough, a rudder as a sickle! This is the habitat of sailors and farmers alike, of fish and oxen alike. You sow where once you sailed, and the land you sow is cultivated sea, for the river comes and goes. The Egyptians sit and wait for it, counting the number of days. The Nile never cheats: the river observes the due period and measures out its water scrupulously, a river unwilling to be convicted of late repayment. It is also possible to see river and land competing: the one strives with the other, the water to deluge such an area of land and the land to absorb such an expanse of sweet sea. The two share victory between them (the vanquished party is nowhere to be seen), and the water merges into the land.

Around the Herdsmen's villages, the Nile is always plentiful. Whenever the whole of Egypt is deluged, lakes are created here;

and, even if the Nile recedes, the lakes remain, filled with silt now that the water level has dropped. The inhabitants both walk and sail on these lakes, although no boat carrying more than one passenger manages to sail: the silt attacks and gets the better of anything alien to the place. Small, light vessels and shallow water are enough for the locals. If an area happens to be completely dried up, the sailors pick up their vessels on their backs and carry them until they reach water. In the middle of these lakes lie some islands, formed at irregular intervals. Some have no houses on them, only crops of papyrus bush. These dense columns of papyrus leave just enough space between them for a single man to stand, and these gaps between the dense parts are covered by quantities of matted papyrus. It is into these shelters that they run to make their plans, to prepare ambushes and to conceal themselves, using the papyri like ramparts. Certain other islands, though, contain huts and are walled in by the lakes, like an improvised imitation of a city. These are the haunts of the Herdsmen. Nearby is an island bigger than the others, and containing more huts. Its name, I believe, is Nicochis. It was here that they had gathered, since it was the best-fortified place, taking encouragement from their numbers and from the topography (for there was only a single, narrow causeway that prevented it from being a complete island: it was one stade long and twelve fathoms wide).° This city was also surrounded by lake.

[13] Now, when they saw the general advancing, they devised a plan as follows. They assembled all the old men and gave them branches of date-palm to indicate supplication, and arranged behind them the most vigorous of the young men, armed with spears and swords. The old men were to raise the branches and conceal those behind them with the shock of foliage, while those following were to trail their spears behind them on the ground so as to minimize the risk of their being seen. If the general acceded to the old men's prayers, the spear-bearers were to do nothing to provoke battle. If he did not, however, they would invite him into the city, as if they were delivering themselves up to death; but when they reached the middle of the causeway, the old men would run apart upon a signal and throw down their suppliant branches, whereupon the armed men would charge into their midst and do whatever they could.

So, they stood there prepared in this manner, begging the general to respect their age, to respect their supplications, and to have mercy on the city. They offered one hundred talents° of silver to him personally, and one hundred men (who had volunteered to give themselves up for the good of the city) to carry it to the satrap's headquarters, so that he might be able to convey further spoils to the latter. This was no lie: the gift would have been made, had the general been willing to accept. But he rejected their terms.

'In that case,' replied the old men, 'since that is your decision, we shall accept our fate. But please, grant us this favour in these terrible circumstances: do not kill us outside the gates and far from the city, but accompany us to our ancestral land and the hearth where we were born. Make the town our tomb. Look: we are leading the way for you, the way that leads to death.'

On hearing this, the general set aside the accoutrements of battle and commanded the army to follow him at ease. [14] Spies had been posted by the Herdsmen in advance to watch these events from afar, with the orders to break down the river dyke, should they see the enemy crossing, and unleash the entire volume of water onto them. For the streams of the Nile are controlled in the following manner: the Egyptians build a dyke along the side of each canal, to prevent the Nile from bursting its banks and inundating the land before it is required. When they need to water the plain, they make a small gap in the dyke and the water is then conducted through. Now, there was behind the city a large, broad canal, and this was swiftly breached by those appointed to the task when they saw the enemy advancing.

Everything happened at once. The old men who were facing the soldiers suddenly parted, and the others all ran forward brandishing spears. The water was now on them: the lakes swelled, tumescent on every side, while the isthmus was submerged, looking everywhere like a sea. The Herdsmen fell upon and speared those in front of them (including the general himself), unprepared and panicked as their victims were by the unexpected events. The ways in which the others died defy description. Some were killed in the first engagement without even brandishing their spears, while others, who had no time to defend themselves, ascertained what was going on even as it happened to them. For others, the events were realized before they realized the events were happening. Others, in shock at the extraordinary turn, simply stood there and awaited death; others slipped as soon as they moved, the river knocking away their legs; while still others attempted to escape by plunging into the deeper part of the lake, and were dragged under. As for those who were still standing on the mainland, the water came up to their navels, washing away their shields and leaving their stomachs unprotected against injury. The water-level in the lake, meanwhile, had risen above the height of a man's head. It was impossible to tell what was lake and what was plain: anyone running along the land out of fear of losing his way was too slow to get away; while anyone who stumbled into the lake, thinking it was land, was submerged. A novel kind of ill-fortune, this: such a terrible shipwreck, with not a ship in sight. Two extraordinary departures from convention: an aquatic infantry battle and a shipwreck on land!

The spirits of the other side, meanwhile, had been lifted by the turn of events: they imagined that it was their manhood, and not a devious trick, that had led them to victory. Thus it is with an Egyptian: in times of fear, cowardice leads him to servility, whereas his bellicosity is exacerbated in positive situations. Both reactions are immoderate: in the former instance he is too weak in the face of misfortune, and in the latter too headstrong in victory.

[15] Ten days had elapsed since the onset of Leucippe's madness, and the illness was not abating. Once, while she was sleeping, she cried out in the voice of a woman possessed:

'You are the reason for my madness, Gorgias!'

When dawn broke, I told Menelaus what she had said, and began to make enquiries as to whether there was a Gorgias anywhere in the village. When we set out, a young man approached me, and said:

'I have come to rescue you and your wife.'

I was stunned, thinking that the man must be a divine emissary.

'You would not happen to be Gorgias, would you?'

'Of course not', he replied. 'My name is Chaereas: Gorgias is the man who has ruined you.'

I shuddered all the more at this.

'What do you mean, ruined?' I asked. 'And who is this Gorgias? Some deity revealed his name to me last night: interpret the divine revelation for me.'

'Gorgias', he said, 'was an Egyptian soldier. He is now no longer: the Herdsmen did for him. He was smitten with desire for your wife. Being skilled in herbs and potions, he prepared a love-drug, and persuaded your Egyptian servant to take it and pour it in with Leucippe's drink; but he inadvertently served it unmixed, and the potion brought on her madness. Gorgias' servant recounted all this to me yesterday: as it happened, he accompanied him on the expedition against the Herdsmen, but Fortune, so it seems, saved him for us. He is asking for four gold pieces in exchange for the antidote (he has another drug prepared that can overturn the first one).'

'May the gods reward you for this service', I replied. 'Please, bring this man that you mean to me.'

He left. I went up to the Egyptian and thumped him in the face two or three times, crying:

'Tell me! What did you give Leucippe? Why has she gone mad?'

Terrified, he confirmed everything Chaereas had recounted to us. We locked him in prison, to keep hold of him. [16] Then Chaereas arrived with the fellow in question.

'You can take the four gold pieces now,' I said to both of them, 'as a reward for this favourable revelation, but hear what I have to say on the issue of the drug. As you see, a drug was also responsible for the woman's present distress: it would not be without risk to subject organs already drugged to a second dosage. So come, tell me the contents of this drug and prepare it in our presence. I shall pay you four more pieces if you do this.'

'Your fear is justified,' said the man, 'but the ingredients are common and all edible. I myself shall taste it, in the same quantities that she takes.'

He then ordered someone to make certain purchases and bring them to him, naming each item aloud. As soon as they were brought, he crushed them all together in our presence and made two servings.

'I shall drink the one first,' he said, 'and then give the other one to the woman. When she has taken it, she will sleep soundly for the entire night. Around dawn, both the sleep and the disease will leave her.'

He himself took the drug first; he told us to give her the remaining portion to drink in the evening.

'I am going away to sleep', he said. 'The drug has that effect.'

With these words, he departed, accepting the four pieces from me.

'You can have the others,' I said, 'if she recovers from her illness.'

[17] When it was time for her to drink the drug, I prayed to it as I poured it:

'O drug, child of the earth, gift of Asclepius,° may the promises made about you turn out true! Bring greater fortune to her than I have done, and save my beloved! Defeat that savage, barbarian drug!'

After negotiating this treaty with the drug, I kissed the cup and gave it to Leucippe to drink. After a while, just as the man had said, she lay asleep. I sat beside her and spoke to her, as though she could hear me:

'Will your sanity really return? Will you ever recognize me? Will I hear that voice of yours? Please, prophesy during this sleep as well: your prophecy yesterday about Gorgias was certainly accurate. How much happier you are in your sleep! When you are awake this unhappy madness grips you, but your dreams are sane.'

As I was conversing thus with Leucippe as though she could hear me, the long prayed-for dawn finally broke. Leucippe spoke—and it was her voice!

'Clitophon!'

At this, I leaped up and ran to her to find out how she was. She seemed to know nothing of her actions, and was astounded to see her bonds, asking me who had bound her. I was overjoyed to see her sane: I untied her excitedly and then told her the whole story. She was embarrassed to hear it, and blushed as if she had been performing those actions now. I comforted her with reassuring words. I was more than happy to pay the price for the drug: all our travelling money was safe, since Satyrus happened to have had it stored in his belt when the ship went down, and neither he nor Menelaus had lost anything to the bandits.

[18] A larger force was now dispatched against the bandits from the capital.° It subdued the bandits, razing the entire city to its foundations. Now that the river had been delivered from the Herdsmen's lawlessness, we made ready to sail for Alexandria. Chaereas, whom we had befriended after he revealed the incident with the drug, sailed with us. His family was from the island of Pharos,° and he was a fisherman by trade. He had served as a mercenary in the naval expedition against the Herdsmen, and, now that the war was over, he had been demobilized. After such a long period when sailing had been difficult, there were travellers everywhere on the river, and there was much pleasure to be had in watching: sailors sang, passengers clapped, the very ships danced. The whole river was a festival, and the river seemed to be revelling as we sailed upon it.

I also drank the water of the Nile unmixed with wine for the first time, wanting to judge the pleasure of its taste (for wine conceals the nature of the water). So I drew some into a cup of translucent glass, and watched the liquid vie with the vessel's limpidity: the vessel was vanquished. It was sweet to drink, no more cold than was pleasant (some of the rivers I know in Greece can cause pain; I noted the contrast with this river). For this reason, Egyptians do not fear to drink this water straight, feeling no need for Dionysus.°

I found equally amazing the way in which they drink it. They are reluctant to drink draught water, and they do not tolerate drinking-cups, since they have their own ready-made cups: they drink out of their hands. Any Egyptian on a sailing trip who feels thirsty leans overboard and puts his face near the river, puts his hand in the water, submerges the cavity, fills it with water and hurls the liquid like a javelin into his mouth, hitting the mark exactly. The mouth awaits the missile agape, and closes when it strikes home, refusing to allow the water to fall out again.

[19] I also saw another beast of the Nile, reputed to be even more powerful than the hippopotamus: its name is the crocodile. In form, it is a mixture between a fish and a beast. It is enormous from head to tail, and too broad to tell of. Its skin is puckered with scales; the colour of its back is a petrous black, while its belly is white. It has four feet, which flare out slightly to the side, like the tortoise. Its tail is long and thick, like a solid body: it is not, as is the

case with other animals, an accessory, but a single bone continuing and completing the vertebra, an integral member. On its upper side, the tail sharpens into pitiless spines, like the teeth of a saw. It actually uses it against its prey like a whip, lashing its adversaries with it and inflicting multiple injuries with a single blow. Its head is interwoven with its back, forming a single straight line: nature has cheated it out of a neck. The head is more rugged than the rest of the body, and the full length of the jaws is usually stretched wide apart, so that this entire part is opened up. During the rest of the time, when the beast is not gaping, it is a head; but when it gapes towards its prey, it becomes one big mouth. It opens its upper jaw, keeping the lower one straight: the distance between them is immense. The gaping chasm reaches back to its shoulders, where the stomach immediately begins. It has many, extremely long teeth. The number they possess is said to be as great as the number of days illuminated by the god in an entire year: that is how great a fence° encloses the plain within their jaws! But if it emerged onto land, you would not believe that it has such strength, to see it struggling to haul its body along.

Book 5

[1] After three days' sailing, we reached Alexandria. As I entered through the so-called 'gates of the Sun', I was immediately confronted with the brilliant beauty of the city, and my eyes were filled with pleasure. Two opposing rows of columns ran in straight lines from the gates of the Sun to the gates of the Moon (these two deities are the city's gatekeepers). Between the columns extended the open part of the city. Many a road crisscrossed this part: you could be a tourist at home. When I had advanced a few stades° into the city, I reached the place named after Alexander,° where I saw another city altogether. Its beauty was dissected as follows: a row of columns ran in a straight line, traversed by another of equal length. I divided my eyes between all the streets, an insatiable spectator incapable of taking in such beauty in its entirety. There were sights I saw, sights I aimed to see, sights I ached to see, sights I could not bear to miss . . . my gaze was overpowered by what I could see before me, but dragged away by what I anticipated. As I was guiding my own tour around all these streets, love-sick with the sight of it, I said to myself wearily:

'We are beaten, my eyes!'

I saw two extraordinary novelties, grandeur competing with splendour and the populace striving to exceed their city. Both sides won: the city was bigger than a continent and the people more numerous than an entire race. When I considered the city, I could not believe that it could be filled with people; when I beheld the people, I was amazed that a city could hold them. The scales were that finely balanced.

[2] By chance (some deity had no doubt willed it), there was a festival going on in honour of the great god whom the Greeks call Zeus and the Egyptians Serapis. There was a torchlit procession, the largest I had ever seen. It was evening and the sun was setting, but there was not a hint of night, since a new sun was dawning,

split into tiny specks. It was then that I saw a city vying with the heavens for beauty. I also beheld Zeus Meilichios and the temple of Zeus Ouranios.° I addressed a prayer to the great god, asking that our sufferings should one day cease. We then returned to the lodgings that Menelaus had procured for us. It seems, however, that the god did not nod his assent to our prayers: Fortune was once again set to put us through our paces.

[3] This is what happened. Chaereas had long ago conceived a secret passion for Leucippe, and this was the reason why he had made the revelation about the drug, both as an opportunity to snare us into his friendship and as a means of rescuing the girl for himself. Realizing that consent would not be forthcoming, he arranged a plot: assembling a band of bandits who shared his trade (he being a man of the sea), he arranged what they had to do; then he invited us to Pharos to share his hospitality, under the pretext of celebrating his birthday.

When we went outside, we encountered a bad omen. A hawk, chasing a swallow, hit Leucippe on the head with its wing. I was disturbed by this, and raised my head to heaven:

'O Zeus,' I said, 'what is this portent you reveal to us? If this bird is truly sent by you, then give us a clearer omen.'

Now, on turning around I saw a picture hanging up (for I happened to be standing next to a painter's studio), and the encrypted meaning it conveyed was a similar one. It told of the violent rape of Philomela by Tereus,° who cut out her tongue. The picture incorporated the entire narrative of the drama: the robe, Tereus, the banquet. The maid was standing holding the unfolded robe; Philomela stood by her with her finger placed upon the robe, indicating the pictures woven into it. Procne had nodded her understanding of this performance: she was staring fiercely, furious at the picture. The embroidery showed the Thracian Tereus wrestling with Philomela for Aphrodite's prize. The woman's hair was torn, her girdle undone, her dress ripped, her chest half exposed. Her right hand was digging into Tereus' eyes, while her left sought to shut away her breasts with the shreds of her dress. Tereus held Philomela in his grip, pulling her towards him with all his bodily strength into a constricting, skin-to-skin embrace. This was the depiction the artist had woven into the robe. The remainder of the painting represented the women, simultaneously cackling and cowering, showing Tereus the leftovers of the feast in a basket, the head and hands of his son. Tereus was depicted leaping from his couch, waving his sword at the women and kicking his leg against the table. This was neither standing nor fallen, a pictorial indication that it was about to fall.

[4] Menelaus spoke up:

'I think we should postpone our journey to Pharos: the two signs have been clearly unfavourable, the bird's wing landing on us and the danger implied by the picture. Interpreters of signs say that if we encounter paintings as we set off to do something, we should ponder the myths narrated there, and conclude that the outcome for us will be comparable to the story they tell. This painting is filled with all sorts of negative aspects: illicit desire, shameless adultery, female misfortunes. For this reason, I advise you to postpone the expedition.'

His words seemed reasonable, and I made our excuses to Chaereas for that day. He went away extremely annoyed, promising to revisit us the next day. [5] Now the female species° is rather fond of myths, and Leucippe said to me:

'What is the meaning of the myth in the painting? What were those birds? Who is that shameless man?'

I began to tell the story.

'The nightingale, the swallow, and the hoopoe: all three humans, all three birds. The hoopoe is the man; of the two women, Philomela is the swallow and Procne the nightingale. The women came from the city of Athens. The man's name was Tereus, and Procne was his wife. It seems that with barbarians one wife will not satisfy Aphrodite's needs, especially when the opportunity to indulge in rape presents itself. Such an opportunity to display his nature was provided to this Thracian by Procne's kindly affection: she sent her husband to collect her sister. He began the outward journey still faithful to Procne, but the homeward one aflame for Philomela. On the way, he made Philomela his second Procne. Out of fear of Philomela's tongue, he gave her as her wedding present the gift of speechlessness, clipping the flower of speech. All to no avail, for artful Philomela invented silent speech:° she wove a robe to be her messenger, weaving the plot into the threads. The hand imitated the tongue: she revealed to Procne's eyes what normally meets the ears, using the shuttle to communicate her experience.

'When Procne heard from the robe of the rape, she sought to exact an excessive revenge upon her husband. Their anger was doubled, since there were two women of a single mind: they plotted a feast more ill-starred than their marriages, blending resentment into a recipe for atrocity. The feast was Tereus' son, whose mother Procne had been before her anger: she had no memory of the birth-pangs now. Thus do the pangs of resentment vanquish even the womb: for when wives desire nothing other than to hurt the husband who has brought grief to the marriage-bed, though they themselves suffer no less pain as they inflict it, they weigh up the pain of suffering against the pleasure of inflicting.° Tereus' feast was served up by the Furies:° the women brought him the leftovers of his son in a basket, cackling as they cowered. When Tereus saw the leftovers of his son, his meal filled him with sorrow: he realized that he was the father of the feast. When this dawned upon him, he flew into a mad rage, drew his sword, and ran at the women. They were whisked into the air, and Tereus was lifted up with them, metamorphosing into a bird. Even now they preserve° the image of their suffering: the nightingale flees, with Tereus in pursuit, retaining his hatred thus even in winged form.'

[6] Now, this was how we escaped from the plot on this occasion, but it bought us only a single day. On the following day, Chaereas appeared at dawn, and in our embarrassment we found it impossible to decline. So we boarded the boat and went to Pharos. Menelaus stayed behind, pleading illness. First of all, Chaereas took us to the lighthouse to show us the mechanism from underneath, and an extraordinary marvel it was. It was a mountain lying in the middle of the sea, touching the very clouds. The water lapped underneath the construction itself, which stood perched over the sea. On the citadel of this mountain shone what was for ships a second steersman. Afterwards, Chaereas led us to his house, which lay on the far side of the island, right on the sea.

[7] When evening came around, he withdrew, citing his stomach as his excuse. After a while there was a sudden shout at the doors, and a large group of well-built men immediately rushed in, dag-

gers at the ready, and they all made a dash for the girl. When I saw my beloved being abducted, I could not bear it and hurled myself among their swords. One of them struck me on the thigh with his dagger, and I collapsed. While I lay there bleeding profusely, they put the girl in the boat and made their escape. What with all the racket, and the shouting that customarily attends banditry, the commandant of the island turned up: I recognized him, as he had been in the camp with us. I showed him my wound and asked him to give chase to the bandits. There was a flotilla of ships moored in the town: the commandant boarded one of these with the detail that was on duty and set off in pursuit. I too embarked, after being helped on board bodily.

When the bandits saw the ship now closing in to attack, they stood the girl on the deck with her hands tied behind her. One of them shouted out in a loud voice:

'Behold your prize!'

Then he cut her head off and shoved the rest of the body into the sea. When I saw this, I screamed and made to throw myself after her. The bystanders restrained me, but I begged them to halt the ship and have someone dive in, in the hope that I might have the girl's body, even if only for burial. The commandant assented and stopped the ship. Two of the sailors hurled themselves overboard, seized the body, and brought it on board. Meanwhile, the bandits were rowing away more vigorously. When we closed in again, the bandits caught sight of another ship, and on recognizing it (they were pirates fishing for murex) called for help. When the commandant saw that there were now two ships, he became afraid and backwatered, since the pirates had turned from flight and were inviting battle.

When we returned to land, I disembarked and embraced the body.

'Now I can truly say you have died a double death,° Leucippe,' I wailed, 'divided between land and sea. I am holding the leftovers of your body, but you yourself I have lost. The allotted division between sea and land is hardly equal: small is the part of you apportioned to me, though it may seem the larger, while the sea holds your entirety in a small part. But since Fortune has begrudged me the chance to kiss your face, let me kiss your carcass.'

[8] With these lamentations I buried the body and returned to Alexandria. The wound healed, despite my wishes, and with Menelaus' consolation I regained the strength to live. Six months had passed, and the larger part of my grief was beginning to wither. Time cures grief, soothing the wounds of the soul. Sunlight is full of pleasure: whatever has grieved us for a while, even excessively, does indeed boil for as long as the soul is stoked, but it is then cooled by the superior pleasures of daylight. Someone walking behind me in the marketplace suddenly grasped my hand, pulled me around, and, without a word, embraced me and began to kiss me profusely. At first I did not know who he was: I stood there astonished, being battered by his celebration, like a target for osculation. Then he stood back a small way and I saw his face: it was Clinias! I cried out with joy and threw my arms around him in turn, returning the same embraces. Afterwards, we retired to my lodging. He told me his story and how he had survived the shipwreck, while I told him the full story about Leucippe.

[9] 'As soon as the ship broke up,' he said, 'I grabbed onto the yardarm and managed to clamber on to the top of it, a difficult task because it was already teeming with men. Then I locked my hands around it and tried to hold on, dangling down the side. We had been in the sea for a short while when a colossal wave lifted up the timber upright and dashed one end against an underwater reef, the opposite end to the one where I was dangling. After the impact, the timber swung backwards with great force, like a catapult, and shot me off like a sling. After that, I had to swim for the rest of that day, with all hope of survival gone. Eventually, I tired and abandoned myself to Fortune. It was then that I saw a ship travelling towards me. Raising my hands as much as I could, I signalled by nodding that I was throwing myself on their mercy. Whether they pitied me or whether the wind carried them, they sailed in my direction, and one of the sailors threw me a rope as the ship ran past. I grabbed onto it, and they dragged me back from the very gates of death. The vessel was sailing to Sidon. Some of them recognized me and tended to me.

[10] 'After two days' sailing, we came to the city. I begged the Sidonians onboard (Xenodamàs the merchant and Theophilus, his father-in-law) to tell no Tyrian they happened to meet that I

had survived the shipwreck, to prevent them discovering that I had travelled abroad with you. I expected to avoid detection, if all went smoothly on their side, as there had been a gap of only five days when I had been out of sight. I had told my household in advance, as you know, to announce to anyone who asked that I had gone to the country for ten solid days. This story, I found, was the one that prevailed about me. It happened that your father had not yet returned from Palestine, and did not return until two days later. There he received a letter from Leucippe's father which, as it happened, arrived a single day after our departure: in it, Sostratus pledged his daughter to you. On reading this letter and hearing of our flight, he found himself in all sorts of troubles, partly because he had foregone the prize promised by this letter, partly because Fortune had arranged events like this in so short a space of time (after all, none of this would have happened, had the letter arrived earlier).

'He decided that it was best not to write to his brother yet about anything that had happened, and he asked the girl's mother to keep her silence for the present. "No doubt we shall find them," he said, "and Sostratus must not find out about this unfortunate occurrence. Wherever they are, they will return as soon as they hear of the engagement, relieved to be able to enjoy openly what they escaped in search of."

'He made exhaustive inquiries about your whereabouts. A few days ago, Diophantus the Tyrian arrived by ship from Egypt, telling him that he had spotted you there. When I learned the news, I boarded a ship at the earliest opportunity, and this is the eighth day I have been touring the entire city in search of you. You need to have a plan to deal with this, as your father is also no doubt on his way here.'

[11] When I heard this, I wailed, berating Fortune for her practical joke:

'O goddess!' I cried. 'Now Sostratus is giving me to Leucippe, and the approval of our marriage has been posted to me from the thick of battle; but the days were carefully reckoned to prevent the message reaching us before we escaped! Alas for this inopportune boon! Oh, how blessed I am—or would have been, but for one day! Marriage follows death, wedding-songs follow dirges. What sort of a bride is this, when Fortune said I could have her, but refused me the whole cadaver?'

'Now is not the time for lamentations', said Clinias. 'Let us consider whether you should put out for your fatherland or stay put for your father.'

'Neither', I replied. 'How could I confront my father, especially given that I have not only eloped so disgracefully, but also caused the death of the charge entrusted to him by his own brother? The only course remaining is to make my escape before he gets here.'

At that point, Menelaus slipped in with Satyrus. They embraced Clinias and learned the events from us.

'The way is open', said Satyrus, 'for you to turn the present situation to your advantage, by taking pity upon a soul that is aflame for you. Clinias should hear this too. Aphrodite has granted a great favour to this fellow, but he refuses to accept it. She has driven a woman crazy for him—a woman of such great beauty that you would think her a statue if you saw her. Her family is from Ephesus,° and her name is Melite. She is extremely rich, and young. Her husband recently died at sea. She wants to take Clitophon as her master (it would be wrong to say 'husband'!), offering him herself and all her wealth. She has wasted two months here on his account, begging him to go with her. For his part, this victim of some delusion scorns her, thinking that Leucippe will be resurrected from the dead to join him.'

[12] 'Satyrus' advice is far from absurd, it seems to me', said Clinias. 'If beauty, wealth, and desire combine against you, you should not dilly-dally: beauty procures pleasure, wealth leisure, and desire respect. Eros hates those who give themselves airs: come on, follow Satyrus' advice and indulge the god.'

With a groan, I replied:

'If this is Clinias' opinion too, then take me where you will. Only do not let this damned woman pester me by pressuring me into the act before we get to Ephesus: I have already taken a vow to abstain from intimacy in the land where Leucippe died.'

On hearing this, Satyrus ran to Melite with the good tidings. A little later he returned, saying that the woman had almost passed out with pleasure when she had heard; and that she begged me to come to her lodgings for dinner that day as a prelude to the marriage celebrations. I agreed, and went.

[13] When she saw me, she leaped up and flung her arms around me, filling my face with kisses. She truly was beautiful: you would have said that her face was daubed with milk, and that roses grew in her cheeks. Her brilliant eyes scintillated with erogenous sparkle, and her hair was thick, long, and golden in colour. It was not without a certain feeling of pleasure that I beheld the woman.

The dinner was extravagant. She toyed with the dishes to give the impression of eating, but was unable to manage whole portions: her eyes were focused entirely upon me. Nothing is sweet to lovers other than the beloved: desire occupies the entire soul, leaving no room therein for thoughts of sustenance. The pleasure of the spectacle floods in through the eyes and settles in the breast, ever drawing with it the image of the beloved. This pleasure is impressed upon the soul's mirror, leaving its form there; then the beauty floods out again, drawn towards the desirous heart by invisible beams, and imprints the shadowy image deep down inside. I understood this, and said to her:

'Come on, you have not touched your food. You look like someone eating in a painting.'

'Yes, but what extravagant provisions, what wine could be worth more to me than the vision of you?'

With these words, she began to kiss me, and I accepted her kisses with no small pleasure. Then she drew apart.

'That', she said, 'is what I call sustenance.'

[14] This is how things went for the time being, but when evening came she tried to keep me there to sleep the night. I refused, telling her what I had already revealed to Satyrus. Reluctantly, and in some distress, she let me go; but we agreed to meet the following day at the temple of Isis, to hold discussions and to make our pledges with the goddess as our witness. Menelaus and Clinias went with us. We took our oaths, I to love her sincerely, she to make me her husband and master of her entire property.

'But', I said, 'our agreement will only begin when we arrive at Ephesus: here, as I told you, you must give way to Leucippe.'

An extravagant dinner was prepared for us, a wedding banquet in name, although the act itself had been shelved by mutual agreement. I remember Melite making a joke during the festivities. As all present were expressing their best wishes for our marriage, she leaned towards me and whispered:

'A novel phenomenon this, one that I alone have experienced. It is like what they do for unrecovered corpses: I have seen the tomb of the unknown soldier, but not the groom with the unknown bride . . . !'

This was a joke, but she meant it.

[15] On the following day, we made our preparations to travel. Fortunately, the wind was also encouraging us. Menelaus came as far as the harbour and embraced me, wishing me better luck with the sea this time. He turned back again, filled with tears: an excellent young man, worthy of the gods themselves. We too all began to shed our tears. Clinias had decided not to leave me, but to sail with us as far as Ephesus and spend some time in the city, before returning if he found that everything was going fine for me.

A following wind got up. It was evening, and after dinner we lay down to sleep. Melite and I shared a cabin on the boat that had been specially fenced off. She put her arms around me and began kissing me and demanding her conjugal rights.

'We have now passed over the borders of Leucippe's land, and reached the borders of our agreement. The appointed time is here. Why must I wait until Ephesus? The vagaries of the sea are unpredictable, and the currents of the winds fickle. Believe me, Clitophon, I am on fire! I wish I could show you this fire of mine. I wish the fire of love shared the nature of normal fire, so that I could have inflamed you by embracing you. As it is, this kind has all the qualities of the normal kind, except that it consumes itself with fire: though it blazes furiously when lovers clasp, it spares those who are clasped. O mystic fire! O fire brandished in occult rites! O fire refusing to escape your own borders! Let us initiate ourselves into the cult of Aphrodite, dearest!'

[16] 'Do not force me to break my pious covenant with the dead', I replied. 'We have not yet passed the borders of the land of that poor girl, not until we set foot on another land. Have you not heard how she died at sea? Even now I am sailing on Leucippe's tomb. Perhaps her ghost is roaming around this ship somewhere! They say that the souls of those killed at sea do not even descend

to Hades at all, but wander around the water in that spot. Perhaps she will manifest ourselves while we are embracing! And does this seem to you a suitable place for conjugals? A marriage on the wave, a marriage tossed around by the sea? Do you want us to have a mobile bridal suite?'

'You are playing the sophist, my dear', she said. 'Any place can be a bridal suite for lovers: nowhere is inaccessible to the god. Is not a seaborne location more appropriate for Eros, and for the mysteries of Aphrodite? Aphrodite is the daughter of the sea.° Let us propitiate the goddess of marriage, and with our marriage pay our respects to her mother. It seems to me that our surroundings betoken marriage, this yoke dangling above our heads and the bonds taut around the yardarm. The omens are good, my master: a bridal suite lying under a yoke° and ropes bound tight. Even the rudder is close to the bridal suite: see, Fortune is piloting our marriage! Our wedding cortège will be joined by Poseidon (for it was here that his own marriage to Amphitrite° also took place) and the chorus of sea-nymphs. The breeze is whistling sweetly around the rigging: it seems to me that the wind's pipings are leading the wedding-hymn. See how the sail billows out like a pregnant belly. I take even this as a favourable omen: you will soon father me a child, too.'

Seeing how worked up she was, I replied:

'Let us remain philosophical about the matter until we reach land, my dear wife. I swear by the sea itself, and by the fortunes of this voyage, that I am as enthusiastic as you. But the sea has its laws. I have often heard it from those of a nautical inclination that boats should be undefiled by Aphrodite's acts, perhaps because they are hallowed ground, or perhaps to prevent anyone relaxing in the midst of such great danger. Let us cause no offence to the sea, dearest: let us not unite consummation with perturbation. Let us set aside an undefiled pleasure for our later enjoyment.'

With these words, which I sweetened with honeyed kisses, I persuaded her. We slept thus for the rest of the night.

[17] When we had completed the following five days' sailing, we came to Ephesus. Her house was huge, the pre-eminent one in the city. She had a large body of servants, and the household was extravagantly furnished.° She gave the orders for the most sumptuous feast possible to be prepared.

'Meanwhile,' she said, 'let us go to my country estate.'

The estate was four stades° from the city. We climbed into a carriage and set off. As soon as we arrived, we began to stroll through the orchard avenues, when suddenly a woman threw herself at our knees. She was bound in heavy irons, carrying a mattock, her head shaven and her body filthy, girt with an extremely shoddy tunic.

'Pity me, mistress!' she cried. 'You are a woman, so am I, and a free woman by birth—though a slave now,° thanks to Fortune's designs.'

With this she fell silent.

'Stand up, woman', responded Melite. 'Speak! Who are you? Where are you from? Who was it who put you in these chains? For even in the midst of misfortune, your beauty proclaims your noble birth.'

'It was your servant,' she replied, 'since I would not serve him in bed. My name is Lacaena,° and my family is from Thessaly. I place my fortune in your hands, pleading for mercy. Free me from the calamity that has befallen me! Grant me safe haven until I can pay back the two thousand pieces! (That was the price that Sosthenes paid the bandits for me.) I assure you, I shall raise it very quickly; if not, you can have me as a slave. But look how he has shredded me with his numerous lashes!'

As she spoke, she parted her tunic and showed us the marks etched onto her back, an even more pitiable sight. When we heard this, I for my part was extremely upset, since she seemed to have something of Leucippe about her; Melite, on the other hand, replied:

'Take heart, woman. We shall get you out of this situation, and grant you a free passage home. Someone have Sosthenes summoned to me!'

Straightaway, she was freed from her chains. Sosthenes arrived, in some distress.

'You wretched specimen! Have you ever seen any of my slaves, even the most useless, so ill-treated? Who is she? Tell me—and no lies!'

'My lady,' he replied, 'I only know that some trader called Callisthenes° sold her to me, saying that he had bought her from some bandits, and that she was freeborn. The name the trader gave her was Lacaena.'

Melite stripped him of the supervising position he held, and put the woman in the hands of her maidservants, telling them to wash her, dress her in clean clothes, and take her to the city. She then sorted out some business on the estate (the reason for her presence), mounted the chariot with me, and the two of us returned to the city and began the feast. [18] In the midst of the entertainment, Satyrus, wearing an earnest expression, gestured to me with his head to get up. I made the excuse that my haste was due to a stomach problem, and got up to leave. When I was outside, he handed me a letter without a word. I took it, but before I read it I was immediately struck with amazement, recognizing Leucippe's handwriting! This was what the letter said:

From Leucippe to Clitophon—to my master, for that is what I must call you, since you are also the husband of my mistress. You know what I have suffered thanks to you; but in the present situation you need reminding. Thanks to you, I left my mother and took up a life of wandering; thanks to you, I was shipwrecked and endured bandits; thanks to you, I was sacrificed as an expiation, and have now died a second time; thanks to you I have been sold and bound in iron, I have wielded a mattock, dug the earth, been whipped—was all this for me to become to another man what you have become to another woman? Never! No, I had the strength to hold out in the midst of so many trials—while you, unenslaved and unwhipped, you are married! So, if you feel any obligation towards me for the pains I have suffered thanks to you, ask your wife to send me away as she promised. As for the two thousand pieces that Sostratus paid for me, please vouch for me that I will send them to Melite. You can trust me: Byzantium is not far. And if you yourself cover the debt, you should count that the compensation paid to me for my pains on your behalf. Farewell. Enjoy your new marriage. As I write this, I am still a virgin.

[19] When I read this, I experienced every sort of reaction at the same time: I burned, paled, marvelled, disbelieved, rejoiced, and brooded. Then I said to Satyrus:

'Have you brought this letter from Hades? If not, what is the meaning of this? Has Leucippe risen from the dead?'

'Exactly', he replied. 'She is the woman you saw on the estate. At that point, no one else who saw her would have recognized her, given her transformation into an ephebe:° the metamorphosis is due entirely to her haircut.'

'And yet,' I said, 'even now, with such good news, you have pulled up short: you cheer only my ears, refusing to reveal the news to my eyes as well.'

'Stop it', replied Satyrus. 'Go inside and control yourself, before you ruin all of us, and until we are in a safer position to take stock of this situation. You can see that the pre-eminent lady in Ephesus is crazed with passion for you, and we are all alone with traps all around us.'

'I cannot', I cried. 'Joy is penetrating every pore of my body! But look how she accuses me in her letter!'

At the same time I scrutinized the letter again as though I were gazing upon her person. I read every single word, and said:

'Your accusation is well founded, dearest! All your sufferings are my fault: I have brought many a trouble upon you.'

When I got to the part about the whips and tortures inflicted on her by Sosthenes, I began to weep as though I were actually witnessing her torture: for when my mind cast the eyes of my soul upon the letter's tidings, the reading-matter became as visible as real matter. I blushed deeply at the reproaches she levelled at my marriage: I felt like an adulterer surprised in the act, such was the shame inspired by the letter.

[20] 'Alas!' I cried. 'How will the defendant respond, Satyrus? I have been caught! Leucippe has brought her charge: she probably even detests me! But tell me, how did she survive? Whose body was it that we buried?'

'She will tell you herself when the time is right', replied Satyrus. 'For now, you must write back and pacify the girl. I myself have given her my word that you married Melite unwillingly.'

'You told her that I married her, too?' I cried. 'You have ruined me!'

'What naivety!' said Satyrus. 'Is it not the case that the whole city knows of your marriage?'

'But I have not actually *married* her,' I replied, 'I swear it by Heracles, Satyrus, and by our present fortunes!'

'Surely you are joking, my friend? You do sleep together!'

'I know it beggars belief to say it, but the deed has not been done. To this very day, Clitophon is undefiled by Melite. But tell

me, what should I write? These events have so stunned me that I
am all at a loss.'

'I am no wiser than you,' said Satyrus, 'but Eros himself will dic-
tate to you. Only hurry!'

I started writing:

Greetings Leucippe, my mistress! I am at once lucky and unlucky: thanks
to the letter, I can visualize you in my presence, but I know that you are
absent. If you have truly survived, do not condemn me before you learn
that I have imitated your virginity, if there be a male equivalent of virginity. But if you despise me already, before I have defended myself, I
swear by the gods who saved you that I shall deliver a defence of my acts
shortly. Farewell, dearest, and set your mind at peace.

[21] I gave Satyrus the letter, and asked him to tell her suitable
things about me. I left to return to the party, full of pleasure, but
also of sadness at the same time: for I knew both that Melite would
not allow me to pass that night without completing our marriage,
and that it was impossible for me even to look at another woman
now that I had recovered Leucippe. I forced my face into an
expression no different to the one it had previously worn. I was,
however, unable to control it entirely: on the occasions when I was
overcome, I gave the excuse that a shudder had run down my
spine. She realized that this was a preamble to getting out of my
promise, but could find nothing in it to convict me. I got up to go
to bed, my dinner untouched; she got up as well, hard on my heels,
leaving her dinner as it was, half-finished. When we entered the
chamber, I tried to extend my impersonation of illness even further, but she was having none of it.

'Why are you behaving like this?' she cried. 'How long will you
carry on killing me? Look, we have crossed the sea! Look, here is
Ephesus, the rendezvous for our marriage! What sort of occasion
are we still waiting for? How long will we sleep together as if in a
temple? You have set before me a mighty river, and you refuse to
let me drink! So long have I been thirsting, though the water is
there for me—though, in fact, I sleep in the very riverhead! I have
the sort of cohabitation that Tantalus° had alimentation!'

While she was saying this sort of thing through her tears, she
leaned her head on my chest so pathetically that I felt compassion

stirring in my soul. I had no idea how to respond, since her accusations seemed justified. So I said to her:

'I swear to you, dearest, by the gods of my fathers, that I too feel the impulse—and how strongly!—to return your passion. But', I continued, 'some affliction has struck me: I have gone down with a sudden illness. You know how there is no Aphrodite without Hygeia.'°

With these words, I began to wipe away her tears, and I tried to regain her confidence with other oaths that what she desired would take place soon. She accepted this for now, although with great difficulty.

[22] On the following day, she summoned the maidservants to whom she had entrusted Leucippe's care, and asked them first of all whether they had looked after her well. They replied that they had neglected none of her needs. Then she ordered them to bring the woman to her. When she arrived, she said:

'It is unnecessary for me to tell you of the benevolence I feel towards you: you already know. You have received only your just due; but return me an equal favour, using the powers you possess! I have heard that you Thessalians bewitch those you desire,° to deprive a man of inclinations towards any other woman, and make him feel that the bewitcher is everything to him. Grant me this drug, my dearest friend—I am on fire! Did you see that young man walking with me yesterday?'

'You mean your husband?' blurted Leucippe, contemptuously. 'That was what the women in the household told me.'

'Husband? Pah!' replied Melite. 'He is more like a stone than a husband. Some dead woman is closer to his heart than I am! He cannot eat or sleep without remembering the name of Leucippe (as she was called). I spent four months in Alexandria on his account, my friend, cajoling and wheedling—what did I not say, what did I not do to please him? But he is as deaf to my demands as iron, wood, or some other inanimate object. In time, and reluctantly, he was persuaded, but persuaded only into my eyesight. I swear to you by Aphrodite herself: this is the fifth day that I have slept with him, only to rise in the morning as if from a eunuch's bed!° It is like loving a statue: I get no more than ocular satisfaction from my beloved. I beg you, one woman to another (just as you begged me yesterday): give me something to use against this man's arrogance! You will save my soul—though in fact it has already been broken.'

When Leucippe heard this, she felt a surge of pleasure that I had not done anything with the woman; but what she said was that, if permitted, she would go to the estate and seek out some herbs. And she went. She thought, clearly, that she would not be believed if she refused: that, I imagine, is why she promised. Melite was assuaged by her mere hopes, for even pleasures not yet arrived delight with their anticipation.

[23] I, however, knew nothing of this, and was at my wits' end working out how I could put off my wife the following night as well, and how I could meet with Leucippe. She too, it seemed to me, was equally enthusiastic to leave for the estate on Melite's errand and return that evening (Melite was to provide the chariot). We, meanwhile, went to a drinking-party. As soon as we had reclined, a mighty hubbub was heard in the men's quarters, then a stampede. One of the servants ran in panting, and said:

'Thersander is alive—and here!'

This Thersander was Melite's husband. He had been presumed dead at sea, since some of the slaves who had been with him, and who had survived when the vessel capsized, had presumed that he had been killed and announced as much. As soon as the slave spoke, Thersander ran in hard on his heels: he had heard everything about me along the way, and was keen to lay his hands upon me as soon as he could.

Melite leaped up, staggered by the extraordinary turn, and tried to throw her arms around her husband. Despite this, he pushed her away with all his strength. Then he faced me, and said:

'Aha! The adulterer!'

He jumped on me and dealt me a blow full of anger on the side of the head; then he grabbed me by the hair and smashed me onto the ground, before attacking me and raining blows upon me. I felt as though I was in a mystery-cult:° I had no idea who the man was, nor what I had done to deserve his blows. I suspected that something grave was afoot, and so I was fearful of defending myself, though I could have done. When he tired of beating me, and I of being philosophical about it, I stood up and said to him:

'Who on earth are you, my man? Why have you assaulted me like this?'

He was even more enraged that I had as much as spoken, and struck me again, calling for chains and fetters. I was bound and escorted into a cell. [24] While all this was going on, unbeknownst to me, Leucippe's letter fell out. I had been carrying it inside my tunic, attached by the tassels of my shirt. Melite picked it up without my knowledge, fearing that it was one of her letters to me. When she read it in private, and discovered Leucippe's name, the recognition of the name immediately struck her in the heart. She did not, however, think that she was still alive, since she had heard so many times that she was dead. But when she read on, perusing the rest of the letter, she learned the whole truth and her soul was simultaneously divided between multiple emotions: shame, anger, desire, and jealousy. She felt shame before her husband, she was angered by the letter, desire withered her anger, jealousy inflamed her lust, and finally desire won out.

[25] It was now towards evening. Thersander had recovered from his initial anger and run off to visit a friend in the vicinity. Melite, meanwhile, negotiated with the man instructed to guard me and visited me without the others' knowledge, setting two servants in front of the cell. She found me lying on the ground. As she stood beside me, she wanted to say everything at once: the expression on her face revealed all that she wanted to say.

'Alas, wretched me: even looking at you causes me suffering! First of all, my desire—foolish, senseless desire—came to nothing; then I am hated, but love my hater, hurt but pity my hurter; then, not even your contumely has put an end to my desire! O man and woman, what a pair of sorcerers united against me: the one mocking me for all this time, the other off to fetch a charm for me! I, ill-starred woman, had no notion that I was asking my bitterest enemy for a drug to use against myself!'

As she spoke, she threw Leucippe's letter down upon me. When I saw it and recognized it, I shuddered and looked down at the ground with the expression of one who had been found out. She started up her tragic wails again:

'O poor me, alas for my woes! Thanks to you, I have lost my husband; nor will I have you for the future, not even the empty pleasure of looking at you (and that was all you could manage). I know that my husband despises me, and has accused me of adultery with you—a fruitless adultery, a sexless adultery, which gained me nothing but insult! Other women gain satisfaction of their craving as compensation for their degrading; I, ill-starred woman, have reaped the fruit of degradation but nowhere that of pleasure. Perfidious barbarian! You had the audacity to cause a woman suffering under Eros' rule to wither away, and when you yourself were a slave of Eros at that! Felt you no fear of his wrath? No shame before his torch? No respect for his mystic rites? Did these tear-filled eyes not crush you? Ah, you are more savage than the bandits—even a bandit feels shame in the face of tears! Nothing could spur you towards Aphrodite, not even once: no entreaty, no lapse of time, no bodily embrace. No, and this is most outrageous of all, when you had stroked me and kissed me, you got up after that as though you had been another woman! What is this shadow of a marriage? She was not old, the woman you slept with, nor reluctant to be embraced by you: no, she was young and loving—another might even have said beautiful. You eunuch! Hermaphrodite! Handsome hex! I call down upon you the most just curse: may Eros avenge himself upon you and your affairs in this same way!'

'Thus she spoke, weeping all the while. [26] After a short period during which I was silent, with my head bowed, she changed her tone and said:

'Those words, dearest, were spoken by my anger and grief; what I will say now will be spoken by Eros. Even in my fury, I am aflame; even outraged, I love. Call a truce, even now! Pity me! I no longer ask for many days together, for the long marriage with you of which the unfortunate woman I was dreamt. One embrace is enough for me: it is a small remedy for so great a disease. Quench a small part of my fire! If I have been too bold and forward with you, forgive me, my dearest: when desire is frustrated it turns even to madness. I know my behaviour is unbecoming, but I feel no shame in divulging mystic secrets when they are those of Eros: the man I address is an initiate, and you know what I am going through. For the rest of humankind, the arrows of the god are unseen, and none may reveal his bow; only lovers know the wounds borne by their like. This one day is all I have left: make good your promise! Remember Isis, honour the oaths you made there. If you had consented to cohabit as you promised, I would not have cared for ten thousand Thersanders; but since marriage with another woman is impossible now that you have found Leucippe, I agree to give up this claim. I know I am beaten, and I ask for no more than I may get.

'All these bizarre events are conspiring against me: even the dead are resurrected. O sea, you saved me when I was sailing, but in saving me you killed me all the more. You have sent two of the dead against me. Leucippe alone was not enough—I am happy for her to live, to stop Clitophon's grief—but now the savage Thersander is among us too. You were struck in front of my eyes, and I—infortunate woman!—was unable to help! It was on this face—O gods!—that the blows rained down! Surely, Thersander must have been blind.

'But I beg you, Clitophon, my master (for you are master of my soul), give yourself to me today for the first and last time. This short span of time will count for me as many days. May you never lose Leucippe again, may she never die again, not even a false death. Do not spurn my passion! It is the source of your greatest fortunes. It gave you back Leucippe: if I had not loved you, if I had not brought you here, Leucippe would still be dead to you. Fortune, Clitophon, also gives out gifts! A man who comes across a treasure trove pays honour to the place where he finds it, building an altar, performing a sacrifice, and garlanding the ground. You found the trove of your love in me, yet you pay no honour to these benefactions. You should reckon that Eros is speaking through me, saying: "Return the favour you owe me, Clitophon: I am the high priest of these mysteries. Do not depart leaving Melite uninitiated: the fire burning her also belongs to me."

'My care for you also manifests itself in other ways. You will be freed from your bonds presently, even if Thersander refuses. You can stay with my fosterbrother, for as many days as you like. And you can expect Leucippe to join you at dawn: she said she would spend the night on the estate looking for herbs, so that she could pick them under the gaze of the moon. This is how she mocked me, for I asked her for a drug to use against her, thinking she was

Thessalian. What could I do when success was eluding me, other than seek herbs and drugs? For that is the last refuge of the unfortunate in love. Now, about Thersander: you can take heart on that score, too, as he has run off to visit his friend, leaving the house to me in his anger. I think some god has driven him away so that I can see to unfinished business with you. Come now, give yourself to me!'

[27] With this philosophical exposition done (Eros even teaches eloquence) she started loosing my bonds, kissing my hands and placing them upon her eyes and heart, saying:

'You see how it pounds, pumps, and persistently palpitates, filled with agony and expectation—please, let there be pleasure too! This pounding is like a kind of supplication addressed to you.'

When she had loosed me, thrown her arms around me, and wept, I felt a natural human reaction. I was also genuinely scared of Eros, that he might visit his wrath upon me; and, what was more, I considered how I had regained Leucippe, how I was about to get rid of Melite, how the act to be performed was a matter not of marriage but of the remedy for a kind of illness of the soul. So I did not resist when she threw her arms around me, and nor did I object to her embraces when she embraced me. Everything that Eros wanted to happen happened: we needed no bed, nor any other of the comforts that Aphrodite offers. Eros is a resourceful, improvising sophist, who can turn any place into a temple for his mysteries. For Aphrodite, the unaffected is sweeter than the ostentatious, for the pleasure it yields is natural.

Book 6

[1] After I had performed my cure upon Melite, I said to her:

'Now it is time to secure me my safe passage, and the other things you promised in relation to Leucippe.'

'Have no fear on her account', she replied. 'You can imagine you already have Leucippe. For your part, get dressed in my clothes and hide your face with the robe. Melantho will guide your way to the door. A young boy will be waiting for you at the door itself, with orders from me to convey you to the house where you will find Clinias and Satyrus. Leucippe will be there for you.'

With these words, she dressed me up as herself and kissed me.

'How much more handsome you have become with this clothing!' she said. 'I once saw Achilles° like this in a painting. But please take care, dearest, and keep this clothing as a memento of me; and leave yours for me, so that I may put it on and be enveloped by you.'

She gave me a hundred gold pieces and summoned Melantho, who was one of her trusted servants, and was guarding the door. When she came, Melite told her of the plan for me, and instructed her to return to her as I soon as I was outdoors.

[2] This was how I made my getaway. The warder of my cell withdrew, thinking I was his mistress when Melantho nodded to him. I proceeded through the empty parts of the house to a back door. The man who had been set there by Melite took me in hand. He was a freedman who had made the sea voyage with us, and I was already fond of him. When Melantho returned, she accosted the guard who had just locked the cell, and ordered him to reopen it. When she opened the door, entered, and told Melite that I had got away, she summoned the guard. As you can imagine, he was stunned at the sight of this most paradoxical spectacle—the proverbial deer in place of the maiden°—and stood there speechless. She then said to him:

'It was not because I could not trust you not to let Clitophon go that I resorted to this deception, but so that you could be absolved of blame in Thersander's eyes, as you were not party. Here are ten gold pieces for you, a gift: a gift from Clitophon if you stay here, and travelling money if you think it better to escape.' Pasion (as the guard was called) replied:

'Whatever you think, mistress, will suit me fine.'

Melite thought it best if he departed for now, and returned when matters with her husband had been sorted out and his anger had been calmed. That is what he did.

[3] As for me, my old friend Fortune attacked again, scripting a new drama for me: enter Thersander, returning forthwith! His friend had persuaded him to change his mind and not to spend the night away from home, and so he was returning to his house after dinner. It was the festival of Artemis and there were drunkards everywhere: throughout the entire night, the market-place was occupied by a mass of humanity. I had thought this my only danger: unbeknownst to me, one more serious had sprung up.

When Sosthenes (the man who had bought Leucippe and had been ordered by Melite to give up his management of the estate) learned that the master was back, he decided not to quit the estate yet but to get his own back on Melite. First of all, he made sure that Thersander was forewarned about me (it was he who had slandered me). Then he told some altogether plausible-sounding lies about Leucippe: having given up on getting her for himself, he offered her to his master like a pimp, seeking to drive him away from Melite.

'I have bought a girl, master', he said. 'She is beautiful, an incredibly beautiful thing. You must believe my words, as you would your own eyes. I was keeping her for you, because I heard and believed the news that I craved, that you were alive. I did not show her before, because I wanted to let you catch the mistress in the act, and to prevent that worthless, foreign adulterer from making a mockery of you. The mistress took her away from me yesterday, and was on the point of sending her away; but Fortune has kept her for you, and you can get your hands on her great beauty. Anyway, she is on the estate, undertaking some mission or other on behalf of the mistress. If you like, before she returns I can lock her up under guard, and make her yours.'

[4] Thersander approved, and told him to do just that. Sosthenes went to the estate with all speed. When he saw the cabin where Leucippe was intending to spend the night, he took a couple of labourers and told them to use underhand methods to distract the maidservants accompanying Leucippe, calling them over and keeping them engaged in conversation as far away as possible. Two others he took with him, and when he saw Leucippe alone he pounced and, holding her mouth, abducted her in the direction opposite to that where the maids had been diverted. He carried her to a secret hut, placed her inside, and said:

'My arrival will bring you a heap of benefits: take care not to forget me in your time of good fortune! Don't be afraid at this abduction, and don't imagine there was any intention to hurt you. After all, it is this abduction that has played the go-between, procuring my master as your lover!'

She was struck silent by the extraordinary nature of this calamity. Sosthenes, meanwhile, went to Thersander and told him what had happened. Thersander happened to have set out back to the house, but when Sosthenes revealed what had happened with Leucippe, dramatically embellishing her beauty, the words filled him with a kind of vision of beauty, a natural beauty. As an all-night festival was taking place, and the distance between them and the estate was only four stades, he ordered him to lead on and resolved to pay her a visit.

[5] At this point I was dressed in Melite's clothes, and I absent-mindedly bumped headlong into them. Sosthenes was the first to recognize me, and cried:

'Look, it's the adulterer! He's playing the bacchant,° attacking us wearing the spoils of your wife!'

The young man who was guiding me spotted them in advance and ran away, and fear robbed him of the opportunity to forewarn me too. On seeing me, they grabbed me. Thersander bellowed, and a mass of festival-goers converged. Thersander listed even more grievances, bellowing both decencies and indecencies: 'Adulterer!' 'Clothes-thief!' He took me to the prison and handed me over into custody, charging me with adultery.° I was unaffected by this, either by the outrage of being chained up or by the verbal assault: I was confident that I would be rescued by the argument that I was no adulterer, that I was openly married to her. But I was fearful for Leucippe, as she was not yet safe in my keeping. Our souls are natural prophets of doom: good news we rarely derive from such prophecy. My thoughts about Leucippe, then, were morbid: full of fear, I suspected the worst. Thus was the suffering of my soul.

[6] When Thersander had thrown me into prison, he put all his energies into going after Leucippe. On arrival at the hut, they found her lying on the floor, thinking through what Sosthenes had said, and betraying grief and fear together upon her face. It is my opinion that the saying that 'the processes of the mind are completely invisible'° is not sound: they are visible in the face as if in a mirror. If the mind is pleased, it beams forth the image of joy through the eyes; if it is saddened, it contorts the face into a vision of calamity. Now, when Leucippe heard the door opening, she raised her head a little (there was a lamp in the hut) and then lowered her eyes again. When Thersander caught a glimpse of her beauty (for beauty resides most of all in the eyes), illuminated as if by a sudden flash of lightning, he abandoned his soul to her and stood there, bound by the spectacle, waiting for the time when she would raise her eyes towards him again. But since she hung her head towards the ground, he asked.

'Why so downcast, woman? Why is the beauty of your eyes flowing away onto the ground? Let it flow into my eyes, instead.'

[7] She was filled with tears on hearing this, and even her tears had their own distinctive beauty: for a tear swells the eye, making it more prominent. If the eye is vulgar and unattractive, it contributes to the ugliness; but if it is sweet, the black dye of the pupil softly garlanded with white, it resembles a fountain's generous breast whenever moistened by tears. When the salt water of tears floods around the eye, the outer part shines, while the black part turns deep crimson: the latter is like the violet, the former the narcissus. The tears laugh as they spin around the eyes. Such were Leucippe's tears: they overmastered her grief, and turned it into beauty. If they could have congealed as they fell, the earth would have had a novel kind of amber.° Thersander gaped at her beauty, while her grief drove him wild: his eyes were pregnant with tears. It is a fact of nature that a tear is most likely to attract pity in its

beholders. All the more so a woman's: in that it is more luxuriant, it has more power to bewitch. If the weeper is a woman of beauty and the spectator her lover, then not even the eye is unmoved, but it imitates the tears. For since it is in the eyes of the beautiful that beauty resides, it flows thence into the eyes of the beholders and stays there, drawing forth from the wellspring of tears. The lover welcomes both sensations. He snatches the beauty down into his soul, but keeps the tears in his eyes, praying that he will be seen; and though he could wipe them away, he does not, but retains the tear for as long as he can, fearing its flight before its due time. And he even checks his eye movements, in case the tears should wish to fall before his beloved has seen, for he thinks that this is a testament to his love. Of this sort was Thersander's reaction. His tears were a performance: he felt, to be sure, the natural human reaction one might expect, but he also displayed ostentatiously to Leucippe that he was crying for the reason that she was. Leaning towards Sosthenes, he said:

'Look after her needs for now. You can see how upset she is: I shall keep out of her way (though with extreme reluctance), so as not to pester her. When she is in a calmer way I shall speak with her. And as for you, woman, cheer up! I shall soon cure you of your tears.'

Then, as he left, he addressed Sosthenes again:

'Make sure you say suitable things about me. At dawn, come and see me after you have succeeded.'

With these words he parted. [8] While this was going on, it happened that Melite, after her encounter with me, had sent a young man to the estate in search of Leucippe, to tell her to hurry back and that the drugs were no longer necessary. Now when this fellow arrived at the estate, he found the maidservants looking for Leucippe in a state of extreme distress. As she was nowhere to be found, he made sure he was the first to tell Melite what had happened. When she heard that the news of how I had been thrown into prison, and then of how Leucippe had disappeared, a cloud of grief descended over her. She had no need to discover the truth: she already suspected Sosthenes. Wishing to search openly for Leucippe with the aid of Thersander, she thought up a verbal artifice that combined the truth with sophistry.

[9] When Thersander entered the house, he began bellowing once again:

'You arranged for the adulterer's escape! It was you who freed him from his bonds and got him out of the house! All your work! Why did you not go with him? Why are you still here? Are you not going to run away to your beloved, so that you can see him bound in stronger chains?'

'Adulterer?' asked Melite. 'What adulterer? What is up with you? If you like, now that the madness has passed, you can hear the whole story. The truth, you will find, is easily learned. I have but one request of you: be a fair jury, purge your ears of the slander, give up the anger in your heart, listen to me with pure reason as a judge. This young man committed no adultery with me—nor was he my husband. His family is from Phoenicia, and he is second to none in Tyre. He too had an unfortunate sea voyage: he lost all his baggage to the sea. When I heard of his fortunes, I took pity, remembering you. I provided him with hospitality, saying: "Thersander is likewise probably wandering somewhere, too. Some woman will probably take pity on him, too. And if he has truly died at sea, as the rumours have it, let us honour all shipwrecks as though they were his."

'And how many other shipwrecked men did I nurture back to health? How many of the sea's dead did I bury, if I found a timber from a shipwreck washed up on land, saying: "Perhaps this was the ship on which Thersander sailed."

'This man was the latest in the line of survivors from the sea. The honour I paid him was dedicated to you. He made a sea voyage, like you: I was honouring the image of your calamity, dearest. Why otherwise did I bring him here with me? The story is true. He was grieving for his wife, but unbeknownst to him she was not dead. Someone told him that she was here, in the service of one of our stewards, meaning Sosthenes. This was right: when we arrived, we found the woman. That's the reason why he was accompanying me. You have Sosthenes, and the woman is on the estate: you can check every detail of my account. If I have told a single lie, I am an adulterer.'

[10] As she spoke, she pretended not to have found out about Leucippe's disappearance. She was also keeping in reserve the

option, if Thersander sought to discover the truth, and if Leucippe had not turned up by dawn, of producing the maidservants with whom Leucippe had departed, who would say (which was true) that the girl was nowhere to be seen; in this way she could commit herself to the search openly, and coerce Thersander into joining her. After this plausible piece of acting, she added:

'Believe me, my husband. You never accused me for all the time we were together, so do not harbour such suspicions now. The rumour spread because of the honour I paid to the young man, since the masses did not know the reason for our association. And you too, after all, are dead according to rumour. Rumour and Slander are two evil sisters. Slander is sharper than a knife, stronger than fire, more plausible than the Sirens; Rumour is more fluid than water, speedier than the wind, quicker than wings. Whenever Slander shoots a verbal shaft, it flies away like an arrow and wounds the person it is meant for, though he be absent. The man who hears is soon persuaded, and is set alight by the fire of anger: he rages against the wounded man. From the arrow wound springs Rumour, which immediately flows in a great flood, deluging the ears of those in the way. The gusts of language disperse it, charging in all directions; it also takes flight, lightened by the tongue's wing. These two are the enemies who wage war against me: it was they who captured your soul, and barred the way for my words to enter the gates of your ears.'

[11] With these words, she touched his hand and tried to kiss him. He was softened: the plausibility of her words was winning him over, and his suspicion was somewhat allayed by the fact that the part about Leucippe chimed with what Sosthenes had told him. Ultimately, however, he was unconvinced: once the drops of jealousy have landed on the soul, they are hard to wash away. He was perturbed to hear that the girl was my wife, and ended up hating me all the more. So for then, he said he would verify her story, and went off to bed on his own. Melite, meanwhile, was upset in her soul, since she had not fulfilled her promise to me.

Sosthenes, who had accompanied Thersander thus far, agreed to some solemn promises about Leucippe and turned back towards her. Feigning an expression of happiness, he said:

'We have succeeded, Lacaena! Thersander has fallen for you, he is mad enough about you to make you his wife soon. This success is all down to me. I was the one who repeatedly extolled your prodigious beauty and filled his soul with imagining. Why are you weeping? Get up, and give sacrifice to Aphrodite in thanks for your good fortune! But remember me, too.'

[12] 'May the same good fortunes befall you,' replied Leucippe, 'as you have come here bringing to me!'

Sosthenes failed to spot her irony, thinking that she meant her words. With a kindly tone, he said:

'I also want to tell you who Thersander is, to add to your pleasure. He is the husband of Melite, the woman you saw on the estate. He is the highest-born man of all Ionia. His wealth exceeds his ancestry, and his integrity his wealth. As for his age, well, you have seen that he is young and handsome (which is what most delights women).'

At this, Leucippe was unable to bear Sosthenes' blathering:

'You wicked beast!' she cried. 'How long will you keep polluting my ears? What does Thersander matter to me? Let Melite profit from his handsomeness, the city from his wealth, and the needy from his integrity and benevolence! I do not care if he is nobler born than Codrus and richer than Croesus!° Why pile up this catalogue of praises that do not belong to him? I shall only approve Thersander as a good man when he stops outraging other people's wives!'

[13] 'Surely you are joking?' asked Sosthenes, seriously.

'Why would I joke?' she replied. 'Leave me alone, man, to be ground down by my fate and the deity who controls me. I know that this is some pirates' den that I am in.'

'It seems to me,' he said, 'that you are incurably mad. You think all this is a pirates' den: wealth, marriage, and luxury? And when Fortune presents you with a man like this, whom the gods love enough to retrieve from the very gates of death?'

At this point he recounted the story of the shipwreck, attributing his salvation to divine causes, as though it were a prodigy greater than Arion's dolphin.° When Leucippe declined to respond to his mythologizing, he said:

'You should consider a course more advantageous to yourself. Make sure that you do not speak like this to Thersander, or you will provoke that man of integrity. He is intolerable when he is angry. When integrity meets with compliance it is increased still further, but when it is scorned it is roused to anger: for one who is exceptionally benevolent is equally passionate in punishment.'

That was how matters stood with Leucippe. [14] Clinias and Satyrus, meanwhile, learned that I had been locked up in prison (Melite had got the news to them), and immediately hurried to my cell, though it was night. They wished to stay there with me, but the warder would not let them, ordering them instead to go away at once. They agreed reluctantly to leave, but only after I had given them some instructions concerning Leucippe—if she turned up, they were to come to see me at dawn—and told them the story about Melite's promises. My soul was poised between hope and fear: the part that hoped was fearing, the part that feared hoping.

[15] When day broke, Sosthenes hurried to see Thersander, Satyrus and the others to see me. When Thersander saw Sosthenes, he asked him how the matter of winning the girl over to him stood. Sosthenes' reply avoided the truth in favour of some highly plausible sophistry:

'Well, she is refusing,' he said, 'but I do not think it is a matter of simple refusal: she seems to suspect that you will use her once and then reject her, and she is reluctant to be abused.'

'On that count she can rest assured,' replied Thersander. 'My feelings towards her are such that they will never die. One thing alone I fear, and am eager to learn from the girl: whether she has actually married that young man, as Melite told me.'

With this exchange, they arrived at Leucippe's hut. When they approached the door, they heard her lamenting. Without making a sound, they halted behind the door.

[16] 'Alas, Clitophon!' she repeated over and over again. 'You do not know where I am, where I am locked up, nor do I know what fate has befallen you. We are cursed by the same ignorance. Oh surely Thersander did not find you in his house? Surely you too have not suffered some outrage? Often have I wished to ask Sosthenes, but I did not know how to phrase the question. If I asked about my husband, the fear was that I would bring some disaster upon you by provoking Thersander against you. If I asked

about some total stranger, then that too would inspire suspicion: why would a woman care to find out about people with no links to her? How many times did I force myself, but fail to persuade my tongue to speak? This alone could I say:

' "Clitophon, my husband, husband of Leucippe alone, faithful and constant: not even the woman who shared your bed could sway you—even though I (heartless woman!) believed she had. When I saw you on the estate, after all that time, I did not kiss you!"

'Now if Thersander comes to me and asks, what am I to say to him? Shall I cast aside the role I have acted and tell him the true story: "Do not think I am a slave, Thersander! I am the daughter of the general of Byzantium, the pre-eminent woman in Tyre. I am no Thessalian, and my name is not Lacaena. Such is the outrage of pirates: they even robbed me of my name! My husband is Clitophon, my fatherland Byzantium, my father Sostratus, and my mother Pantheia."

'But you would not believe my words; I also fear that you may believe the part about Clitophon, and that my untimely release may bring about the death of my darling. Come, it is best to reassume my dramatic role, to wear once again the costume of Lacaena.'

[17] When Thersander heard this, he withdrew a short distance and said to Sosthenes:

'Did you hear that incredible speech, crammed with passion? What powerful words! What grief! How she reproached herself! That adulterer gets the better of me everywhere. He must be an outlawed alchemist, in my opinion! Melite loves him, Leucippe loves him. O Zeus, I wish I were Clitophon!'

'Come,' replied Sosthenes, 'we need none of this effeminacy if the deed is to be done! You must go in and confront the girl! If she feels passionate about that accursed adulterer for the time being, that will last only as long as she knows him alone and has slept with no one else. As soon as you find yourself in the same position, she will eventually forget him: you are much more handsome than him. An old desire wilts when new desire arises: a woman loves best what she has to hand, and only remembers what is absent for as long as she has found no replacement. When she has found another, she wipes the former from her soul.'

When he heard this, Thersander was roused to action, for when language inspires hope that amatory success awaits, it persuades with ease: desire takes what it wants as an ally, and arouses hope. [18] Leaving a short interval after Leucippe's soliloquy so as not to seem to have overheard her words, he entered, arranging his appearance in a way that (he thought) would be most agreeable to behold. When he saw Leucippe, his heart was inflamed: she seemed to have grown more beautiful on this occasion. He had nurtured the fire all night, for the entire period he had been separated from the girl, but it suddenly flared up again when the flame was fuelled by the sight of her. He very nearly fell upon the girl and threw his arms around her; but he controlled himself, sat down next to her, and struck up a conversation, stringing together various nonsensical themes. This is what lovers are like, whenever they seek to chat with their beloveds. Reason has no authority over their language, and their entire soul is instead focused upon the beloved: they blather with the tongue alone, without reason at the reins.

As he spoke with her, he placed his hand on her neck and ran it around, as if he were about to kiss her. She foresaw the route the hand was taking and bowed her head, pressing it into her bosom. He continued nonetheless to encircle her neck, then tried to force her to push her head upwards; she in turn pressed it down and hid away her kisses. When this round of hand-wrestling was over, Thersander was seized by a spirit of erotic competition: he shoved his left hand under her face, and grabbed hold of her hair with his right, dragging her head backwards with the latter and driving it up with the former by pushing upwards on her chin. When he finally ceased from this violence, whether because he had won, because he had failed, or because he was exhausted, Leucippe said to him:

'You are not acting like a free man, nor like a nobleman. You are doing nothing more than imitating Sosthenes: the slave is suited to his master. Keep your distance in the future, and do not expect to succeed unless you turn into Clitophon.'

[19] When Thersander heard this, he did not know which way to turn, consumed as he was with desire and anger. Fury and Desire are two torches. Fury is a different kind of fire, with a fundamentally opposed nature (although it has a similar force): for the

one provokes hatred, the other compels love, and the spring of fire lies in the vicinity of each. The one resides in the liver, the other is enshrouded in the heart.° So whenever both seize a person, the soul finds itself weighing up the two, and each one's fire lies in the balance. Both fight to tip the scales. Generally, Desire wins when his appetite is successfully satisfied; but if the beloved spurns him, he summons Fury to an alliance. The latter, being a neighbour, agrees, and the two join their fires. Once Fury has Desire harnessed by his side, exiled from his familiar position, he does not treat the alliance as a friendly one aiming at the satisfaction of Appetite, for he is not by nature given to pacts; instead, he overpowers him, then overmasters and shackles Appetite like a slave. He does not allow Desire (assuming that he should even want to) to sue for peace with the beloved. Desire sinks down, swamped by Fury, and though he wishes to recoil to his own position of power, he is nevertheless forced to hate the beloved. When Fury, full of his own power, bubbles up to capacity and overflows, he is satisfied and tires, and subsides in his tiredness; then Desire gets his revenge, arms Appetite, and overcomes Fury while he is still asleep. When he sees the outrageous abuses he has committed against his dearest beloved, he is pained, makes his defence speech from the dock, issues invitations to share time together, and promises that Fury is softened by Pleasure. If he achieves what he wants, he is pacified; if he is spurned again, he sinks once more into Fury, who wakes from his sleep and acts in the now-familiar way, for Fury is an ally of spurned Desire.

[20] When Thersander had initially hoped that his erotic ambitions would be fulfilled, he was totally enslaved to Leucippe; but when he failed to get what he had hoped for, he abandoned the reins of his soul to anger. He beat her around the side of her head, and said:

'You wretched slave, you really are lovesick! Oh yes, I heard everything you said. You do not like it that I even speak to you? You do not think it a great blessing to be kissed by your master? No, you pretend to be shocked, and put on an air of desperation. I reckon you are a whore: after all, you *are* in love with an adulterer. Alright then, since you are unwilling to try me as a lover, try me as your master!'

'Even if you want to be tyrant over me,' replied Leucippe, 'I am happy to be tyrannized, if only you refrain from violence against me.'

Then she looked towards Sosthenes, saying to him:

'You can testify to the way I endure outrages, since you committed even greater wrongs against me.'

Sosthenes was ashamed to be proven guilty, and said:

'This woman should be torn with lashes, master, and submit to ten thousand tortures, to teach her not to despise her master.'

[21] 'You should do as Sosthenes says,' replied Leucippe, 'it is good counsel. Prepare the tortures! Someone bring in the wheel and stretch my hands: here they are! Someone bring in the whips, too, and beat my back: here it is! Someone bring in fire and burn my body: here it is! Someone bring in a blade and slice up my skin: here it is! You will behold a novel kind of contest: one woman competes against all your tortures, and conquers them all!

'You dare to call Clitophon an adulterer, when you yourself are one? Tell me, do you not fear that Artemis° of yours? Do you rape a virgin in the virgin's city? Lady goddess, where are your arrows?'

'A virgin?' cried Thersander. 'What audacity! How amusing! You, a virgin, after passing so many nights with pirates? Were these pirates of yours eunuchs? Or was it a sect of piratical philosophers? Or did none of them have eyes?'

[22] 'I am indeed a virgin,' replied Leucippe, 'despite even Sosthenes: you can ask him. He acted like a real pirate towards me: the others were more temperate than you lot, and none of them attempted such outrage. If you act in such a way, then this is the real pirates' lair. Are you not ashamed to do what the bandits shied away from? You do not know it, but your shameless deeds will redound all the more to my praise. Even if you kill me in your mad passion, someone will say: "Leucippe was a virgin after the Herdsmen, a virgin even after Chaereas, a virgin even after Sosthenes . . ." (that will be the moderate version, but the more glorious praise will continue as follows) ". . . a virgin even after Thersander, who was even more lecherous than the bandits: because he could not commit his outrage upon her, he even killed her."

'So, arm yourself, bring on the whips, the wheel, the fire, the knife, and use them on me! Let your counsellor Sosthenes fight by your side! I am unarmed, alone, a woman: freedom is my only weapon, but it will not be battered by your blows, nor cut up by your knife, nor scorched by your fire. My freedom I will never renounce—not I! Even if you set it ablaze, you will find the fire is not hot enough.'

Book 7

[1] When Thersander heard this, he went through the full spectrum of reactions: grief, fury, and plotting. He was furious because he had been insulted, his grief was due to his failure, and his plotting was motivated by his passionate desire. His soul was torn apart, and without a word to Leucippe he ran out. On the surface, it was an exit in anger, but in fact he was giving his soul the opportunity to dissipate the threefold wave that had struck him.

Now, with Sostratus' help he came up with a plan: he approached the prison warder, asking him to have me killed by poison. The warder refused, fearing the reaction of the town: the previous official had been put to death when it had been discovered that he had administered such a poison. So Thersander tried a different route, asking him to throw someone else into the cell where I was bound, as though he were another prisoner (he made this request under the pretence that he wanted to use him to learn my story).

The warder agreed, and the man was presented to him. This man, instructed by Thersander, was to introduce with great artifice the story that Leucippe had been murdered, and that Melite had arranged the murder. Thersander had invented this artifice so that I would despair at the news that my beloved was no longer alive, and so that even if I were acquitted at court I would give up my search for her. Melite had been implicated in the murder so that, thinking Leucippe dead, I would not marry Melite for the reason that she was in love with me, and thus by remaining in Ephesus cause him to fear that he could not enjoy Leucippe with impunity; rather, I would presumably despise Melite as the murderess of my beloved, and leave the city for good.

[2] So when this fellow found himself in my presence, he did indeed assume this dramatic role. Scoundrel that he was, he wailed:

'What twists does life still have in store for me? Whom must I guard against to ensure a life free from danger? For it is not enough that we should behave righteously: our fortunes assail and submerge us. I should have had to be a prophet to guess who my travelling companion was, and what he had done!'

This and the like he repeated to himself, trying to set the linguistic trap for me, by getting me to ask what was wrong. But I for my part was wrapped up in my own thoughts, with little care for his wailings. But another man chained up with us (for a man who is down on his luck is an inquisitive being, curious to hear about the problems of another: sharing in another's suffering is a remedy for the grief caused by one's own suffering) asked:

'What have you suffered at Fortune's hands? If you have done nothing wrong, you must have encountered an evil spirit. I can testify to that from my own experience.'

With that he recounted his own reasons for ending up in chains. I paid no attention to them. [3] When he stopped, he demanded to be repaid for the story of his misfortunes.

'You too must tell your story', he said.

'I happened to be walking along the road away from the city yesterday,' the other began, 'travelling towards Smyrna.° When I had advanced four stades,° a young man joined me, coming from the countryside, engaged me in conversation and walked alongside me for a while. "Where are you headed?" he asked.

' "To Smyrna", I replied.

' "I am going the same way", he said, "may Fortune smile on us!"

'From then on we travelled together and conversed, as one does on the road. When we arrived at a tavern, we breakfasted together. Four other men converged on the same tavern, sat down next to us, and pretended that they too were breakfasting, although they were in fact scrutinizing us carefully and nodding to each other. I suspected that the men had designs against us, but I could not comprehend the meaning of their nods. My companion gradually turned pale and began to eat more sluggishly. Before long, he was also seized by a trembling. When they saw this, they leapt up, grabbed us, and immediately bound us with leather straps. One of them beat him around the side of the head. When he was struck, as if he had undergone ten thousand tortures, he confessed before anyone asked him:

' "Yes, I am the one who killed the girl! And I accepted a hundred gold pieces from Melite, Thersander's wife: it was she who hired me. But here, you can have the hundred pieces: why kill me and deny yourselves a nice profit?" '

Although I had been paying no attention beforehand, when I heard the names of Thersander and Melite I was stung by the words as if by a gadfly. Alert, I turned around to him and said:

'Who is this Melite?'

'Melite', he replied, 'is the pre-eminent woman in this city. She was smitten with desire for some young man (a Tyrian, I think they say he was). As it happened, he was also smitten with a girl, whom he discovered to be a slave in Melite's household. Melite, burning with jealousy, grabbed this girl when she found her and handed her over to the wayfaring companion I was talking about (Fortune did not smile on me!), with instructions to murder her. He performed the unholy act. And I, alas, without having ever seen him before, without having had any part in the act or the agreement, was marched off with him in chains, as if I had aided and abetted the act. The worst thing of all is that when we had travelled a small distance from the tavern, they accepted his hundred pieces of gold and let him escape, and brought *me* before the prefect of the city.'

[4] When I heard this fiction, which spelled disaster for me, I neither wailed nor wept: I had neither voice nor tears. A sudden trembling enveloped my body and my heart dissolved; only a tiny fragment of my soul remained intact. When I had sobered up a little from this speech-induced intoxication, I asked:

'What means did this hireling use to kill the girl? What did he do with the corpse?'

But now that he had stung me with his gadfly's sting and inflicted upon me the mischief he was there for, he kept his silence, refusing to say anything. When I asked him again, he said:

'Are you suggesting that I had a hand in the murder? All I heard from the murderer was that he had killed the girl. He did not say where and how.'

It was then that the tears came to me, and I allowed my eyes their grief. Just as, when one's body is lashed, the weals do not spring up at once and the skin does not bloom under the lash straightaway, but it swells up after a short while; and just as when someone is gored by a boar's tusk he seeks the wound immediately and cannot find it, because it is still sunk deep and concealed (it forms the scar at its leisure, then afterwards the white trace dawns suddenly, the advance party announcing the arrival of the blood, which comes a while later in a copious stream); just so, when the soul has been struck by the arrow of grief loosed by language, it is wounded and pierced at once, but because of the speed of the blow the wound does not yet gape, and tears are driven far from the eyes (for tears are the blood of the wounded soul). As the tusk of grief gradually gnaws away the heart, the soul's wound is torn apart, the gateway of the tears is opened in the eyes, and the tears surge forth a short time after the opening. So it was with me: the first shocks of hearing these words struck my soul like arrows, silencing me and stopping up the well of tears; but afterwards, when my soul had had some respite from the barrage of misfortunes, the tears flowed freely.

[5] I started speaking:

'What deity deceived me with a brief moment of joy? What deity presented me with Leucippe, only to begin a new tale of disaster? The only enjoyment of her I had was with my eyes, and I did not even satisfy them: my hunger even for gazing was not allayed. That truly was but the pleasure of dreams! Alas, Leucippe, how many times death has torn you from me! Have I ever ceased lamenting you? Am I always to mourn you, as death follows death? All those other deaths were just Fortune's jokes at my expense, but this one is no joke on Fortune's part. How did you die, Leucippe? There was some small comfort for me after those false deaths, in the first instance because your body was whole, in the second because I could bury you, though I thought I was missing your head. In this case, though, you have died a double death,° in body and in soul! You escaped two lairs of banditry, to be murdered by Melite's piracy! What unholy impiety it was for me to kiss your murderess so many times, to accept her polluted embraces, to bestow upon her before you the pleasures of Aphrodite!'

[6] In the midst of my lament, Clinias entered. I told him everything, and that I had resolved to end my life once and for all. He tried to console me:

'Who knows whether she has come back to life? Has she not died many times before? Has she not been resurrected many times before? Why are you so keen to die? You will have plenty of leisure to do so when you discover for sure that she is dead.'

'Nonsense! What more incontrovertible evidence could you discover than this? I think I have found the best means of death—and not even that godforsaken Melite will get out of this one altogether scot free. Listen how. As you know, I prepared a speech of defence on the charge of adultery, in case the matter came to court. I have now decided to do quite the opposite: to confess to the adultery, and to how Melite and I jointly killed Leucippe. In this way, she will share in the punishment, and I shall leave behind this accursed life.'

'Hush now,' said Clinias. 'Will you go so far as to die in such disgraceful circumstances, with the reputation of a murderer—the murderer of Leucippe, at that?'

'Nothing is disgraceful', I replied, 'that harms one's enemy.'

A little while after these exchanges of ours, one of the jailers released the man who made the revelations about the false murder from his chains, saying that the magistrate had ordered him to bring him to give his account of the crimes with which he was charged. Clinias and Satyrus continued to console me, trying to persuade me not to respond to the accusation in the way I intended. Their words were to no avail. They rented a house on that very day and moved in, so as to stop lodging with Melite's fosterbrother.

[7] On the following day, I was led into the courtroom. Thersander had prepared meticulously for the prosecution, hiring no fewer than ten orators. Urgent preparations had also been made for the defence of Melite. When they stopped speaking, I also made a request to speak.

'They are all talking nonsense,' I said, 'both Thersander's team and Melite's. I shall tell you the whole truth. A long time ago I fell for a Byzantine woman called Leucippe. I thought she had died (she had in fact been abducted by bandits in Egypt), and I met Melite. We hooked up with one another, and left Egypt to come here together. Then we found Leucippe enslaved in the service of Sosthenes, a manager of Thersander's property. How Sosthenes had ended up with a free woman as his slave, and what was the deal he struck with the bandits, I leave to you to ponder. Now, when Melite learned that I had discovered my former wife, she was terrified that my attentions might be diverted in her direction, so she plotted to kill her. I concurred—why deny the truth?—since she promised to make me lord and master of her property. I hired someone to murder her, and the reward for the murder was one hundred gold pieces. When he had committed the act, he was off, and thereafter disappeared. As for me, well Eros took immediate revenge: when I learned that she had been killed, I changed my mind and began to weep out of love for her. I still love her. Hence this self-accusation, in the hope that you may send me to meet my beloved. I can no longer bear life, polluted with murder and loving the woman I killed.'

[8] At these words of mine, all were stunned by the extraordinary turn of events, especially Melite. Thersander's orators were delighted and gave a shout of victory, while Melite's began asking the meaning of my words. Her reply was made up of confused protestations, denials, vigorous but incoherent assertions: she said that she knew Leucippe and agreed with everything I had said, but not about the murder. Since this mostly chimed with my account, her lawyers also began to harbour suspicions about Melite, and to be unsure how they should conduct the speech for the defence.

[9] At this point, amidst the mighty hubbub in the courtroom, Clinias stepped up.

'Please,' he said, 'allow me a word too: after all, a man's life is at stake in this trial.'

When he took the stand, he burst into tears.°

'Men of Ephesus,' he said, 'do not impetuously condemn to death a man who desires to die: death is naturally sought as a remedy by those down on their luck. He has falsely confessed the guilt that belongs to the real criminals, aiming to bring on himself the penalty of the unfortunate. I shall give you a brief account of his misfortunes. As he said, he had a girlfriend. This was no lie. And the assertion that bandits abducted her, and the parts about Sosthenes, and the entire story he told up until the murder, this all happened as stated. Then she suddenly disappeared. I do not know where, whether someone killed her, or whether she has been kidnapped alive. The one thing I do know is that Sosthenes was struck with desire for her, and inflicted numerous abusive tortures upon her when he did not get his way with her. He also has bandits for friends.

'Now, Clitophon thinks the woman has been killed and has no more will to live: this is why he has brought this false accusation of murder upon himself. Even he admits that he desires death, and that it is because of his grief at what has happened to the woman. Think about it: does someone who has really killed someone want to join him in death, and find life too much to bear because of the pain? What murderer is so compassionate? What kind of hatred so loving? Do not believe him, by the gods! Do not kill a man who needs pity more than punishment! If he himself plotted her death, as he says, let him tell us who the hireling was! Let him show us her corpse!

'But if there is no murderer and no corpse, well then, whoever heard of such a murder? "I was in love with Melite," he says, "that is why I killed Leucippe." Why then does he accuse Melite, the woman he loves, of murder? Is it for Leucippe's sake that he now wishes to die—the woman he killed? Who on earth could show such hate for what he loves and such love for what he hates? Would he not have been far more likely to have denied the murder under cross-examination, so as to save his beloved, and to avoid a pointless death on behalf of the slain woman?

'So, why has he accused Melite if she has not done anything of the sort? I shall tell you the reason for this, too. But, by the gods, do not think that I am making this speech out of a desire to slander the woman: this is simply how it all happened. Melite was rather amorously inclined towards him, and had had words with him on the subject of marriage (before this fellow, this corpse from the sea, was resurrected). Clitophon disapproved: in fact, he rejected the marriage with paramount force. Then he discovered (as he stated) that his sweetheart, whom he had considered dead, was alive and in Sosthenes' hands, and he became even more estranged from Melite. Now, before Melite learned that his beloved was Sosthenes' slave-girl, she pitied her and freed her from the chains that Sosthenes had put on her; she welcomed her into her house, and treated her with every other kind of respect that one would a free woman who had fallen on hard times. But when she found out, she sent her onto the estate on an errand for her; and it was at this point that they say she disappeared. If you need proof that I am not lying, Melite will agree, as well as the two maidservants she sent to the estate with Leucippe. This was one event that led Clitophon to suspect her of killing Leucippe out of jealousy; the other occurrence that served to confirm his suspicion happened in prison, and exacerbated his fury against both himself and Melite. One of the inmates was bewailing the disaster that had befallen him, saying that he had fallen in unawares with someone on the road, an assassin who had committed the murder of a woman for pay. He named names: Melite was the hirer, Leucippe the victim. I do not know whether these events actually happened as stated, but it is open to you to find out. This inmate is to hand, as are the maidservants and Sosthenes: the latter will tell you the source from which he acquired Leucippe as a slave, the maids will tell you how she disappeared, and the inmate will have the details of the contract-killer's crimes. Before you have each of these pieces of information, it is unholy and impious to believe this poor young man's raving words and put him to death. His madness is caused by grief.'

[10] Clinias finished speaking. His speech persuaded the masses, but Thersander's orators and all his friends who were present cried for the death of the murderer who had been steered by divine providence to accuse himself. Melite offered to produce the two maidservants, and requested Thersander to produce Sosthenes, saying that he was no doubt the one who had killed Leucippe. Her lawyers put forward this challenge with great enthusiasm. Thersander was perturbed, and secretly sent one of his supporters to Sosthenes on the estate, with orders to him to disappear as quickly as possible, before the men sent to fetch him should arrive. This man mounted a horse and went to him with all haste, telling him of the danger: if he was caught there he would be dragged off to be tortured. Sosthenes happened to be in Leucippe's hut, trying to charm her. When Thersander's man summoned him with his shouts, he went out deeply disturbed. On hearing the facts he was filled with fear and imagined that the townsfolk were already upon him. He mounted a horse and rode with all haste in the direction of Smyrna, and the messenger returned to Thersander. The

saying is true, it seems, that fear is prone to stun the memory:° in his fear for his own person, Sosthenes was so stunned as to forget absolutely everything incidental, and he did not even remember to shut the door to Leucippe's hut—so vile is the servile class in times of fear.

[11] Meanwhile, when the first challenge had been issued by Melite, Thersander came forward.

'This fellow,' he said, 'whoever he is, has blathered enough fictional accusations. For my part, I am amazed at your obtuseness: you have caught this murderer in the act (and a confession counts for more than having caught someone at it), but you do not summon the executioner, instead you sit there listening to a charlatan with his oh-so-plausible theatricals and tears. In my opinion, he too must have been an accomplice in the murder, and must be fearing for his own safety. I do not know why we still need tortured slaves when the matter is so clearly proven.

'I think that there has also been a second murder. This man Sosthenes, whom they demand that I produce, has been missing for three days now: it is not difficult to suspect, therefore, that he has become the victim of their plotting. After all, it was he who denounced the adultery to me: so it seems likely to me that they killed him, and, knowing that I would be unable to bring him forth (vicious scoundrels that they are!), they have issued this challenge to produce him. But suppose he were to turn up, alive: what on earth would he tell you, even if he were present in this court? Whether he bought some girl? Let us say, for the sake of example, that he did buy her: is he supposed to tell you that she was in Melite's service? "Yes," he replies (speaking through me). After telling you this, Sosthenes now leaves the court. From now on, I address Melite and Clitophon. When you took my slave, what did you do with her? For she was indeed my slave, since Sosthenes bought her, and if she were still alive and not murdered at the hands of these people, she would certainly be slaving for me.'

Thersander had added this argument out of extreme malice, so that even if Leucippe were later discovered alive, he could make her his slave. Then he continued:

'Now, Clitophon admits to having killed her, and accepts the penalty, while Melite denies it. The torture of the maidservants will

convict her. If they turn out to have taken the girl from her and
failed to bring her back, what should we conclude to have happened? Why was Leucippe sent out of the house at all? And to
whom? Is not the matter plain, that they had briefed some men to
kill her? The maids, no doubt, did not know the men: that way, the
act could be committed without the increased risk of superfluous
witnesses. Although they did not know it, the place where they left
her was a haunt of bandits: and so they managed to avoid observing the outcome. And as for this part about some prisoner who is
supposed to have told them about the murder, this is also sheer
nonsense. Who is this prisoner, then, who has not said a word to
the prefect, who divulged the secrets of the murder to Clitophon
alone? Unless, that is, someone who recognized him as an accomplice . . . !

'Come on, stop tolerating this vapid babble and treating a matter of such importance as a game! Can you believe that this man
accused himself without divine prompting?'

[12] Thersander finished speaking and swore an oath that he did
not know what had become of Sosthenes. It was decided by the
president of the jury—a man of royal descent, who tried cases of
murder using as advisors, in accordance with the law, certain of the
senior men, who assessed his judgement—It was decided, then, by
him, after consultation with his colleagues, to condemn me to
death in accordance with the law, which stated that anyone who
confessed to murder should be executed; while in Melite's case,
they decided on a retrial, using the evidence of the tortured maids;
they also decided that Thersander should sign a written oath concerning Sosthenes, swearing that he did not know what had happened to him; and that I should be tortured (since I was now a
condemned man°) concerning the matter of Melite's complicity in
the murder.

I was bound in chains, my body was stripped of clothes and suspended in mid-air from ropes, and the whips, fire, and wheel were
brought in by various figures. Clinias let out a wail and called upon
the gods. Just as this happened, the priest of Artemis was seen
approaching, wreathed with laurel. This was the signal that the pil-
grimage to the goddess had arrived. Whenever this happens, all
judicial punishments are to be put on hold for as many days as it

takes for the pilgrims to complete their sacrifice.° For this reason, I was freed from my chains for now.

The leader of the expedition was Sostratus, Leucippe's father. There had been an epiphany of Artemis during the war against Thrace, and when the Byzantines had emerged victorious, they had reckoned it incumbent upon them to send a victory sacrifice to the goddess in thanks for her support. In fact, it had been to Sostratus that the goddess had appeared in private, during the night: the dream had signalled that he would find his daughter and his nephew in Ephesus.

[13] Around the same time, Leucippe spotted that the door of her hut was open and that Sosthenes was not around. She peered about to check that he was not outside, and when he was nowhere to be seen, her courage and her hope of old returned to her. The memory of how she had often in the past been rescued contrary to all expectation inspired this hope amid her present danger. She took full advantage of her fortune. Close to the estate lay the precinct of Artemis: she ran out to it and took sanctuary in the temple. Since ancient times, entry to this temple had been forbidden to free women, and open only to men and virgins. If any woman should enter it, the penalty was death, except in the case of a slave with a complaint against her master: such a woman was permitted to supplicate the goddess, and the city officials arbitrated between her and her master. If it turned out that the master had done nothing wrong, then he regained his serving-woman, after having sworn not to hold her escape against her; but if the serving-woman seemed to have just cause for complaint, she remained there in the service of the goddess. Sostratus had only just fetched the priest and proceeded to the courtroom to suspend the processes when Leucippe arrived at the temple, and so she narrowly missed coinciding with her father.

[14] When I was released from the tortures, the court was dissolved and a tumultuous crowd gathered around me, some in pity, others claiming divine intervention, and others trying to work out what had happened. It was then that Sostratus saw me and realized who I was. As I stated at the beginning of my story,° he once came to Tyre for religious reasons during the festival of Heracles, and stayed in Tyre for a long period (at a time well before our

escape). As a result, he easily recognized my face, and, in the light of the dream, naturally enough assumed he would find both of us. Approaching me, he said:

'Here is Clitophon—but where is Leucippe?'

On recognizing him, I hung my head and stared at the ground; the bystanders, meanwhile, recounted all the accusations I had levelled against myself. He gave out a wail, beat his head, and made for my eyes, very nearly tearing them out (for I made no attempt to prevent him—in fact, I offered him my face to assault). It was Clinias who came forward and restrained him, while trying to appease him:

'What are you doing, man?' he said. 'Why this pointless savagery against a man who loves Leucippe even more than you do? He has submitted to death because he thinks she is dead.'

He carried on at length in this vein, attempting to calm him. Sostratus, however, invoked Artemis in his grief:

'Was it for this that you brought me here, mistress? Was this the meaning of your nocturnal prophecies? To think that I trusted your dreams, expecting that you would help me find my daughter! A fine gift this is that you have given me! You have helped me discover her murderer!'

When Clinias heard about the dream of Artemis, he was delighted and said:

'Take heart, father: Artemis is no liar. Your Leucippe is still alive: you can trust my prophecies. Can you not see how she has rescued Clitophon too? I mean from the tortures: just now he was dangling on high.'

[15] At that point, one of the temple attendants ran up to the priest at great speed, and announced, so that everyone could hear:

'A foreign girl has taken refuge with Artemis!'

When I heard this, I was all aflutter: I raised my eyes, and the life began to return to me. Clinias said to Sostratus:

'My prophecies were true, father.'

Then at once he asked the messenger:

'She is, I presume, beautiful?'

'I have never seen such beauty,' he replied, 'only Artemis outdoes her.'°

At this, I leapt up and cried:

'You are talking about Leucippe!'

'I certainly am', he replied. 'That was the name she gave, saying that her fatherland was Byzantium and her father Sostratus.'

Clinias clapped and burst into a triumphant paean,° and Sostratus fell to the ground in joy; I jumped into the air, chains and all, and flew towards the temple, as if hurled by a catapult. The guards gave chase, thinking that I was trying to escape, and cried out to people on the way to grab hold of me. My feet, however, were like wings: it was only with great difficulty that certain bystanders managed to grab me as I raced madly. The guards arrived and tried to beat me (and I, newly heartened, defended myself), then started dragging me off to prison.

[16] At that point, Clinias and Sostratus arrived. Clinias cried out:

'Where are you taking that man? He did not murder the woman to whom the conviction pertains!'

It was then Sostratus' turn to agree, adding that he was the father of the presumed victim. When those who were present learned the full story, they praised Artemis and surrounded me, refusing to let them take me to prison. The guards protested that they were not empowered to release a man who had been condemned to death, until finally the priest, at Sostratus' request, pledged that he would 'watch over the man, and hand him over to the people as soon as they ask for him.'

I was thus released from my chains, and I hurried to the temple with all speed. Sostratus was at my heels: I have no idea whether his joy matched mine. But there is no man so fleet of foot that the wing of Rumour fails to outstrip him; and on this occasion too, Rumour reached Leucippe before we did, with the whole story about Sostratus and about me. When she saw us, she rushed out of the temple and embraced her father, though her eyes were fixed upon me. I stood there, restraining myself, out of respect for Sostratus, from throwing myself at her, gazing continually on her face. This was how we greeted one another: with our eyes.

Book 8

[1] Just as we were about to sit down and discuss these events, Thersander arrived at the temple in great haste with some witnesses in tow.

'I protest,' he shouted to the priest in a loud voice, 'with these people as my witnesses, that you acted improperly by releasing a man legally condemned to death from his chains and from the death-penalty. And you are also in possession of my slave, that rampant, man-mad° woman! Make sure you keep her safe for me!'

I felt a searing pain in my soul at the words 'slave' and 'rampant woman'. I could not stand the wounds caused by these utterances, and while he was still mid-rant, I cried:

'No, you are the one who are mad, rampant, and a slave three times over! She, on the other hand, is freeborn, a virgin, and worthy of the goddess!'

When he heard this, he replied:

'You dare to abuse me, you a convicted prisoner?'

He punched me in the face with extreme violence, and then brought down a second blow. Fountains of blood spurted from my nostrils, since all his fury had gone into the blow. As he punched me unthinkingly a third time, he accidentally landed his hand in my mouth and against my teeth. He injured his fingers, and with a scream he withdrew his hand in pain. My teeth avenged the assault on my nose: they injured the knuckles that delivered the punch, and his hand reaped what it had sown. In consequence, Thersander gave an unmanly shriek at the blow and withdrew his hand, and was thus stopped in his tracks. Although I saw how hurt he was, I pretended not to have noticed: instead I began a tragic declamation about the tyrannical abuse I had suffered, and the temple was filled with my cries.

[2] 'Ah, whither must we yet flee, to escape the violence of men? Whither must we hasten for protection? To some god other than

Artemis? For in her very temple I am struck! In this place of inviolable sanctuary I am punched! Normally, such events occur only in deserted places, where there is no witness, indeed no person at all: but not in your case, for you tyrannize under the eyes of the very gods! The refuge of the temple offers a haven to criminals, but I, who have committed no crime, a suppliant of Artemis, am beaten by her very altar, under the gaze—alas!—of the goddess! Those blows were directed against Artemis! What is more, your drunken madness is not even confined to punches: you actually go so far as to inflict facial wounds, as though in a military battle! The ground has been desecrated by human blood! What man pours libations of this kind to the goddess? Is this not what goes on among barbarians? Among the Taurians, in the case of the Scythians' Artemis?° No temple other than theirs is bloodied in this fashion. You have turned Ionia into Scythia! The blood that flows in Tauris flows in Ephesus as well! Go on, use your sword against me too! And yet what need do you have for a blade? Your hand does the job of a sword! That right hand of yours is guilty of murder and murderous desecration, for performing such actions as murder involves!'

[3] At these cries of mine, those who were in the temple gathered around in a crowd. These people, among them the priest himself, reproached him for his shameless perpetration of such blatant actions, in a temple of all places. I was encouraged, and said:

'This is the sort of treatment to which I have been subjected, gentlemen, though I am freeborn and from a city of no small note: this man has plotted against my life, but Artemis has saved me and exposed the malice that lay behind his accusations.° Now I must venture forth and wash my face clean outside: heaven forbid that I should do so inside, and that the sacred water should be polluted by the blood caused by this outrage.'

Then they dragged Thersander forcibly out of the temple. As he left, he cried out shocking words:

'You wait! You have already been tried, and you will soon suffer the penalty! But this fake virgin, this whore, she will soon be punished . . . by the panpipes!'

[4] When, eventually, he had departed, I too went outside and cleansed my face. It was time for supper, and the priest entertained us extremely hospitably. I was unable to look Sostratus directly in

the eyes, knowing how I had treated him. Sostratus, in turn, was ashamed to look at me when he saw the scratches that he had inflicted on me in the area of my eyes. Leucippe, meanwhile, stared at the ground for much of the time. The banquet was all embarrassment. As the drinking progressed, and Dionysus° (the father of free speaking) gradually melted the embarrassment, the priest was the first to speak, and he addressed Sostratus:

'Why not tell us your adventures? I imagine that the twists and turns you have undergone would be a pleasure to hear. Stories of that sort go particularly well with wine.'

Sostratus was delighted to take the opportunity.

'My part in the story,' he said, 'is simple: my name is Sostratus, my family is from Byzantium, I am this man's uncle and this girl's father. As for the rest of it, the fantastic adventures—well, speak up, Clitophon, do not be shy. After all, if events have caused me a certain amount of grief, it is certainly not your fault but Fortune's. And, anyway, a narrative of events past provides more entertainment° than grief for one whose sufferings are over.'

[5] I narrated everything: the passage from Tyre, the sea voyage, the shipwreck, Egypt, the Herdsmen, the abduction of Leucippe, the fake belly beside the altar, Menelaus' artifice, the general's infatuation and Chaereas' drug, the bandits' abduction, the wound in my thigh. I showed them the scar.° When I came to the part about Melite, I omitted my performance of the act,° reshaping the story into one of chaste self-control, although I told no actual lies: I told of how Melite was smitten with desire, and how I controlled myself, of all the time she spent beseeching me, and failing, of all her promises and all her laments. I narrated the part about the ship, the sea voyage to Ephesus, how we had both passed the night together, and how—'with Artemis here as my witness!'—she had risen as if from another woman's bed.° Only one of my actions in the course of the drama did I overlook, namely the services I subsequently rendered Melite. Then I told of the dinner and of how I falsely accused myself, and when I reached the sacred embassy, I concluded my account.

'That is my story told', I said. 'But Leucippe's outdoes mine. She has been sold into slavery, she has tilled the soil, and the beauty has been pillaged from her head: look at her haircut!'

Then I narrated the story, every detail of it. Then, when I reached the part about Sosthenes and Thersander, I excerpted her story even more than I had done mine, in an amorous attempt to gratify her, given that her father was listening. I told of how she had endured having every kind of violent outrage inflicted upon her body except one, and that it was for the sake of the last-mentioned that she had tolerated all the others.

'. . . and she remains up until the present day, father, in the same state as she was when you sent her on her way from Byzantium. This tale redounds to the praise not of myself, in that after making my escape I refrained from the acts for the sake of which I had escaped, as much as of her, in that even in the midst of bandits she retained her virginity, and she even overcame the chief bandit—I mean Thersander, that shameless rapist. Our peregrination bespoke philosophical moderation. Eros was in pursuit: we escaped a smitten man and a smitten woman. During our travels, we became like brother and sister. If there be such a thing as virginity in a man, I have retained it up to the present day, as far as Leucippe is concerned. As for her, well, she has desired for a long time now the temple of Artemis. O lady Aphrodite, do not be angry at us for spurning you! We did not want the father of the bride to miss the marriage. The father is now here: o come to us too, we pray, and look favourably upon us!'

As they listened to this, the priest sat agape with wonder at each of the events in the story, while Sostratus wept whenever the plot included Leucippe. When I finished, I said:

'You have heard our story. There is one single thing that I should like to learn from you, reverend priest. What on earth was Thersander talking about when he added his final words about Leucippe as he was leaving? What are the panpipes?'

'Well might you ask,' he replied, 'and it is fitting that we who know about the panpipes should oblige all present with a response: I shall tell you a fabulous tale, in return for yours. [6] Do you see that grove behind the temple? There is a cave there which it is forbidden for women to enter, but which is not forbidden for pure virgins. The panpipes hang a small way within the portals of the cave. Now, if your Byzantine culture embraces this instrument, you know what I am talking about; but if any of you is less familiar with this kind of music, then come, let me tell you its properties, and the entire fable about Pan and the pipes.

'The panpipes comprise a series of flutes, and each of the flutes is made from a reed. All the reeds sing out like a single flute. Tied one next to another, they form a row. It is identical from the front and from the rear. The reeds gradually decrease in size: each is bigger than the one it follows, the second being bigger than the first by the same amount as the third is bigger than the second, and, according to this proportion, each in the remaining troupe of reeds bears an equal relation to the one before. The central reed is of mean length, thanks to the odd total.° The reason for such an arrangement is the harmonic distribution: the top reed is the shrillest, just as at the other end the first one is the lowest, and the outermost flute at either end is allotted one of these two pitches. As for the harmonic intervals that lie between the extremes, each of all the intervening reeds produces a lower pitch than the next, down to the final baritone affixed.

'All the sounds that Athena's flute° makes within the tube, Pan's pipe also makes through the openings at the end of the reeds. In the former case, the fingers govern the pitch of the sound; in the latter, the artist's mouth plays the part equivalent to the fingers. In the former, the flautist closes all the holes bar the one through which his breath escapes; in the latter, he lets all the other reeds alone, placing his lip only upon the one to which he refuses silence, then he leaps from one to another, wherever the note harmonizes sweetly. In this way, his mouth dances from flute to flute.

'Originally, the panpipes were neither a flute nor a reed, but a maiden, of such beauty as to excite hopes and prayers. Now Pan° set off in pursuit of her in an erotic race. As she fled she entered a woody thicket, and Pan, bounding at her heels, lunged towards her with his hand. He thought he had bagged his quarry, and that he was holding onto her by the hair: but his hand was, in fact, clutching a thatch of reeds. They say that she sank into the ground, and that the earth sprouted reeds in her place. Pan hacked down the reeds, furious that they had stolen the object of his desires. When afterwards he was unable to find her, he concluded that the girl had dissolved into the reeds, and burst into tears of regret at having cut them down, thinking that the object of his desires was dead.

So he gathered together the fragments of reeds, as though they were the limbs of a body, and recomposed them into a single body. Then he held the cut up reeds in his hands and kissed them, as though they were the girl's wounds. He gave out a lover's moan as he placed his lips upon them, and breathed into one end of them, into the flutes, as he kissed. As his breath flowed through the channels in the reeds, it made the sounds of a flute: the panpipes acquired a voice.

'They say that Pan dedicated these panpipes here, enclosing them within the boundaries of this cave, and that he frequents the place and habitually blows on the panpipes. In later time, he gave the space over to Artemis, after making a compact with her that no female with experience of womanhood should enter therein. So, whenever anyone is accused of not being a virgin, the people send her forth as far as the portals of the cave, and the panpipes try the case. The girl enters alone, dressed in the robe required by tradition, and someone else closes up the portals of the cave. If she be a virgin, a sweet, divine tune may be heard, either because there is a musical breeze in the place itself, stored up within the panpipes, or perhaps even because Pan himself plays the pipes. After a short while, the portals of the cave open of their own accord, and the virgin emerges, her head garlanded with the foliage of the pine tree.

'If, on the other hand, she has lied about her virginity, the pipes are silent and a wail is emitted from the cave instead of the music. The people withdraw immediately, and abandon the woman in the cave. On the third day, the virgin priestess of the place enters, and discovers the panpipes on the ground and no sight of the woman. So, now you know: make your preparations for this event, so that you yourselves may succeed. If, as I hope, Leucippe is a virgin, you will receive the blessing of the panpipes and you can leave happily (the judgement of the pipes never errs); if not—after all, you yourselves know full well, what is likely to have happened to one who found herself, albeit unwillingly, caught up in the midst of so many intrigues . . .'

[7] Before the priest could say the next word, so it seemed to me, Leucippe spoke up:

'Do not even say it! I for one am ready to be locked into the cave of the panpipes, even without a formal summons.'

'Excellently spoken,' replied the priest. 'I am delighted by your chastity, and by the way matters have turned out for you.'

Then, when evening fell, each of us departed to sleep in the place that the priest had arranged for us. (Clinias did not join in the meal, in case we should seem vulgar enough to abuse our host's hospitality, preferring to remain during that time in the quarters he had occupied the previous day.) I had observed, however, that Sostratus was secretly worried by the story of the panpipes, in case the part about her virginity might have been a lie told out of embarrassment at his presence. I signalled to Leucippe with an unseen nod of the head that she should allay her father's fears (she was the one who knew the way most likely to persuade him). She seemed, I thought, to share my intuitions, and as a result she was quick to comprehend: even before my nod, she had been pondering what might be the most acceptable means of convincing him. Now, when she was about to retire to sleep, she kissed her father, and whispered to him:

'Have no fear on my account, father: you can believe what you heard. I swear by Artemis, not a single lie has been uttered by either of us.'

On the following day, Sostratus and the priest were busy with the sacred embassy, and the sacrifices were duly performed. The city councillors° were present too, to take part in the sacrificial rites. Many prayers were offered up to the goddess. Thersander, who also happened to be present, approached the president of the council, and said:

'Make a public declaration that the case concerning my complaints will be tried tomorrow. Certain people have already released the man whom you condemned yesterday, and Sosthenes is nowhere to be seen.'

The trial, then, was declared for the following day. We were all set, and made our preparations. [8] When the appointed day came, Thersander spoke as follows:

'I do not know what to say or where to start, whom to denounce first and whom second: for many acts of wickedness have been perpetrated by many men, and no one is any the less wicked than any other. All these acts are independent of one another, and there may be some I miss out in my accusation. I fear that my speech may turn out to be incomplete, given that I am in the grip of my emotions, and my tongue is guided from point to point by memories of other crimes. If one hurries on to what has not yet been said, one foreshortens the entire account of what has already been said. When adulterers murder the slaves of others, when murderers commit adultery with the wives of others, when pimps interrupt our sacred embassies, when whores pollute the most holy of our temples, when these whores fix the trial days for slave and master alike—what crimes are left to commit, when corruption is intermixed with adultery, impiety, and sacrilege? You have condemned a man to death on some grounds or other (it makes no difference which), you have packed him off to the prison in chains to be guarded until the sentence is carried out—and now this man stands before you, wearing a white robe instead of chains! The prisoner now stands in the ranks of the free! No doubt he will even have the effrontery to speak up, to make some rhetorical speech against me—and against your vote!

'Now, read out the decision reached by the president and his advisors.

[The decree is read]°

'Hear how you voted! Hear the sentence you pronounced against him, in my favour! You decided that Clitophon should be put to death! So where is the executioner? Let him seize this man and take him away! Give him the hemlock,° now! According to the laws, he is already dead: the penalty conferred on him is a day overdue! What is that that you say, O most august and reverend priest? Where in the sacred laws is it written that you may take those condemned by the council and the magistracy to be imprisoned and killed, and rescue them from their penalty, release them from their bonds, and raise your authority above that of presidents and juries? Step forward from your seat, president, yield your offices and juridical functions to this man! You no longer have authority in any sphere! You have no power to condemn villains: what you decide this very day is overruled. Why, O priest, do you stand alongside us as if you were one of the masses? Step forward, sit in the president's chair, and you try our cases in the future—or, rather, give out your edicts like a tyrant! Let no law, no judicial verdict be read out to you! In fact, do not even think of yourself as human at all! Allow us to prostrate ourselves before you along with Artemis! It is, after all, her privilege that you have usurped: she alone is entitled to rescue those who have fled to her, and even then only before a juridical trial. The goddess has never released a man in chains, nor has she freed a man condemned to death from his penalty. Her altars are for unfortunates, not for reprobates: but you go so far as to free prisoners and release convicts! In this way, you set yourself above Artemis.

'And who was this man residing in the temple instead of the prison? A murderer and adulterer, cohabiting with a pure goddess! Alas: an adulterer with a virgin! And there was with him a rampant woman, who had run away from her master. We know that you received her as well, that you shared your hospitality and a drinking-party with them. You probably even slept with them, reverend priest: you turned the temple into a bordello. The abode of Artemis has become a bedroom for adulterers, for a whore! Such things hardly happen in a penny brothel!

'My first suit covers both men: I propose that the one should be punished for his insolence, and the other submit to the penalty decreed. My second action is for adultery against Melite. I need make no speeches to charge her: it has been decreed that the enquiry should proceed via the torture of the maidservants. So, I request these maids to be produced: if under torture they state that they are unaware that this convict consorted with her over a long period of time, assuming what is more the position of husband (and not just that of adulterer) in my house, then I acquit her of all blame. If, however, the opposite is the case, then I say that she must, in accordance with the law, pay me her dowry in forfeit, and that he must undergo the punishment that is due to adulterers. That punishment is death: as a result, no matter how he dies, whether as an adulterer or as a murderer (he is liable to both penalties), he will have a penalty left to pay when he has paid the penalty, for though dead he will owe us another death.

'The third of my suits is against this slave of mine and this venerable man who is playing the part of her father. I shall save this one for later, after you have condemned these people.'

With these words, Thersander concluded. [9] The priest then came forward. He was a speaker of no slight ability, and in particular emulated the style of Aristophanic comedy.° He delivered his own speech, opening with an extremely suave exordium in the style of the comic poets, accusing Thersander of renting his body:

'To insult those who have lived decent lives in this ill-befitting way, in the presence of the goddess, is the sign of an impure mouth. And this is not the only time this has happened: wherever he goes, his tongue is an instrument of all kinds of abuse. When he was a boy, he consorted with many of society's more upstanding members, and expended all his youthful beauty on such activities. He acted the part of piety, he made a show of self-control: he pretended that his desire was to open himself up to a good pedagogy, ever bending to, always submitting to men who wished to see him attain this end. When he left his father's house, he rented a place for himself up a narrow passageway. He set up house there, indulging for the most part his passion for Homer (Homer-eroticism,° you might call it), and he hooked up with and entertained everyone who might be of any use for the purposes he had in mind. He reckoned that he was training his soul in this way, but it was in fact all an act to cover up his wickedness. Then in the gymnasia, too, we saw how he rubbed the oil into his body, how he clamped the pole between his legs,° and how when it came to wrestling with young men, he grappled particularly with the ones whose manhood was more pronounced. This is how he treated his body.

'That was when he was in the flower of youth. When he came to manhood, all was revealed that previously had been concealed. Now that his youth was past, he neglected the rest of his body, but sharpened his tongue alone for indecency, using his mouth for shameless activities, abusing everyone, bearing the stains of his shamelessness on his face. This is the man who felt no shame at pronouncing this ill-educated, sacrilegious slander against the man whom you have honoured with the priesthood, in your very presence! If I had lived somewhere other than among you, I should have needed to make a reply on behalf of myself and the way I have lived my life; but since you all know as well as I do the gulf between the way I live and these sacrilegious slanders, I shall turn now to address you on the subject of the accusations brought against me.

' "You freed a man condemned to death!" he cries, levelling terrifying reproaches at me for this, with accusations of tyranny and all the other bluster straight from the stage which he used against me. But the tyrant is not the man who guards victims of false prosecution, but the man who keeps under guard men who have done nothing wrong, though neither the city council nor the people have condemned them! Or can you tell me under which laws you locked up this young foreigner in prison in the first instance? Which of the magistrates condemned him? Which jury ordered the fellow to be bound? Even if we grant that he is guilty of all the crimes you have listed, he still needs to be judged first, to be cross-examined, to put forward his own side of the story. Let it be the law that binds him, the law that is master of everyone—including you! For no one has power over another without a legal judgement. Close the courts, then! Pull down the council chambers! Expel the prefects! It seems more appropriate to pronounce everything that you said to the president a true indictment of your own behaviour: stand up, president, make way for Thersander! You are president in name only: this man does your job for you. Or, rather, his actions go beyond even your powers: for you have advisors, and you may do nothing without them; nor may you do anything before you reach this seat; nor have you ever condemned a man to be bound when in your own home. But this fine fellow has become his own people, council, president, and magistrate all at the same time! In his own home, he hands out punishments, he tries cases, he orders men to be bound. The time of the trial is the evening: and what an excellent nocturnal juror he is, too!

'Now he is shouting out repeatedly: "You have freed a convict condemned to the death-penalty!" What death-penalty? What convict? Tell me the grounds for the death-penalty! "He is convicted of murder", he replies. So he has committed murder, has he? Tell me, who is the victim? The girl he killed, said by you to have disappeared, you can see here living: you would not dare to accuse him of this same murder! For this is not the girl's ghost: the Lord of Hades did not allow a dead girl to rise from the dead to testify against you!

'You are liable for two murders: your words have pronounced the girl dead, your deeds have willed the man dead. Or, rather, you

intended to do away with her, too: oh, I have heard about the little drama on the estate! But Artemis, great goddess that she is, rescued both of them, snatching one from Sosthenes' clutches, and
the other from yours. Ah yes, Sosthenes: you snatched him away to
prevent the exposure of your own complicity. Are you not ashamed
that you have been proven guilty of bringing malicious actions,
even as you indict these two foreigners?

'Enough of my replies to this man's sacrilegious slanders: I hand
over to the foreigners to make their own defences.'

[10] As an orator (a man of no slight reputation, a member of
the city council) was about to speak on behalf of Melite and myself,
another orator by the name of Sopater, a lawyer hired by
Thersander, interjected:

'Hold on, my excellent Nicostratus'—that was my orator's
name—'it is my turn to speak next against these adulterers, then
yours afterwards. Thersander's words accused the priest alone,
touching lightly on the case against the prisoner, only enough to
skim the surface. The time for *you* to refute the charges will come
when I have demonstrated that he is liable for two deaths.'

Thus he spoke, gesticulating wildly and slapping his face.°

'We have listened to the priest's comic performance,' he continued, 'all these innuendoes directed against Thersander, acted out
in a base and shameless manner. The prologue to his oration consisted of reproaches aimed at Thersander, on the very points on
which the latter had accused him. Not a single word spoken
against him by Thersander, however, was untrue: he did indeed
release a prisoner, entertain a whore, and conspire with an adulterer. As for his malicious and rather more shameless accusations
disparaging the way Thersander has lived his life, well, there was
no malicious accusation from which he refrained. A priest should
have, if nothing else, a tongue undefiled by outrage (to use his own
words against him). After the comedy came a bombastic performance in the tragic mode, spoken explicitly now, with no more rid-
dles: he rebuked us for binding an adulterer we had captured. At
these words, I was flabbergasted that anyone could afford to hire
him for such a display of zeal. The truth of the matter may be
divined. He saw the faces of this rampant pair, the adulterer and
the prostitute: she is young, in the bloom of her youth; the lad is

also in his bloom, not yet hard on the eye, and still useful for the priest's pleasures. Which of the two was it that bought you off? After all, you all bed down together, you get drunk together, and there was no one there to witness what you did during the night . . . I fear you have turned the temple of Artemis into that of Aphrodite: we shall have to judge whether it is proper that you should hold the privileged position of the priesthood.

'As for Thersander's life, everyone knows that from his earliest youth it has been one of orderly self-control, and that when he arrived at manhood he married in accordance with the laws, even if he did err in his choice of wife, since she did not turn out as he had hoped: he had put his trust in her ancestry and property. In all probability, she has in times gone by been unfaithful with other men, too, but kept these peccadilloes hidden from her excellent husband. In this, final act of the drama, however, she has divested herself of all decency, and steeped herself in shamelessness. When her husband set off on a lengthy voyage, she deemed this a perfect opportunity for adultery. She found a rent-boy—yes, this is even more unfortunate: the object she found for her desires was of the type that plays the man's role for women, but turns into a woman for men! And so brazen was she that it was not enough to consort with him publicly in a foreign land, but she even brought him here, sleeping with him the entire length of that sea journey, even having her rampant way in public, while everyone watched! O adultery shared between land and sea! O adultery stretching from Egypt right to Ionia!

'Now I grant you, adultery does occur in marriages—but usually only on a single occasion. If the crime occurs a second time, one covers up the deed, hiding it away from all. But this woman commits adultery and proclaims it, not just with a fanfare but even with a public declaration! The whole of Ephesus knew the adulterer! She felt no shame in importing these goods from abroad, when she arrived with a cargo of purchased beauty and an adulterer as her wares. "But I thought that my husband was dead!" she says. Well now, if he is dead, you may be acquitted of the charge: for the adultery has no victim, and a marriage with no husband cannot be violated. But if (since the male partner still lives) the marriage has not been annulled and another man has despoiled the female partner, then the marriage has been downright pillaged! Put simply, if the marriage no longer stands, he is no adulterer; if it does stand, he is an adulterer.'

[11] While Sopater was still speaking, Thersander cut short his speech.

'Stop,' he said, 'there is no need for words. I issue two formal challenges, to Melite here and this supposed daughter of the sacred ambassador (I no longer intend to torture her, as I suggested a little earlier°), who is in reality my slave.'

He then started reading:

'Thersander issues a challenge to Melite and Leucippe (this, so I heard, is the whore's name). I challenge Melite, on the question of whether she shared Aphrodite's pleasures with this foreigner during the time when I was abroad, to enter the water of the holy Styx,° to take an oath and acquit herself of the charges. As for this one, I call on her, if she happens to be a woman and not a virgin, to resume her position as her master's slave, since it is open only to women of servile status to enter the sanctuary of Artemis; and if, on the other hand, she says she is a virgin, to be enclosed within the cave of the panpipes.'

Leucippe and I immediately accepted the summons: we had known that it would come. Melite, meanwhile, took heart, since she and I had shared nothing but words for all the time that Thersander had been abroad.

'I too accept the challenge, and I volunteer a further addition: it is a crucial one, that I permitted no man at all, whether citizen or foreigner, to approach me for the purpose of a relationship during the time you mentioned. But what of you? What should your punishment be, if you are proven to have brought these accusations out of malice?'°

'Whatever the jurors decide is a suitable penalty', he replied.

Thereupon the court was dissolved, and it was ordained that the matters to do with the challenge directed at us should take place on the following day. [12] The story of the water of the Styx goes as follows. There was an attractive maiden by the name of Rhodopis, who had a passion for the chase and the hunt, with her swift feet, her sure hands, her girdle and headband, her tunic hitched up to the knees, and her hair cut in a man's style. Artemis beheld her in admiration, and invited her to be her hunting companion; and most of the time they hunted together. Rhodopis swore that she would always remain by her side, flee relationships with men, and never submit to Aphrodite's outrages. This was Rhodopis' oath; but Aphrodite heard, grew angry, and wished to avenge herself upon the girl for this slight.

There was a young man of Ephesus, as distinctively beautiful among the boys as Rhodopis was among the maidens. His name was Euthynicus. He too was a hunter like Rhodopis, and he was equally unwilling to know Aphrodite. So the goddess launched herself against both, crossing the paths of their hunting (up until now they had been apart). Artemis was not present at that time. Aphrodite sent her archer son° down to join them, saying:

'My son, do you see this pair who spurn Aphrodite, who despise us and our mystic rites? Even more brazen, the maiden even cursed me in an oath! Do you see how their paths have met as they chase the hind? Now it is your turn to start hunting, beginning with that bold girl. Your arrow is altogether surer than hers.'

Both aimed their bows, the girl at the hind, and Eros at the maid. Both hit the target, and the huntress, having trapped her prey, herself became the prey. The arrow entered the hind on his back, and the maid in her heart (the arrow being the love of Euthynicus). Eros let fly a second arrow, this time against the boy. Euthynicus and Rhodopis beheld one another. At first, the eyes of each were fixated, and neither was willing to give ground in either direction; gradually, however, the wounds flared up in each, and Eros led them to the cave in question (where there is now a spring), and there they betrayed the oath. When Artemis saw Aphrodite laughing and realized what had happened, she rendered the girl into water on the spot where she had surrendered her virginity.

For this reason, whenever an accusation is levelled at anyone in matters concerning Aphrodite, she enters the spring and washes. The spring is low, and reaches only as far as the middle of the shin. The adjudication proceeds as follows: she inscribes her oath on a tablet with a cord attached to it, and hangs it around her neck. If she tells the truth in her oath, the spring remains at ground level; but if she lies, the water rises in anger right up to her neck, and submerges the tablet. When we had discussed this and evening had come upon us, we departed to our own beds.

[13] On the following day, the entire populace was present. Thersander led the way, his face beaming as he looked towards us and laughed. Leucippe was dressed in the sacred garb: a tunic made of linen that came down to her feet, a girdle tied around the middle of the tunic, a dyed scarlet ribbon around her head, and bare feet. She entered with absolute serenity. As I watched her, I stood trembling, saying to myself:

'I have every faith that you are a virgin, Leucippe; but, my dearest, I fear Pan! The god is a lover of virgins, and I am afraid that you may become a second set of pipes! Only she escaped his pursuits on the plain, she was pursued in the open air; while you we have shut up within the portals, as if in a besieged city, so you will be unable to escape if he pursues you! O Lord Pan, look favourably on us, do not transgress the law of the place! We, after all, have observed it. Let Leucippe re-emerge to us a virgin! Such is the deal you struck with Artemis: do not cheat the virgin goddess!'

[14] As I was rambling to myself in this way, a musical melody began to be heard, and it was said that none sweeter had ever been heard. At once, we saw the portals open. When Leucippe ran out, the entire populace gave a cry of pleasure, and began to chide Thersander. Words alone could not describe how I felt. With this sweetest of victories behind us, we departed; now we progressed to the second adjudication, to the Styx. As before, the populace travelled to see the spectacle. All the rituals were followed there, too: Melite hung the tablet around her neck, the spring was low and translucent, and she entered it and stood there, her face radiant. The water remained as it was, at ground level: it did not rise even the slightest distance above its usual mark. When the time ordained for her enclosure had elapsed, the president took her by the hand and helped her out of the water. Thersander had lost two bouts. Since he was about to be worsted a third time, he slipped away and ran off to his house. He was fearful that the people might stone him to death, since four young men had turned up dragging Sosthenes behind them (two were relatives of Melite, two her servants: Melite had sent them to look for him). When Thersander, standing at a safe distance, perceived this, knowing that Sosthenes

would reveal the whole business if he were tortured, he pre-empted this eventuality by running away and slipping out of the city at nightfall. The magistrates ordered Sosthenes to be thrown into jail, since Thersander had escaped. Then, finally, we were acquitted: we had won the war in an open confrontation, and were hailed by all and sundry.

[15] On the following day, those entrusted to do so led Sosthenes before the magistrates. When he saw that he was being taken to be tortured, he confessed everything in clear detail, all Thersander's audacity and all his own complicity. He did not even omit the private conversation they had held concerning Leucippe outside the doors of her hut.° He was thrown back into prison pending sentencing, while Thersander was condemned to exile in his absence. As for us, the priest entertained us in his accustomed manner. While we dined, we exchanged tales of the adventures of the previous day, and any aspects of our experiences that remained unshared. Leucippe, no longer so very shy in front of her father now that she had been clearly proven a virgin, narrated what had happened to her with great pleasure. When she arrived at Pharos and the bandits, I said to her:

'Please, tell us that fabulous story about the bandits of Pharos, and the mystery of the decapitation there, so that your father can hear it too? That is the only part of the whole plot that remains unheard.'

[16] 'The bandits', she replied, 'hoodwinked an unfortunate woman, one of those who make money by selling Aphrodite's wares, into believing that, if she came aboard and slept with a certain shipowner, then he would make her his wife. They kept this woman on the ship, in ignorance of the true purpose for her presence, drinking quietly down below with one of the pirates, who pretended a desire for her. When they abducted me, as you know, they put me on the deck, then took flight, making their getaway by rowing. When they saw the ship in pursuit, they stripped the jewellery and clothing from the poor woman and put it upon me, then my frock upon her. Then they stood her up on the stern, where she would be visible to you as you pursued: they cut off her head, throwing her body into the sea, as you saw, and keeping the head, when it tumbled, on board the ship for the time being. A short

while later, when they were no longer being pursued, they got rid of this too, throwing it overboard in like fashion.

'I do not know whether they had arranged for the woman's presence in advance for this purpose, or whether they had originally decided to make a slave of her and sell her, just as they also sold me later on. It was because they were being pursued that they slaughtered her, to deceive their pursuers; and they chose her instead of me because they thought that they would make more by selling me than her. As a result of these events, I also saw Chaereas pay an appropriate penalty (he was the one who had advised them to kill the woman instead of me and throw her overboard). The rest of the gang of pirates said that they would not hand me over to him alone: after all, he had already taken the other body from them, which if sold would have given them an opportunity for profit; I, they argued, should be sold in place of the woman who had died as the common booty of all of them, rather than of him alone. He began to protest, with a display of self-righteousness, citing their agreements that they had not abducted her to be sold for their own profit but because he himself desired her. Then he said something rather rash, and one of the bandits—good on him!—stood up behind him and cut off his head. So he paid the perfect penalty for the kidnap, and was himself thrown into the sea. The bandits sailed for two days, then took me somewhere or other and sold me to their regular slaver, and he sold me to Sosthenes.'

[17] Sostratus then spoke up:

'Now that you have recounted your own adventures, my children, you must hear from me what happened at home concerning Calligone (your sister, Clitophon): I do not want to turn up at the banquet of tale-telling altogether empty-handed!'

When I heard my sister's name, I gave him my full attention.

'Yes, father,' I said, 'do tell! Only please let the subject of the story be alive!'

He began by telling everything that I have already related: Callisthenes, the oracle, the sacred embassy, the boat, the abduction. Then he continued:

'During the sea voyage, he learned that it was not my daughter, and that he had made a mess of the whole business; but he fell for

Calligone anyway, and deeply. He threw himself at her knees, and said:

' "Lady mistress, do not think of me as some bandit, some criminal! I was, after all, born into the nobility: my family is from Byzantium, and I am second to none in rank. Eros scripted my role as bandit, Eros made me weave these artful wiles to get you. So, from this day on consider me your slave! For a dowry, I give you first of all myself, then an amount that your father would never have given. I shall also respect your virginity for as long as you see fit."

'With these words, and many more that were even more alluring, he won the girl over to his side. He was, moreover, handsome to behold, eloquent, and extremely persuasive. When he came to Byzantium, he made a public statement promising her an enormous dowry, and made all the other preparations with extravagance: clothing, gold, everything that goes to adorn women blessed by fate. He treated her as a gentleman would, respecting her purity as he had promised. As a result, he now even captured her heart. In other ways, too, he showed himself extremely decent, proper, and moderate: there was a sudden, miraculous transformation in the young man. He got up and offered his seat to older men, he took care to be the first to greet those whom he met, his hitherto indiscriminate extravagance was transmogrified from prodigality into prudence, and he cultivated a benevolence towards those forced by poverty to accept charity. As a result, all marvelled at this sudden metamorphosis of a lesser being into an altogether excellent one.

'It was me, however, that he won over most of all. I was extremely fond of him, and counted his former prodigality as the fantastic excesses of his nature, not as an inability to control himself. The story of Themistocles° came to mind: he too had a great reputation for licentiousness in his earliest youth, but later surpassed all the Athenians in wisdom and manly excellence. I began to regret having told him to go to hell when we had discussed my daughter's marriage. He paid much attention to me, calling me "father" and serving as my bodyguard in public. Nor did he neglect his military training: he distinguished himself with particular vigour in the equestrian exercises. During the time of his prodigality, too, he had taken pleasure in practising such things, but as a self-indulgent game; even so, his manliness and experience had been nourished, unbeknownst to him. He made it his ultimate goal to distinguish himself for his fortitude and versatility in military encounters. He also gave quite acceptable sums of money to the city. They made him joint general with me. For this reason, his devotion to me increased still further, and he subordinated himself to me on every issue.

[18] 'When, thanks to the divine epiphany, we had triumphed in the war, we turned back towards Byzantium. We praised Heracles and Artemis: I was elected to give thanks to Artemis here, and he to Heracles in Tyre. Before we set off, Callisthenes took me by the hand and recounted for the first time what he had done concerning Calligone.

' "Of my actions," he said, "the aggressive ones were motivated by youthful nature, violent as it is, but others latterly by personal choice. I have respected the girl's virginity to this very day, in the middle of a series of wars at that, when no one foregoes his pleasures. Now, therefore, I have decided to take her back to her father in Tyre, and to obtain legal permission for the marriage from him. If he is willing to give me his daughter, I shall accept her and count my blessings; if, on the other hand, he turns difficult and bad-tempered, then he will receive her back a virgin. But since I offer no mean dowry, I hope to win her with goodwill."

'I shall also read out to you the statement that I wrote before we sailed, recommending the girl should marry Callisthenes, citing his ancestry, his status, and his military accomplishments. That is the content of my statement. I have already taken the decision that if we win our appeal I shall sail first to Byzantium and afterwards to Tyre.'

After sharing these marvellous adventures, we went to bed, following the usual arrangement. [19] On the following day, Clinias turned up, saying that Thersander had made his getaway during the night. He had lodged an appeal with no intention of fighting it, simply wishing to use this pretext to delay the cross-examination of his overweening actions. We stayed for the next three days (the stipulated period), then approached the president and read out the laws that stated that Thersander had no case against us. Then we embarked upon the ship, met with a following wind, and put in at Byzantium. There we concluded the marriage for which we had so often prayed; then we voyaged to Tyre. We arrived two days after Callisthenes, and found my father about to perform the sacrifices for my sister's wedding on the following day. So we were there to share with him in the sacrifices, and to pray to the god that my marriage and Callisthenes' would be overseen by good fortunes. Then we decided to spend the winter in Tyre before returning to Byzantium.

Explanatory Notes

1.1   *Assyrian*: i.e. Syrian. Syria was often referred to in antiquity by the archaic but inaccurate name of Assyria: the use of the word here strikes an antiquarian tone.

     its people fathered the Thebans: Greek myth told that Agenor (usually king of Tyre, but here transplanted to Sidon) sent his son Cadmus to search for his missing daughter Europa, who had, however, been abducted by Zeus in the form of a bull (the story is the subject of the picture that Achilles will proceed to describe). Whilst in Greece, Cadmus is said to have founded Thebes.

     Astarte: the Phoenician goddess Ishtar, thought of by the Greeks as equivalent to Aphrodite and Selene, the goddess of the moon.

     picture: like Longus' *Daphnis and Chloe*, this novel begins with a set-piece description of a painting (often, but somewhat inaccurately, referred to by modern scholars as an *ecphrasis*). Descriptions of art-works have a long history in Greek literature (cf. especially Homer, *Iliad* 18. 478–613; 'Hesiod', *Shield of Heracles*; Apollonius of Rhodes, *Argonautica* 1. 721–73), but are particularly important in the novels (see also 3. 6–8; 5. 5).

     The meadow: descriptions of gardens and sculpted landscapes are common in Greek literature from Homer onwards, especially in contexts where there is at least a hint of eroticism (*Odyssey* 5. 63–75; 7. 112–32; Apollonius of Rhodes, *Argonautica* 3. 219–27; Longus, *Daphnis and Chloe* 2. 12; 4. 2–3).

     A man was pictured . . . : modelled on Homer, *Iliad* 21. 257–9.

1.2   *What power . . . sea!*: the all-conquering power of Aphrodite and Eros is a common theme in ancient literature (e.g. Sophocles, *Women of Trachis* 497–506; Euripides, *Hippolytus* 439–81; Petronius, *Satyricon* 83).

     swarm of stories: similar phrase at Plato, *Republic* 450a.

     grove: reminiscent of the site of Socrates' and Phaedrus' disquisitions on desire and rhetoric in Plato's *Phaedrus* 230b–c (a key text for Greek erotic writers of the Imperial period).

1.3   *Her eyes . . . snakes*: the iconography of the figure in the dream suggests that she is a Fury (see e.g. Euripides, *Orestes* 256), an aveng-
ing deity (oddly, as there is no suggestion of Clitophon's having
committed a crime; but an epicizing travel narrative is best motivated by divine wrath).

1.4   *Selene*: the goddess of the moon (see also n. on 1.1). One manuscript reads 'Europa', which would link this picture directly to the
one at the beginning of the work.

      the purple pigment . . . ivory: the phrase derives from Homer, *Iliad*
4. 141–2, 'just as a Maeonian or Carian woman stains ivory with
scarlet' (also imitated by Heliodorus, *Aethiopica* 10. 15. 2).

      towed by the lure: this translates 'dragged by the *peisma*' (both 'cable'
and 'persuasion').

1.5   *Daphne*: the Greek word means 'laurel'. This 'aetiology' of the laurel is best known from Ovid, *Metamorphoses* 1. 452–567.

1.6   *The others had measured . . . bellies*: an imitation of Demosthenes, *On
the Crown* 296.

      drunken with desire: echoing the same phrase in a fragment of
Anacreon's lyric poetry (fr. 19 Bergk = fr. 376 Page/Campbell
(Loeb)).

      I could not get to sleep: the lover's sleeplessness is traditional (see e.g.
Plato, *Phaedrus* 251e; Longus, *Daphnis and Chloe* 1. 13, 2. 8 etc.).

      To be sure . . . at rest: this section recalls Plato, *Republic* 571c–d.

      drenched myself with desire: the same phrase at Plato, *Phaedrus* 251e.

1.7   *It was straight to him that I went*: Clitophon visits Clinias as an *eroto-
didaskalos*, a 'teacher of desire'. The phenomenon is familiar in
ancient literature (Diotima in Plato's *Symposium*, Ovid in his *Ars
amatoria*), including the novels (Longus, *Daphnis and Chloe* 2. 3–8;
3. 17–19).

1.8   *slandering the entire female species*: misogynist rants are a frequent feature in ancient literature (see Hesiod, *Theogony* 585–612;
Semonides 7; Euripides, *Hippolytus* 616–17; Juvenal, *Satire* 6). The
phrase 'female species' evokes Hesiod, *Theogony* 590, and the
Hesiodic tone of the entire passage is underlined by the ensuing
quotation.

      I shall give . . . bane?: a quotation from Hesiod, *Works and Days* 57–8.
The first woman, Pandora, was created by Zeus in revenge for
Prometheus' theft of fire.

Sirens: mythical female creatures who lured sailors to land with their song, only to kill them. See Homer, *Odyssey* 12. 39–54; 165–200.

Eriphyle's necklace . . . murder: a list of famous female deceivers of the tragic stage. Eriphyle betrayed her husband, Amphiaraus, for a necklace; Sthenoboea slandered Bellerophon to her husband Proetus; Aerope stole the golden fleece from her husband. Philomela's presence in the list is anomalous: after she was raped by Tereus, who also cut her tongue out so that she could not testify against him, she wove the story and sent it to her sister Procne, who exacted horrible revenge (the story is told at 5. 5). The anomaly is explicable: Clinias' blind rage and misogyny obscure the difference between villains and victims with grievances.

If Agamemnon . . . wife: more female literary figures, with varying degrees of responsibility for the crimes of which Clinias charges them. Agamemnon's abduction of Chryseis, the daughter of a priest of Apollo, brought down the plague in vengeance (in the opening section of the *Iliad*: 1. 92–102). When he had to return her, he took Achilles' prize, Briseis; Achilles sulked, and as an indirect result his best friend Patroclus was killed. The story of Candaules, who was smitten with desire for his wife (!), and died as a result, is found in Herodotus (1. 12). Helen's abduction from Sparta inspired the Greek force to attack Troy; according to the *Odyssey*, Penelope's refusal to marry the suitors ended up in a bow contest for her hand, in which her husband Odysseus revealed himself and slaughtered them; Phaedra fell in love with her stepson, Hippolytus, but killed herself for shame and accused him in a note of raping her (see Euripides, *Hippolytus*); Clytemnestra took another lover, Aegisthus, while Agamemnon was at Troy, and murdered her husband on his return (see e.g. Aeschylus, *Agamemnon*).

as to . . . in thunder: cited from Homer, *Iliad* 2. 478.

1.9   *effluxion of beauty*: from Plato, *Phaedrus* 251b; see also below, 5. 13.

reciprocal desire: another allusion to Plato's *Phaedrus* (255d).

1.10   *a self-taught sophist*: see also 5. 27, 'Eros even teaches eloquence'. The idea of Eros as a teacher comes in Euripides' first *Hippolytus* (fr. 430 Nauck); he is then called a 'sophist' by Plato (*Symposium* 203d) and Xenophon (*Education of Cyrus* 6. 1. 41).

pregnant with his first desire: this extended metaphor of childbirth recalls Plato's discussion of philosophical gestation at *Symposium*

206b–7a (see also Plato *Theaetetus* 150a–151d; Aristophanes, *Clouds* 137).

1.13   *a double death*: an echo of Homer, *Odyssey* 12. 22, where Circe calls Odysseus' men 'twice-dying' (as they have visited the underworld whilst alive).

Your bridal . . . tomb: the funeral and the wedding were closely associated in Greek culture, on the grounds that each was a social ritual to mark radical and unalterable transition from one state (life, virginity) to another (death, marriage). See, most famously, Sophocles, *Antigone* 806–16.

1.15   *earth's purple flower*: the violet.

Eos . . . Tereus: figures from mythology. Eos (Dawn) asked for immortality for her lover Tithonus, but forgot to ask for eternal youth (*Homeric Hymn to Aphrodite* 218–98); later tradition has him turned into a cicada. For the story of Tereus, Procne, and Philomela, see above, note on 1. 8; the allusion here is to the subsequent fate of Philomela, who was metamorphosed into a nightingale.

1.16   *Satyrus*: Clitophon's slave, introduced (as Clio, Leucippe's slave, will be) without warning.

peacock: a common subject for description, such as the one which follows, in Imperial literature (Dio Chrysostom, *Oration* 12. 2–3; Aelian, *On Animals* 5. 21; Lucian, *The Hall* 11).

1.18   *a transmarine marriage of waters*: the story of the desire of Alpheus (a river in the Peloponnese, on the Greek mainland) and Arethusa (a spring in Sicily) was well known in ancient times (e.g. Pindar, *Nemean Odes* 1. 1–2; Vergil, *Aeneid* 3. 694–6; Ovid, *Metamorphoses* 5. 577–641).

Yet another mystery of desire arises: the passion of the viper and the lamprey, another oddity recorded elsewhere (Aelian, *On Animals* 1. 50; 9. 66; Oppian, *The Art of Fishing* 1. 554–79).

1.19   *pretexts*: in all the manuscripts there follows a sentence which means: 'After a little while, it was time for supper, and once more we got together to drink as before.' Scholars consider that this sentence interrupts the narrative, and that it has entered the text erroneously.

2.1   *the battle . . . in Homer*: *Iliad* 16. 823–6.

Dionysus of the Vintage: Dionysus is the god of the vine (also of theatre and licence), represented in Greek literature (most notably in

Euripides' *Bacchants*) as a visitor from the East. A Dionysiac wine festival also takes place in Longus' *Daphnis and Chloe* (2. 1–2).

the dark wine . . . Icarus: references to famous wines of Greek literature: the 'dark wine' is referred to most notably by Aristophanes (*Wealth* 807); the Biblian wine is mentioned by Hesiod (*Works and Days* 589) and Theocritus (14. 15; see also Athenaeus, *Sophists at Supper* 31a–b); the 'Thracian wine of Maro' is that used by Odysseus to intoxicate the Cyclops (*Odyssey* 9. 196–7); the 'Chian wine from the Laconian cup' is found in Aristophanes (fr. 216 Geldart–Hall, from *The Banqueters*); the 'island wine of Icarus' is the famous 'Pramnian' wine (e.g. Athenaeus, *Sophists at Supper* 30b–c).

Icarius: the mythical founder of the eponymous Athenian deme, who received Dionysus when he visited Attica (Apollodorus, *Library* 3. 14. 7; Nonnus, *Dionysiaca* 47. 34–69).

2.3 *mixing-bowl . . . of Glaucus of Chios*: that described by Herodotus (1. 25) as 'worth seeing above all the other offerings at Delphi'.

2.4 *Athena*: goddess of craft and technology, but also of cunning plans. She is Odysseus' patron in Homer's *Odyssey*.

2.6 *Omphale*: Heracles was ordered to serve the Lydian queen Omphale in expiation for his slaying of Iphitus. The 'certain one of the gods' mentioned by Clitophon is, of course, Eros.

Hermes: Hermes oversaw, amongst other things, exchange, profit, and communication. In this capacity, it was Hermes who was mandated by Zeus to find a buyer for Heracles (Apollodorus, *Library* 2. 6. 3).

2.11 *purple*: the purple dye of Tyre was extremely famous and prestigious in antiquity (see esp. Strabo, *Geography* 16. 2. 23).

the shepherd's dog discovered: no earlier version of this story is known.

2.12 *The event . . . view*: to make better sense of the text, I have brought forward this sentence from its position in the manuscripts after the words meaning 'in which the bird had flown'.

Zeus Xenios: Zeus in his aspect as protector of relationships of hospitality between foreigners. He is also invoked at 3. 17 and 3. 21.

2.13 *orphan*: i.e. he had inherited.

a law: no such law is known of.

2.14 *There is . . . to Heracles*: this oracle is also preserved amongst the epigrammatic collection known as the *Greek Anthology* (14. 34), with an extra line.

as I mentioned: there is, in fact, no earlier mention of this in the text as we have it.

phoenix: the word *phoenix* is the Greek for 'date-palm' (and, incidentally, the English genus-word for 'palm').

narrow neck: a causeway (which still exists) was built between Tyre and the mainland by Alexander the Great during his siege of the city.

Hephaestus . . . Athena: the paradox in the oracle depends upon the knowledge that Athena famously rejected Hephaestus' sexual advances, the latter's semen spilling onto the soil of Attica to beget the Athenian people; for Hephaestus to 'possess' Athena, then, is a surprise. Hephaestus' sphere was the forge, hence the reference to fire; Athena, goddess of (amongst other things) craft and technology, was associated with the olive tree.

the Sicilian spring: no one has convincingly linked this passage to any other phenomenon discussed in ancient literature.

river in Spain: again, unattested elsewhere.

a lake in Libya . . . India: this remarkable story is recorded, with a certain degree of scepticism, by Herodotus (4. 195), who locates the lake on an island off the North African coast. The soil of India was famous for being rich in gold (see e.g. Herodotus 3. 98–105).

2.15 *that praised by Homer . . . Thrace*: this refers to Dolon's account of the horses of Rhesus at *Iliad* 10. 436–7: 'His are the most beautiful and largest horses I have seen: | they are whiter than snow, and they run like the winds.'

the myth of Europa: see above, 1. 1 and note.

2.17 *Sarapta*: a small village some 8 miles (13 km) south of Sidon.

Rhodope: not attested elsewhere. Some manuscripts read 'Rhodopis', the name of a famous travelling courtesan (see Herodotus 2. 134–5; Heliodorus, *Aethiopica* 2.25) also mentioned at 8. 12.

2.20 *Gnat-man*: the Greek word *kônôps* (homonymous with Conops' name) means 'gnat'. This information is important for the fables that follow.

a fable about a gnat: this fable is also found in the corpus of Aesop's fables, as numbers 267 and 292 (Hausrath).

2.21 *Prometheus*: the mythical creator of humankind and here, by extension, of animals too. The idea that the lion is afraid of the cock is found elsewhere in classical literature, e.g. Pliny, *Natural History* 8. 52; Aelian *On Animals* 3.31.

2.23   *Odysseus*: Satyrus is punning on the name of Conops, which resembles 'Cyclops'. In Homer's *Odyssey* Odysseus and his men ply the Cyclops Polyphemus with drink before blinding him by plunging the stake into his eye (9. 345–94). The potential sexual connotations of stake-plunging may also be exploited here (cf. the obscene reference at Lucian, *False Critic* 27).

naked blade: grammatically, it could equally well be the daughter who is 'naked'.

2.24   *the coercion . . . the stigma of shame*: the idea that rape is preferable to consensual extramarital sex is found elsewhere in Greek literature (notably at Lysias 1. 32–3), and has been preempted by Clinias at 1. 10.

of the more truthful kind: the reference is to the Homeric belief in true and false dreams (*Iliad* 2. 1–34; *Odyssey* 19. 562–7).

2.25   *torture*: slaves were routinely tortured for forensic purposes in the ancient world.

2.29   *barking*: an allusion to Odysseus' 'barking heart' at Homer, *Odyssey* 20. 13.

2.30   *my father happened to be abroad*: it later turns out that he has been searching for Calligone (5. 10. 3).

2.31   *the first watch of night*: the night was divided, according to various conventions, into three, four, or five 'watches'. Achilles seems to follow the Roman custom of having four watches of three hours, so the first watch is about 6.00–9.00 p.m., the second 9.00–12.00.

Sidon: the distance from Tyre to Sidon is around 20 miles (30 km), and that from Sidon to Beirut around 25 miles (40 km).

2.32   *the gods of salvation*: probably the 'Dioscuri', i.e. Castor and Pollux, the protectors of sea-travellers.

2.34   *ill-starred hunt*: recalls Herodotus' story of Atys' death, accidentally speared by his would-be protector Adrastus (Herodotus 1. 34–45).

apparently for Patroclus: an explicit reminiscence of Homer, *Iliad* 19. 302, where captive Trojan women mourn 'apparently for Patroclus, but in fact each for her own woes'. The line is recalled by other novelists in slightly different forms (Chariton 8. 5. 2; Heliodorus 1. 18. 1).

2.35   *his oration against women*: paired rhetorical speeches on the relative merits of pederasty and heterosexuality are commonplace in the Greek literature of the Principate. See Introduction, p. xxix.

the draught of Tantalus: Tantalus' punishment in the underworld was to suffer perpetual thirst, only to have the waters in which he was chained recede as he leaned down to drink.

2.36   *heavenly . . . vulgar*: clearly recalling Pausanias' famous speech at Plato, *Symposium* 180d–181c, which distinguishes between the 'heavenly' Aphrodite (i.e. the love of men for boys) and the 'vulgar' (love between the sexes).

Him the gods . . . immortals: cited from Homer, *Iliad* 20. 234–5, of Ganymede.

Alcmene . . . flames: Alcmene, the mother of Heracles by Zeus, was harried into exile by Eurystheus, according to Euripides' *Children of Heracles*; Danaë, the mother of Perseus by Zeus, was locked into a chest which was set out to sea by Acrisius, her father; Semele, the mother of Dionysus by Zeus, was consumed by flame when she asked Zeus to reveal himself to her in all his divinity.

Phrygian boy: Ganymede. See Homer, *Iliad* 20. 231–5.

The former servant: Hebe (the personification of youth), who ceded the honour of pouring the gods' wine to Ganymede.

2.37   *lowed*: i.e. turned into a bull, alluding to Zeus' metamorphosis into a bull in the story of his rape of Europa (see 1. 1, above).

satyr's dance: Zeus approached the Theban Antiope in the guise of a satyr (a comical rustic divinity, half-human and half-goat, usually depicted drunk and sexually aroused).

converted himself into gold: Zeus impregnated Danaë by covering her with a shower of gold.

that is how Heracles ascended: according to one version of the myth (best-known through Sophocles' *Women of Trachis*), Heracles was cremated on Mt. Oeta.

why so silent about Perseus?: Perseus was also locked in the chest, so (Clitophon concludes) Zeus' actions were not aimed specifically at the female.

he robbed the world of three days: Zeus was enjoying himself so much he prevented the sun from rising for three days, according to one version (Diodorus of Sicily, *Library of History* 4. 9. 2; Apollodorus, *Library* 2. 4. 8).

my own experience with women is limited . . . : an ironic variation on the standard rhetorical *captatio benevolentiae* 'unaccustomed as I am to public speaking . . .'.

2.38   *the fable*: the reference is to one of Aesop's fables (fable 103 Hausrath). The jackdaw stuck on some feathers in order to try to pass himself off as a peacock; the peacocks, however, pecked at his plumage so much that they ruined his own feathers, and he was excluded by the jackdaws too.

3.2   *the air blared with bugle-sounds*: recalling Homer, *Iliad* 21. 388, 'all around the great heavens, the bugle sounded'.

3.4   *impaled like fish*: Greek fishermen sometimes used javelins. Achilles is here recalling Homer's description of the Laestrygonians impaling Odysseus' men: 'impaling them like fish they caught themselves a joyless banquet' (*Odyssey* 10. 124).

3.5   *Pelusium*: now Tineh, near the easternmost outlet of the Nile.

3.6   *Zeus Casius*: the most famous cult site of Zeus Casius was in Syria, at Mt. Casius near Antioch. There was, however, also a Mt. Casius near Pelusium, and Strabo confirms that Zeus Casius was worshipped there too (*Geography* 16. 2. 33).

mystic meaning: this meaning is debated, but it is not necessarily clear that Achilles has anything precise in mind. For discussion, see G. Anderson in *American Journal of Philology*, 100 (1979), 516–18.

Euanthes: otherwise unknown, this painter may be fictitious.

Andromeda and Prometheus: famous mythological victims. Andromeda was an Ethiopian girl fastened to a rock and molested by a sea-monster in reparation for her mother's boasting that she was more beautiful than the sea-nymphs, before being rescued by Perseus, who married her. The Titan Prometheus was punished by Zeus for stealing fire from the gods and giving it to mortals: he was chained to a rock in the Caucasus with an eagle pecking at his liver, until Heracles delivered him by shooting the eagle.

related to each other: Heracles was Perseus' grandfather.

3.7   *wrist*: there is an untranslatable pun here, since *karpos* means both 'wrist' and 'fruit'.

a bride for Hades: see above, note on 1. 13.

moths' wool . . . strands: i.e. silk, from silkworms. Herodotus (3. 106) tells us that Indians weave clothes from wool found in trees.

helmet of Hades: a magic helmet that rendered its wearer invisible (Homer, *Iliad* 5. 845; 'Hesiod', *Shield of Heracles* 227).

Gorgon's head: the head of Medusa turned onlookers into stone.

Andromeda: Andromeda, or *Andromeda*, alluding to Euripides' famous play of the same name? The Greek could be taken to mean either.

3.9 *Alexandria*: the famous city near the westernmost outlet of the Nile. The intended itinerary involves travelling up to the apex of the delta then back down towards the coast.

Herdsmen: the celebrated *boukoloi* of the coastal areas of the Nile. They are the stock baddies of the novels (Xenophon of Ephesus 3. 12. 2, 'Shepherds'; Heliodorus 1. 5. 1–2, etc.), but may have been based, partly at least, on real pirates in the Roman period (see Cassius Dio 71. 4; Introduction, p. xvi).

3.10 *Sirens*: see above, n. on 1. 8.

3.13 *two stades*: about a quarter of a mile or 400 m.

3.15 *Marsyas*: a satyr who challenged Apollo to a musical composition on the terms that the winner could do whatever he liked with the loser. Apollo, the winner, flayed Marsyas alive.

Niobe: having given birth to a large number (variable in different sources) of children, she boasted that she was superior to Leto who had only had two, Apollo and Artemis. The latter two therefore killed all her children, and Niobe was metamorphosed into stone. In the literary tradition, the name of Niobe becomes a byword for grief through bereavement.

3.17 *Zeus Xenios*: Zeus in his aspect as guardian of relationships between foreigners (Menelaus being Egyptian and Clitophon Syrian). See also n. on 2. 12.

3.18 *Hecate*: the goddess of magic.

3.20 *sitting by the sea . . .*: the proper place for literary characters to grieve (cf. Achilles at Homer, *Iliad* 1. 348–50; Odysseus at Homer, *Odyssey* 5. 81–3).

performer of Homeric songs in the theatre: he is a 'Homerist', as described by Petronius (*Satyricon* 59).

3.21 *Zeus Xenios*: see n. on 3.17.

3.24 *Heliopolis*: modern Materea, in lower Egypt.

3.25 *phoenix*: the legendary bird, a favourite subject for paradoxographers. Achilles' version resembles in certain details the sceptical account of Tacitus, *Annals* 6. 28. Achilles puns here on the homonyms *phoenix* (the bird) and *Phoenix* ('a Phoenician'); see also n. on 2. 14.

4.1 *Artemis*: the patron of hunters, women in labour, etc., but most pertinently a virgin goddess.

4.2 *horse of the Nile*: a hippopotamus (*hippos* = 'horse', *potamos* = 'river').

4.4 *except in paintings*: a characteristically Euripidean touch (see *Trojan Women* 687; *Hippolytus* 1004–5), but probably alluding primarily to Herodotus' claim only to have seen the phoenix in paintings (2. 73).

Hesiod's crow: an allusion to a fragment of Hesiod (fr. 304 Merkelbach–West), 'the cawing crow, mark you, lives on while nine generations of men flower' (lines 1–2).

Ethiopian: 'Ethiopian' in Greek simply means 'burned face', i.e. black, so this expression could in theory refer to an Indian. 'Ethiopia' was, however, the regular name for the part of Africa south of Egypt, which makes it much more likely that Achilles is referring to an African here, even though the episode is set in India. Ethiopia and India were held to have many things in common (see esp. Philostratus, *Life of Apollonius* 6. 1), sometimes including even population exchanges (ibid. 3. 20).

4.5 *a bloom*: attempts to identify this flower have been unsuccessful, and no doubt misguided.

4.7 *Aphrodite . . . Ares*: the goddess of sex and the god of war respectively, who had an extramarital liaison, recorded by Homer (*Odyssey* 8. 266–366).

4.8 *satiation and culmination*: an echo of Homer, *Iliad* 13. 636–7, 'satiation can be reached in all things, in sleep, sex, sweet song and excellent dancing . . .'.

4.10 *when the blood . . . reason*: a parody of a contemporary medical theory which attributed all illnesses to a surfeit of blood. See A. M. G. Macleod, 'Physiology and Medicine in a Greek Novel: Achilles Tatius' *Leucippe and Clitophon*', *Journal of Hellenic Studies*, 89 (1969), 97–105.

4.11 *satrap*: a provincial governor. This Persian word is used by Greek writers of Achilles' time to refer to any local official, especially the governor of a Roman province: thus it cannot be determined from this passage whether Achilles imagines Egypt to lie under

Persian dominion (sixth–fifth centuries BCE) or Roman (31 BC–Achilles' present day).

Thebes . . . Cercasorus: Thebes (not to be confused with the Greek city of the same name: hence Achilles' qualifier 'Egyptian') is the site of modern Luxor, some 500 miles up the Nile from the coast. The city had been extremely important under the Pharoahs, but was largely insignificant by Achilles' time: the mention here is an archaizing touch. Memphis was a large city, the capital of lower Egypt until Alexandria was built, lying just south of modern Cairo.

4.12 *one stade . . . twelve fathoms*: i.e. about 220 × 36 yards (200 × 33 m).

4.13 *one hundred talents*: one talent was the equivalent of 6,000 drachmae, an enormous amount.

4.17 *Asclepius*: the god of healing.

4.18 *capital*: it is unclear whether Alexandria or Heliopolis is meant.

Pharos: the island a little way out from Alexandria, site of the famous lighthouse.

Dionysus: i.e. wine. See 2. 2 and n.

4.19 *fence*: a clear echo of a distinctively Homeric expression, 'the fence of the teeth' (e.g. Homer, *Iliad* 4. 350; *Odyssey* 10. 328).

5 1 *a few stades*: 1 stade = approx. 200 yards (180 m)

place named after Alexander: it is unclear what Achilles is referring to here (obviously, the entire city is named after Alexander). No other ancient author gives us any hints, although there is no reason to doubt Achilles, especially if he is indeed an Alexandrian himself.

5.2 *Zeus Meilichios . . . Zeus Ouranios*: cult-titles of Zeus. The former means 'honeyed', referring to the god's favourable treatment of those who make offerings to him; the latter, meaning 'heavenly', refers to both his heavenly abode and his ancestor Uranus ('heaven'). Here, though, Achilles (as he has told us) is alluding specifically to the cult of the Alexandrian god Serapis.

5.3 *Philomela . . . Tereus*: mythological characters; see 5. 5 and n. on 1. 8 for the story. The 'drama' referred to in the following line may (but need not) refer to a specific play, Sophocles' *Tereus* (now lost).

5.5 *female species*: see n. on 1. 8 above.

silent speech: an echo of Simonides, who referred to painting as 'silent poetry' (fr. 47b Campbell (Loeb)).

they weigh up . . . inflicting: an echo of Euripides' *Medea*, the paradigmatic drama of female revenge. 'JASON: You are hurting yourself too, and sharing in this grief. MEDEA: Know it well! But it salves the pain if you laugh no more' (1361–2; see also 569–73).

Furies: personifications of revenge.

preserve: there is an untranslatable etymological pun here. The birds, including Tereus (*Tēreus*), 'preserve' (*tērousin*) their former states. Tereus is singled out in the following sentence as a 'retainer' of anger.

5.7   *a double death*: see n. on 1. 13.

5.11   *Ephesus*: a place rich with novelistic connotations. Petronius' Latin novel, the *Satyrica*, contains the bawdy story of the widow of Ephesus, while Xenophon's *Ephesian Tale* starts and ends in the city.

5.16   *Aphrodite . . . the sea*: Aphrodite was born when drops of blood from Uranus' lopped-off genitals fell in the sea. Some Greek writers derived her name from *aphros*, 'foam'.

yoke: a symbol of marriage (the image is variously of two beasts yoked together and of the 'breaking in' of the girl with the yoke of adulthood and domestic responsibility). Melite is referring metaphorically to the ship's yardarm.

Amphitrite: a sea-nymph.

5.17   *a large body of servants . . . furnished*: the description of the house recalls Xenophon's description of the house of Theodote the courtesan (*Memorabilia of Socrates* 3. 11. 4).

four stades: about half-a-mile or 800 m.

a free woman . . . slave now: in Greek, these words have the metrical pattern of an iambic trimeter. They may be cited from a lost tragedy; alternatively, Achilles may be using the metrical form to create a tragic subcurrent for this passage.

Lacaena: literally 'Spartan woman'. The name suggests a connection with Helen, the mythical wife of Menelaus and Paris, who is frequently referred to in Greek literature as 'the *Lacaena*'.

Callisthenes: no doubt a different Callisthenes from the one who attempts to abduct Leucippe (2. 13; 8. 17–18).

5.19   *ephebe*: an adolescent male, who would have his hair cut short.

5.21   *Tantalus*: above, n. on 2. 35.

Hygeia: the goddess of good health.

5.22   *you Thessalians . . . desire*: Thessalians were famous for their magic. See e.g. Apuleius, *Metamorphoses* 2. 1.

       as if from a eunuch's bed: an echo of Plato, *Symposium* 219c: 'I had no more *slept with* Socrates than if I'd been sleeping with my father or elder brother.'

5.23   *mystery-cult*: initiation into the mysteries involved defamiliarization and disorientation.

6.1   *Achilles*: Achilles was dressed as a maiden and secreted on the island of Scyros by his mother, Thetis, in a vain attempt to hide him from the commanders who were commissioning soldiers for the Trojan War.

6.2   *the proverbial deer . . . maiden*: in some (notably, Euripides') versions of the story, Agamemnon's daughter Iphigenia was miraculously metamorphosed into a deer when he was compelled to sacrifice her.

6.5   *bacchant*: in Euripides' *Bacchants* Pentheus dresses up as a bacchant (female follower of Dionysus) in order to observe the Dionysiac rituals.

       adultery: a civil offence (against the husband) in many Greek cities.

6.6   *the saying that . . . invisible*: e.g. Euripides, *Hippolytus* 925–7; *Medea* 516–19.

6.7   *amber*: in myth, the daughters of the Sun mourning for their brother Phaethon, metamorphosed into amber-dropping trees.

6.12   *Codrus . . . Croesus*: Codrus was an Athenian king of legendary antiquity, and Ephesus was said to have been founded by his son, Androclus; Croesus is the enormously wealthy Lydian tyrant who figures so heavily in the first book of Herodotus' *Histories*.

6.13   *Arion's dolphin*: according to Herodotus (1. 23–4), the bard Arion was saved by a dolphin when thrown overboard by conspiring sailors. Herodotus himself refers to this event as a 'miracle' (1. 23).

6.19   *liver . . . heart*: the liver and the heart were traditionally the seats of desire and anger respectively (see e.g. Plato, *Timaeus* 70a–71d).

6.21   *Artemis*: patron goddess of Ephesus, a virgin goddess. See also 4. 1 and n.

7.3   *Smyrna*: one of the wealthy and important cities of Asia Minor, halfway down the Turkish coast (now Izmir).

       four stades: about half-a-mile or 800 m.

7.5   *double death*: see n. on 1. 13.

7.9   *he burst into tears*: a hackneyed rhetorical ploy, designed to gain the jurors' pity.

7.10   *fear . . . memory*: a slightly revised quotation from Thucydides ('fear stuns the memory', 2. 87).

7.12   *since . . . condemned man*: normally, Greek lawcourts reserved torture for slaves. See also 1. 25 and n.

        all judicial punishments . . . sacrifice: a reminiscence of the sacred embassy that delayed Socrates' execution in Athens (Plato, *Crito* 43c; *Phaedo* 58a–c).

7.14   *as I stated . . . story*: see 2.14 and following, although Sostratus is not there said to be among the travellers to Tyre.

7.15   *only Artemis . . . her*: the attendant's praise of Artemis' beauty is understandable, given the goddess he serves; but Achilles is also recalling Homer's comparison of the beautiful young Nausicaa with Artemis (*Odyssey* 6. 102–9; 151).

        paean: a song of victory (originally a hymn to Apollo).

8.1   *man-mad*: in Homer's *Iliad*, Paris is described by Hector as 'woman-mad' (3. 39).

8.2   *the Taurians . . . the Scythians' Artemis*: the Scythians of Tauris (in the modern Crimea) were best known among the Greeks (especially from Euripides' *Iphigenia in Tauris*) for their supposed human sacrifices in honour of Artemis. The Scythians were thus reckoned to be especially barbarous.

8.3   *malice behind his accusations*: in a Greek court, a man could be prosecuted for *sycophantia* ('sycophancy'), i.e. bringing a suit against someone out of malicious intent rather than genuine grievance or public interest.

8.4   *Dionysus*: i.e. wine. See n. on 2. 2.

        a narrative of . . . entertainment: the idea that narration provides a therapeutic relief from suffering is common (e.g. Heliodorus, *Ethiopian Story* 1. 9. 1), and goes back at least to Hesiod (*Theogony* 98–103).

8.5   *thigh . . . scar*: recalling the famous scar on Odysseus' thigh, revealed and recognized by his nurse Eurycleia when she washes his feet (Homer, *Odyssey* 19. 386–475).

        I omitted . . . the act: just as Odysseus, when recounting his own encounters to Penelope, seems to gloss over his sexual relationship with Circe (Homer, *Odyssey* 23. 321).

as if from another woman's bed: see more on 5. 22.

8.6 *The reeds gradually decrease . . . the odd total*: this passage is extremely garbled in the manuscripts, and makes little sense. The translation represents the likely meaning.

Athena's flute: i.e. a regular flute, with which variations in pitch are produced by changing the position of the fingers over finger-holes. (Athena was said to have invented the *aulos* or flute.) The sound of Athena's flute is dictated by the finger-holes ('within the tube'), whereas that of the panpipes is determined by the choice of reed (hence emerging from the 'ends of the reeds').

Pan: the woodland god was well known for his pursuit of virgins. The story of the origin of the panpipes is also told in Longus' *Daphnis and Chloe* (2. 34).

8.7 *city councillors*: in oligarchic cities of Achilles' day, the primary decision-making body at local level was the civic council.

8.8 *The decree is read*: these words do not appear in the Greek. Achilles is imitating the practice of scribes of Greek lawcourt speeches, who do not reproduce citations of actual laws, etc. The translation here imitates the practice of modern translators of lawcourt speeches.

hemlock: a poison used for the execution of convicts (most famously, Socrates) at Athens.

8.9 *emulation of Aristophanic comedy*: the Aristophanes in question is the famous author of bawdy and vituperative comedies, who composed in Athens in the fifth and fourth centuries BCE.

Homer-eroticism: the Greek word *homērizein* means literally 'to perform the works of Homer', but also suggests the intercrural penetration of boys (*ho mēros* = 'the thigh').

how he clamped the pole between his legs: the precise gymnastic process described here is unclear, the innuendo less so.

8.10 *gesticulating wildly and slapping his face*: an allusion to Aeschines' characterization of the performance of his arch-enemy, Demosthenes. 'Finally, Demosthenes stood up, gesticulating wildly with his body (as is his custom) and slapping his head' (Aeschines 2. 49).

8.11 *I no longer intend . . . earlier*: there is no such suggestion in the text as transmitted. The crucial point, however, is that only slaves could be tortured in court (see nn. on 2. 25; 7. 12): without explicitly conceding that she is freeborn, Thersander is holding no hostages to fortune.

Styx: one of the rivers of the underworld. To swear by the Styx, according to Hera in Homer's *Iliad*, 'is the greatest and most fearful oath for the blessed gods' (15. 37–8).

brought these accusations out of malice: see n. on 8. 3.

8.12   *her archer son*: Eros.

8.15   *He did not even omit . . . hut*: this detail is inserted to explain how Clitophon could know of the private conversation between Sosthenes and Thersander (6. 17). This device of providing a plausible explanation for the possession of otherwise inaccessible information goes back to Homer (*Odyssey* 12. 389–90).

8.17   *Themistocles*: the Athenian statesman of the fifth century BCE. For the story of his transformation, see Plutarch, *Life of Themistocles* 2. 7.

Glossary: Names in Leucippe and Clitophon

This section contains a brief guide to the prominent names found in the text. It focuses exclusively on the fictional names invented by Achilles (and on his own name); that is to say, it excludes mythological and literary references. Many of these are 'speaking names', i.e. they have strong etymological or literary connections.

The pronunciation of the names in English is to an extent a matter of taste: English speakers, even specialists in ancient languages, rarely pronounce or accentuate the words in the ways that ancient Greeks would have or modern Greeks do. The following is thus merely a guide to pronunciation, and does not reflect ancient phonology.

Achilles Tatius	*A-kill-ees Tay-shus* (or *Tat-tee-us*)
Calligone	*Kall-igg-onn-ee*, 'Beautiful-birth'.
Callisthenes	*Kall-iss-thenn-ees*, 'Beautiful-strength', also the name of a philosopher who accompanied Alexander the Great.
Chaereas	*Kye-ree-ass*, 'Pleasurable', the name also of the hero of Chariton's earlier novel *Chaereas and Callirhoë*.
Chaerephon	*Kye-re-fon*, 'Pleasurable-voice'.
Charicles	*Karr-ick-lees*, 'Famous-joy'.
Charmides	*Kar-mid-ees*, 'Son-of-pleasure', the name also of the sexy young boy in Plato's dialogue of that name.
Clinias	*Kly-nee-ass*, 'Famous' (fame-giving), the name also of both the father and the son of the Athenian voluptuary Alcibiades.
Clio	*Klee-oh*, 'Famous/fame-giving', the name of the eldest muse.
Clitophon	*Kly-toh-fon*, 'Famous-voiced', the name of the subject of a Platonic (or pseudo-Platonic) dialogue.
Conops	*Koh-nops*, 'Gnat'.
Gorgias	*Gor-jee-ass*, 'Shining-bright', also the name of a celebrated Sicilian sophist of the fifth century BCE.

Hippias   *Hipp-ee-ass*, 'Horsey', the name of a sophist, the subject of a Platonic dialogue.

Lacaena   *Lak-aye-nah*, 'Spartan woman'.

Leucippe   *Lyoo-kipp-ee*, 'White-horse', possibly suggesting a slang term for 'penis'. (J. Henderson, *The Maculate Muse: Obscene Language in Attic Comedy*, 2nd. edn. (New York, 1991), 127.)

Melite   *Mel-it-ee*, 'Honeyed' (implying allure and persuasion); also the name of a sea-nymph in Homer (*Iliad* 18. 42).

Menelaus   *Men-er-lay-us*, 'Leader of the people', the name of the cuckolded husband of Helen of Troy.

Nicostratus   *Nik-oss-trat-os*, 'Victory of the army'.

Pantheia   *Pan-they-ah*, 'All-divine', the name of both the love-heroine in Xenophon's *Education of Cyrus* and the girlfriend of the Roman emperor Lucius Verus.

Pasion   *Pass-ee-ohn*, 'Totally Ionic', also the name of a slave-turned-businessman in Athens at the fourth century BCE.

Satyrus   *Sat-eer-us*, 'Satyr', an allusion both to the ithyphallic sexual predators of myth and to the genre of comical 'satyr plays'.

Sopatrus   *Soh-pat-trus*, 'Father-saver', also the name of a parodic poet of the fourth century BCE.

Sosthenes   *Soh-sthen-ees*, 'Strength-saver'.

Sostratus   *Soh-strat-us*, 'Army-saver'.

Theophilus   *Thee-off-ill-us*, 'God-lover (or -beloved)', also the name of an Athenian comic poet of the fourth century BCE.

Thersander   *Thur-sand-er*, 'Manly-courage'.

The Oxford World's Classics Website

www.worldsclassics.co.uk

- Browse the full range of Oxford World's Classics online

- Sign up for our monthly e-alert to receive information on new titles

- Read extracts from the Introductions

- Listen to our editors and translators talk about the world's greatest literature with our Oxford World's Classics audio guides

- Join the conversation, follow us on Twitter at OWC_Oxford

- Teachers and lecturers can order inspection copies quickly and simply via our website

www.worldsclassics.co.uk

American Literature

British and Irish Literature

Children's Literature

Classics and Ancient Literature

Colonial Literature

Eastern Literature

European Literature

Gothic Literature

History

Medieval Literature

Oxford English Drama

Poetry

Philosophy

Politics

Religion

The Oxford Shakespeare

A complete list of Oxford World's Classics, including Authors in Context, Oxford English Drama, and the Oxford Shakespeare, is available in the UK from the Marketing Services Department, Oxford University Press, Great Clarendon Street, Oxford OX2 6DP, or visit the website at www.oup.com/uk/worldsclassics.

In the USA, visit www.oup.com/us/owc for a complete title list.

Oxford World's Classics are available from all good bookshops. In case of difficulty, customers in the UK should contact Oxford University Press Bookshop, 116 High Street, Oxford OX1 4BR.

A SELECTION OF   **OXFORD WORLD'S CLASSICS**